THE FORT McKAY MÉTIS NATION

Fort McKay, Circa 1920. Karl Clark, Provincial Archives of Alberta, A3517b, PR1968.0015.

UNIVERSITY OF CALGARY
LCR Publishing

THE Fort McKay Métis Nation

A COMMUNITY HISTORY

PETER FORTNA

© 2025 Peter Fortna

LCR Publishing Services
An imprint of University of Calgary Press
2500 University Drive NW
Calgary, Alberta
Canada T2N 1N4
press.ucalgary.ca

All rights reserved.

This book is available in an Open Access digital format published under a CC-BY-NCND 4.0 Creative Commons license. The publisher should be contacted for any commercial use which falls outside the terms of that license.

LIBRARY AND ARCHIVES CANADA CATALOGUING IN PUBLICATION

Title: The Fort McKay Métis Nation : a community history / Peter Fortna.
Names: Fortna, Peter, author
Description: Includes bibliographical references and index.
Identifiers: Canadiana (print) 20240528263 | Canadiana (ebook) 20240528301 | ISBN 9781773855912 (hardcover) | ISBN 9781773855929 (softcover) | ISBN 9781773855943 (PDF) | ISBN 9781773855950 (EPUB) | ISBN 9781773855936 (Open Access PDF)
Subjects: LCSH: Métis—Fort McKay First Nation—History. | LCSH: Métis—Alberta, Northern—History. | LCSH: Fort McKay First Nation—History.
Classification: LCC E78.A34 F67 2025 | DDC 971.23/2—dc23

The University of Calgary Press acknowledges the support of the Government of Alberta through the Alberta Media Fund for our publications. We acknowledge the financial support of the Government of Canada. We acknowledge the financial support of the Canada Council for the Arts for our publishing program.

  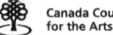

Copyediting by Kaitlin Littlechild
Cover image: "Fort MacKay, Alberta.", [ca. 1917-1919], (CU181632) by Unknown. Courtesy of Glenbow Library and Archives Collection, Libraries and Cultural Resources Digital Collections, University of Calgary.
Cover design, page design, and typesetting by Melina Cusano

Contents

Preface	VII
Acknowledgements	IX
Introduction: Steps toward a Fort McKay Métis Community History	1
1 Early History of the Fort McKay Métis: Origins to 1899	21
2 Fort McKay, Treaty, Scrip and the Immediate Aftermath: 1899 to 1920	35
3 The Bush Economy and the Registered Trapline System	49
4 Land Tenure in Fort McKay: "Split Our Very Identity into Two"	65
5 A Community Turned "Upside Down": Fort McKay's Response to Extractivism	107
Epilogue: From Community to Nation — The Evolving Relationship between the Métis Nation of Alberta and the Fort McKay Métis Nation	135
Appendix: The Fort McKay Métis Nation Position Paper on Consultation and Self-Government	149
Notes	159
Bibliography	205
Index	219

Preface

We are happy to share our history with our people and the broader public. This book documents our community's story and shows how we came to grow into the Fort McKay Métis Nation, rooted in kinship and place.

We would specifically like to thank all the community members who lived this history and fought to ensure our community is still here today against all odds. That is our collective legacy, and it is on that firm footing our Nation is built for today and for the future.

Finally, we would like to dedicate this book to both our Elders and our children. It is our hope that sharing and knowing this history will help to ensure the continued success of our Métis Nation.

Marsi Cho, Kinanâskomitin, Thank you

Fort McKay Métis Nation Council

Loretta Waquan
Felix Faichney
Brenda Paquette
Janice Richards
Lana Huppie

Acknowledgements

A heartfelt thank you to all the Fort McKay Métis members for sharing your knowledge, memories, and insights over the years. Hopefully, by documenting your perspectives on Fort McKay's history, identity, culture, and land use, we can help sustain the Métis way of life for future generations.

Thank you to Fort McKay community members for sharing so graciously. Thank you to the Fort McKay Métis Nation staff and Fort McKay Métis Nation councillors for their continued support.

Thank you to Laura Hanowski for providing detailed information about the Fort McKay Métis community's genealogy. Also, thank you to Terry Garvin, Rod Hyde, Barb Faichney, and Hereward Longley for providing access to their collections of archival photographs and other material about the community. Also, thank you to Emily Boak and Dawn Piche Wambold, who provided research assistance and to Michael Robson, who, with Emily, developed the manuscript's maps. Additional thanks to Heather Devine, Neil Reddekopp, and Patricia McCormack for reviewing and providing comments on earlier drafts of this manuscript.

Finally, thank you to the many Fort McKay Métis Nation staff and community members who helped make this project a reality. They include Barb Faichney, Rachel Richards, Rod Hyde, Dayle Hyde, Lina Gallup, Cort Gallup, Holly Fortier, Billie Fortier, Ron Quintal, Lauretta Waquan, Felix Faichney, Janice Richards, Glen Faichney, Eddison Lee Johnston, Daniel Stuckless, Jenifer Vardy, Maggie Butts, Contessa Short, and many, many others.

I want to thank my family (Gretchen, Patrick, and Jacob) for their continued patience and support as this project took form. Finally, and perhaps most importantly, I want to dedicate the work to the people of Fort McKay, whose histories have changed me in more ways than they will ever know.

Funding for this project has come from the Fort McKay Métis Nation and the Alberta government.

While many have helped with this book, any errors are solely my responsibility and likely a direct result of me not spending enough time in the bush visiting with Elders sharing stories about what really happened.

Introduction: Steps Toward a Fort McKay Métis Community History

"What am I getting myself into?" was my thought as I sat outside of the Fort McKay Industrial Relations Corporation (IRC) office, twenty minutes early for my first day on the job in March 2009. I had taken on a new position as "Métis Liaison." My role was meant to improve Métis participation in the corporation, representing Fort McKay's collective interactions with governments and the multibillion-dollar oil sands companies launching the latest phase of massive industrial projects. Formed in 1998, the IRC was initially owned equally by the Fort McKay Métis and Fort McKay First Nation, but by the mid-2000s, the Métis governing body of had run into trouble. Fort McKay Métis Local 122 had folded, and a new organization, Métis Local 63, had been organized to represent the Métis community's interests, though their ownership of the IRC was not renewed. While Métis Locals were affiliate organizations of the Métis Nation of Alberta, they were independent bodies within their communities and looked after their own affairs. By the time I had arrived, the new Local had virtually no money, no community-owned businesses, and was only hanging onto its assets based upon the strength of the community's leadership and limited support provided by the Fort McKay First Nation.

While the Fort McKay Métis struggled to reconstitute their representative organization, the First Nation had benefited from recent successes. Fort McKay First Nation concluded its treaty land entitlement in 1995, which provided a significant influx of money and land.[1] It was able to leverage the new federal and provincial regulatory requirements based on the ever-evolving "duty to consult" case law to sign a series of impact benefit agreements and business contracts with local industries. The agreements and business arrangements proved highly lucrative, providing the First Nation access to money and resources that community members would have only dreamed about a generation earlier. The band's administration undertook an aggressive community development program over the same period and was able to provide members with new houses and community infrastructure, including a hockey arena, daycare, and Elders' centre. By the early 2010s, the First Nation boasted that only 7 percent of its funding came from the federal government, with the rest coming from their impact benefit agreements and successful business ventures.[2]

In my new role in the IRC, I was expected to support the Métis leaders as they sought to rebuild their administrative capacity so they could take advantage of the opportunities that were, at long last, beginning to present themselves in the community. In the position, I was quick to learn about the important relationship between the Fort McKay First Nation and the Fort McKay Métis — and quick to learn that the colonial legal division between the two entities was not based on the community's history and extensive kinship relations. At the time, the IRC was wholly funded through agreements with the area's industrial developers and the provincial government, which — through its recently completed and misnamed "Aboriginal" consultation policy — had committed itself to ensuring that First Nations potentially impacted by resource extraction projects could participate in regulatory processes and be meaningfully consulted. The policy was not "Aboriginal" in the sense that it provided no direction for how industrial developers should consult with Métis communities (although a limited number did).[3] Yet Fort McKay First Nation used its funds to represent the interests of the First Nation and Métis in the community, showcasing a commitment to a single Indigenous entity and resisting government definitions of difference.

Perhaps inevitably, by 2009, the growing economic imbalance between the two sides of the community led to tension in Fort McKay. This tension was exacerbated by the fact that key members of the band's administration did not fully understand the historic nature of the relationship between Métis and First Nation members in Fort McKay, which stretched back to the founding of the community in the mid-nineteenth century. Increasingly, the First Nation's administrators encouraged the Chief and Council to work independently of the Métis to maximize the leverage offered by the government, which strongly encouraged the region's industrial developers to consult and negotiate with First Nations but not with Métis. The administrators believed their constituents were the members of the Fort McKay First Nation and that the lack of clarity in terms of government policy regarding Métis communities was not their problem. However, the First Nation's Chief and Council understood the importance of the relationship and pushed back against such advice. They wanted to maintain a close and supportive relationship with the Fort McKay Métis. In fact, almost all members of the Band Council were legally Métis themselves before the creation of Bill C-31 or were connected through kinship, marriage, or friendship. Through what they termed the Moose Lake Accord, the First Nation agreed to provide the new Métis organization with start-up funding and support while it re-established an administrative infrastructure and community-based businesses.

While I was hired to provide support to the Métis through the IRC, everyone involved quickly recognized that the needs of the Métis were more fundamental. They needed to develop new operating policies, procedures, and administrative structures that would allow for effective community governance. Within six months, I had left the IRC and moved over to the Fort McKay Métis administration full-time, reporting directly to the Métis Local 63 board of directors. My initial tasks included establishing a community strategic plan, identifying and stabilizing funding sources, and (re-)establishing relationships with external stakeholders.

As with any new community administrator, I soon began to uncover the community's many challenges. As I tried to understand them, my original training as a historian led me to ask questions about how those situations had come to be. Among the first issues that confronted us were the limited harvesting rights of Fort McKay Métis members versus the comparatively open rights available to First Nations members. This difference proved to be extraordinarily difficult to comprehend. How was it that Fort McKay First Nation members could hunt virtually without restriction in the community's traditional territory while their Métis brothers and sisters-in-law, cousins, aunts, uncles, and even parents — most of whom had also lived in Fort McKay their whole life — could not? Leaders at Fort McKay watched with interest as numerous Métis harvesting rights cases wound their way through the legal system, and many long internal debates were had about how the interests of Fort McKay Métis members could be defended if they were charged for "illegal" harvesting.[4] Fortunately, the close connection between the Métis and First Nations community members helped to avert disaster, as more often than not, these interrelated community members would hunt and fish together. If a Fish and Wildlife officer ever asked, it was always the First Nations member who had pulled the trigger or hooked the fish (though I often wondered whether the officers believed the Métis were such bad shots and fishers compared to their First Nations companions). It was all overwhelming at first, and I sought pragmatic "solutions," although the overall situation remained unresolved and continued to take up space in my subconscious.

Another pressing question that emerged shortly after my appointment related to the community's land and housing situation. Housing is an overriding issue in many Indigenous communities and one that is rarely easily solved or even understood, as the circumstances contributing to housing crises are often multilayered and complex.[5] In Fort McKay, the situation was no different. Many houses on the Métis side of the community had fallen into disrepair and were often overcrowded, leading to health concerns.[6] No one seemed to know how the situation had come to pass. As I began to review the issue, my initial question was, "Who owned the houses?" Perhaps foolishly, I thought the question would lead to a simple response, but a simple response was not forthcoming. As it turned out, the Métis houses were on land leased from the provincial government and renewed every five years. The Métis had lived in "their" houses, in some cases for over twenty years, without paperwork in the form of subleases or rental agreements to support their claims. As a result, most occupants did not pay rent, often leaving the "community" responsible for paying the government land taxes and other costs associated with the lease. The bankrupted Métis Local 122 had failed to keep up with these payments, and the relatively new Métis Local 63 was now suddenly responsible. While I appreciated that there was obviously a long history regarding the land, the administrative crisis had to be my focus. We started the difficult process of developing the policies and procedures necessary to manage a land base effectively, which ultimately led to the purchase of the land from the government approximately ten years later, in 2018.[7]

Understandably, given the challenges outlined above, Métis community members increasingly began transferring their membership to the First Nation. This was prompted by ongoing changes to the Indian Act, starting with Bill C-31 in the mid-1980s, which allowed individuals (particularly women) who had lost their status through marriage to claim back membership in the First Nation. Over the next thirty years, disenfranchised First Nations people continued to challenge the misogynistic and racist policies enshrined in the Indian Act, allowing generations of people to qualify or requalify for their status.[8] In Fort McKay, the better access to housing for First Nation members, coupled with per capita distributions from their growing community-owned businesses, proved enticing for many Fort McKay Métis members who had neither secure land tenure nor financial independence. By 2009, the community's population — which was once estimated to be approximately 50 percent Métis and 50 percent First Nation — had transformed. The First Nation now comprised over 80 percent of the community's population.

Finally, in my new administrative position, I maintained the connection with the Fort McKay IRC, which was reconstituted as the Fort McKay Sustainability Department in 2011. That meant I would become intimately involved in various negotiations and managing agreements with industrial developers in partnership with the Fort McKay First Nation. This role required me to become conversant in the language and to gain at least a rudimentary understanding of the community's history related to industrial expansion, which often left me with more questions than answers. Through reviewing historic agreements and related documents, I started to see the Fort McKay leadership's long-standing vision of a single, united community. However, the agreements provided few clues as to why that vision had yet to be realized.

While the Métis leaders recognized the need to record and understand their history — a task that even became a core pillar of their 2009 strategic plan — the pressing needs of the day occupied most of my time. Over two years, we focused on stabilizing the Métis community. We laid the groundwork for a reformulated social enterprise to help finance the community's goals; began negotiations with the Alberta government to secure land for Métis either through a long-term lease or ownership; developed bylaws for a new organization that would help to modernize governance in the community and provide the tools necessary to manage land and membership; and worked to ensure the Métis' place within negotiations conducted in partnership with the First Nation and the region's developers.

By 2012, my career took a different trajectory, and I established my own consultancy. The new company allowed me to continue working for Fort McKay on strategic initiatives while also assisting other communities in the region. This shift allowed me to combine the skills I had learned as an administrator with my academic training as a historian helping Indigenous communities guard themselves against the challenges of massive industrial development and constantly evolving government policies. Along with my colleagues in this new business, I wrote reports about how industry impacted Indigenous and community land use, conducted studies regarding

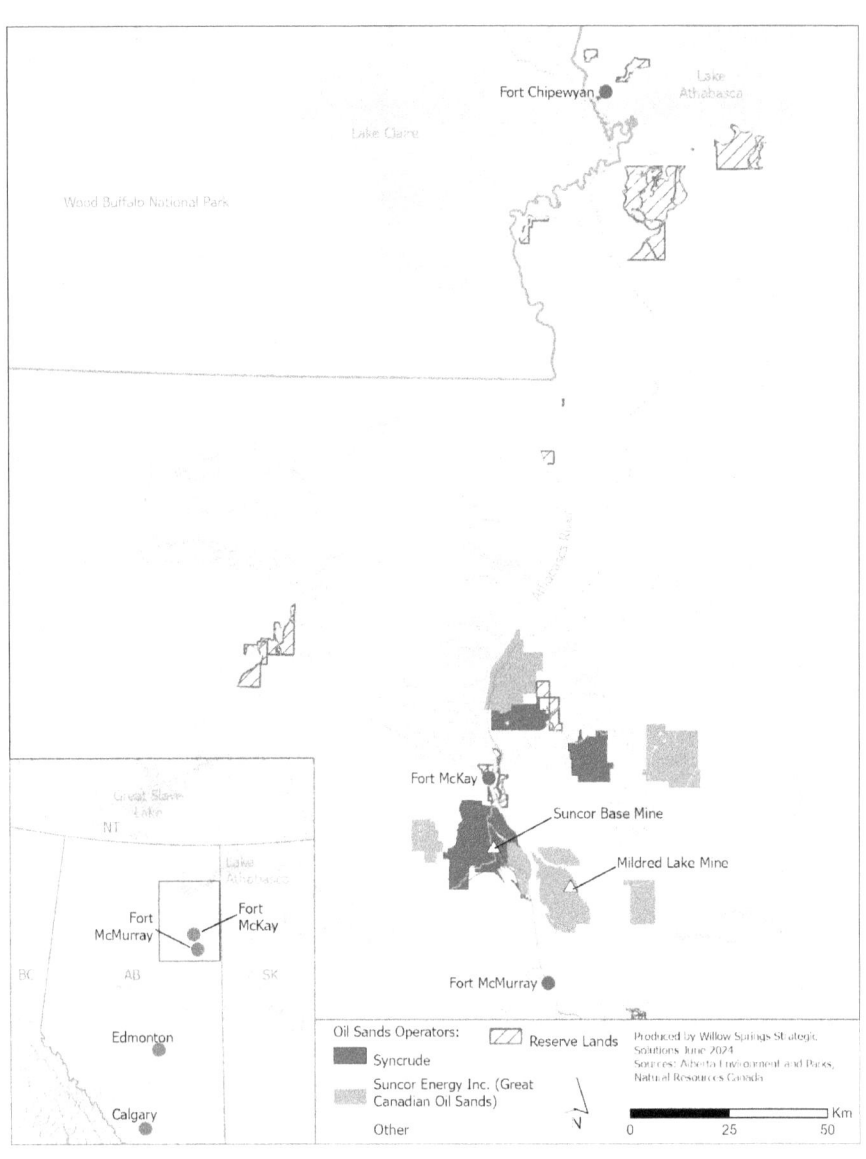

MAP 0.1
Fort McKay Regional Map

homelessness, and participated in a wide range of committees and focus groups that advised government and industry about how projects might be better conceived to limit or avoid negative outcomes.[9]

My practice increasingly involved legal questions regarding consultation and how it should apply to Métis communities. I began researching historical and contemporary issues that Fort McKay Métis and other northern Alberta Métis had to deal with after the *Powley* decision and Alberta's development of its "credible assertion" policy.[10] It was this process that eventually led to this book.

As Métis groups in northeastern Alberta became more organized, they requested that government and industrial developers consult with their organizations in the same way they engaged with the region's First Nations. First Nations had benefited from a consultation policy that involved capacity funding and increasingly led to negotiated long-term impact benefit agreements. However, the Métis requests were often met with silence, obstruction, and a general unwillingness to cooperate. I would joke with my Métis clients that it felt like we were characters in our own dystopian Kafkaesque novel, where we didn't even know the rules of the processes we were being asked to undertake. Frustrated, two Métis groups — Fort McMurray and Fort Chipewyan Métis — brought the issue of Métis consultation forward in the courts.

The *R. v. Powley* (2003) decision had opened a new playing field, and the landmark Métis-rights case affirmed that Métis harvesting rights are protected under section 35(1) of the Constitution Act, 1982. Perhaps most importantly, the *Powley* case established ten criteria, known as the Powley test, by which Métis rights and those eligible to exercise them can be determined. While the extent and the ability of a court to determine what is and is not a "Métis community" or a "Métis person" has been called into question, particularly in academic circles,[11] the decision laid out the basic tenets of what legally defined a Métis community, most notably whether the community has historic roots in a specific geographic location, whether community members self-identify as members of that "Métis community," and whether the community accepts and can represent those members.[12] The line of argumentation adopted by the government in *Fort Chipewyan v. Alberta Government* and *Fort McMurray v. Alberta Government* followed the *Powley* decision and questioned whether either group had the authority to represent the Métis rights-holders in the communities.

In both cases, the Crown argued that it was reasonable for Alberta *not* to require consultation with either the Fort McMurray or Fort Chipewyan Métis because neither group had provided the government information about who they represent, nor did they establish "any authority to act, and cannot demonstrate in any objectively verifiable manner that its members can establish Métis identity for the purpose of claiming section 35 rights."[13] The issue in both cases turned on whether the government owed a duty to consult to Métis groups in Fort McMurray and Fort Chipewyan and what Métis had to do to be recognized as rights holders for consultation purposes. While the cases were linked by the court, the facts in each were different. In *Fort McMurray*, the court found that the government had not fully considered the evidence provided by the community and, therefore, overturned the decisions and forced the government to reconsider whether Fort McMurray Métis were an affected party. In the *Fort Chipewyan* case, as outlined by Moira Lavoie, "the court set out two requirements for Métis organizations seeking to enforce the duty to consult under the Haida test, but whose governance structures are not statutorily recognized by the Crown. First, the organization must provide credible evidence that the organization's members meet the requirements of the Powley test for Métis identification. Second, the organization must provide credible evidence of its representative authority to enforce the duty to consult."[14]

Upon reviewing the *Fort Chipewyan* decision, while the Fort McKay Métis were confident in their own identity and authority to represent themselves, they were worried they did not have the evidence to communicate this effectively in a legal proceeding. Specifically, they understood they needed to explicitly define their own membership and ensure that membership authorized the local leadership to represent them and clearly demonstrate, through genealogy and history, that the contemporary membership was connected to the historic Fort McKay Métis community that held section 35 rights. Specifically, they were worried that if the provincial government did not recognize the authority of individual communities to represent themselves, there was the possibility that even more companies might refuse to consult with them or, even worse, that companies with existing agreements might rip them up until proof of representation was provided. The court made clear that Métis communities had to provide detailed information about whom they represent, establish authority to act on behalf of those people, and show that their constituents hold section 35 rights.[15] While many question whether

Fort Chipewyan v. Alberta Government fundamentally alters the consultation tests set down by the Supreme Court, the decision sent shockwaves throughout Alberta. Métis communities throughout the province considered how they should respond.

Though the Fort McKay Métis recognized they had the resources internally to deal with questions of membership, they knew they also required a community history to validate community knowledge. In the end, they decided they needed at least two expert reports, one detailing the Métis genealogy of the community and a second about Fort McKay Métis' historical development. In 2017, I conducted the historical study, and Laura Hanowski completed the supporting genealogical study.

The project provided a unique opportunity to revisit many of the questions that had originally occurred to me when I had been an employee. The community wanted the report to be prepared independently and without interference to ensure it could be relied upon in court. The parameters provided to me were broad, with the research questions following *Powley*: "Was there a historic Métis community in Fort McKay? And if so, how did that community develop and change over time?" In addition, Fort McKay wanted me to explore the question: "If historic and contemporary Métis communities exist in Fort McKay, how are they connected to one another?" I was asked to complete original research that included archival and primary materials and information already amassed by the community, such as interviews conducted during other projects, their cultural impact assessment, and traditional land-use studies. Though I worked independently, community members reviewed and verified my findings.

After the final reports were submitted, they were used as part of a larger submission that concluded with the recognition of "credible assertion" by the provincial government.[16] This meant that the government acknowledged that it had a duty to consult with the Fort McKay Métis in appropriate situations. Meanwhile, my conversations with the Métis leaders and administrators regarding the project continued. We both saw an opportunity to contribute to a broader conversation regarding the history of Indigenous people in the region and how government and industrial incursions have shaped the development of communities throughout the twentieth and early twenty-first centuries. Those conversations would eventually lead to the genesis of this book.

In the process of completing the project on behalf of Fort McKay, a few key themes began to emerge. First, the sources confirmed one of the first observations I had made as an employee, that there was a clear and demonstrable interconnectedness between the Fort McKay First Nation and Fort McKay Métis that underlies the whole of the community's history and confounds attempts to place the community's "Métis" population within a tidy *Powley* narrative. Similarly, the Fort McKay Métis history also misaligns with national Métis narratives, which propose a singular nation with close ties throughout the "Métis homeland" with demonstratable evidence of shared "spirituality, history, territory, values, traditions, laws, language, music, dance, art, customs, practices, and institutions."[17] Such narratives are predicated on establishing separate and discrete First Nations and Métis groups, which would erase the realities of the connectedness that existed between Indigenous communities like Fort McKay in the time before treaty and that still persist today.[18] The Fort McKay Métis Nation (FMMN) research aligned with that of other established scholars, including Heather Devine, Nicole St.-Onge, Arthur Ray and Kenichi Matsui, Neil Reddekopp, and Patricia McCormack (amongst others). Collectively, they show that in the nineteenth century, a robust society built around the fur trade had developed in Athabasca country that included many ancestors of the people whose descendants would later become Fort McKay First Nation and Fort McKay Métis members. The historic interconnections of these members have been maintained and, in some cases, strengthened into the "modern" era of the twentieth and twenty-first centuries.[19]

At the turn of the twentieth century, as the Treaty 8 Commission, followed by the Half-Breed Scrip Commission, travelled through Fort McKay and other communities in what became northern Alberta, these families divided themselves into two segments by opting for either "treaty" or "Halfbreed scrip." Yet it is doubtful that their decisions hinged upon allegiance to a unique First Nation or Métis identity and heritage. Even the accounts of the treaty party pointed to the general lack of cultural differences and distinctive identities.[20] More often, people living in the Fort McKay region, like many people in northeastern Alberta, decided to enter into treaty or apply for "Half-breed" (Métis) scrip based on their individual — and presumably more pragmatic — concerns.[21] This historic pragmatism has continued to the present day when members of the broader Fort McKay community continue to make economically informed choices about their "status." Kinship ties among community members have strengthened over time as First Nation and Métis community members continue to marry one another and work together to build Fort McKay throughout the modern period. That means it is virtually impossible to disentangle the First Nations and Métis history throughout the study. While the book proports to be a Fort McKay Métis history, much of it actually tells the history of the larger community as a whole in an attempt to avoid arbitrary "obsolete statutory distinctions" that might distort or ignore the community's interconnectedness. Far from being enveloped by a pan-Métis identity, the Métis of Fort McKay are better understood as part of a unique Fort McKay *Indigenous* community — one that belies the significance of ethnic division into "First Nation" and "Métis." The collective Fort McKay community existed and was self-governing long before the Canadian and Albertan governments established control in the region, and that unity still exists today.[22]

A related theme that I had observed as an administrator and that emerged more clearly during the research was the importance of the land, both at Fort McKay itself and in the surrounding region, or "environs," as many of the Métis court cases describe the lands traditionally used by the Métis. The processes by which lands were and are used, managed, and defended provide a key to understanding the community's evolution since the 1960s. The following chapters will show how the struggle over control of the land provided the community its *raison d'être* and helped to forge its identity, ultimately laying the groundwork for the community's prosperity in the modern era. In this sense, the research provides further insight into the creation of what Ian McKay has called the "liberal-order framework" that has come to be known as Canada. Specifically, through undertaking a detailed local history of Fort McKay, we come to learn a little about how Canada is, in fact, better understood as a "project of rule, rather than either an essence we must defend or an empty homogenous space we must possess."[23] The localized history of the community provides a lens through which we can see how Canada's expanded "liberal dominion" moved into the region, supplanting the "aliberal entities" such as Fort McKay, whose "alternative logics" challenged the liberal order and forced governments to forcefully put down alternative ways of knowing, organizing, and managing territories.[24]

For example, by studying the processes that took control of the land away from the Fort McKay people, they transferred it first to the federal and provincial governments and later to the massive industrial developers who promised those governments that they would make previously "unproductive" land "productive." For this question, the concept of "settler colonialism" is helpful, especially its assertion that this form of colonialism involved "eliminating the Native." However, the concept is far from perfect for describing what happened in Fort McKay, particularly as Indigenous land was not privatized, but rather set aside as "Crown Land" to be leased to multinational companies (often with significant national ownership) specializing in oil sands extraction.[25] As such, and as will be shown below, the situation in Fort McKay is perhaps better understood as "extractivism" where companies, empowered by policies approved by provincial and federal governments, were able to take control of Indigenous land, often damaging it beyond repair.[26] Through this process, governments repeatedly minimized the importance of Fort McKay community members' use of the land, while at the same time downplaying the massive impacts that industrial resource expansion had on community's health and development.

Another area to which this research contributes is through the use of genealogy and the construction of an Indigenous community's interconnections. In recent years, Métis history has come to be intertwined with the study of genealogies, primarily traced through governmental scrip records, which often allow scholars to see the scrip takers family interconnection at least one generation forward and back.[27] Genealogies are the specific evidence of kinship, showing how families are constituted and connected to one another over time. While the methods pioneered by the likes of Heather Devine and Brenda Macdougall have undoubtedly made an important contribution to the field, they also have limitations that can contribute to a misrepresentation of Métis history. The first challenge with a genealogical approach that uses scrip records as their primary form of evidence is that this research typically ends in the nineteenth century and remains virtually silent as to what happens to Métis communities in the twentieth and twenty-first centuries. If, following the detailed research of Ens and Sawchuk, many Indigenous communities were transformed to become "Métis" following the somewhat arbitrary ascription of the 1899 Treaty and Scrip commissions, then twentieth-century history is as, if not more, important to determining the existence of a Métis community than the nineteenth century.[28] As will be shown, it was over this period of roughly one hundred years that the Fort McKay Métis were forged and came to create their own Nation.

A second challenge that researchers focused on Métis scrip records can encounter is failing to recognize the interconnectivity that existed in northern Indigenous communities in the nineteenth century and continued into the twentieth and twenty-first centuries. As pointed out by scholars such as Robert Alexander Innes, nationalist histories are prone to finding connections that may not actually exist.[29] Additionally, such approaches tend to minimize the impact of government policies on localized communities, which enshrined the creation of distinct "Métis" and "Treaty" populations. However, these distinctions were often little more than a colonial fiction, as evidenced in Fort McKay's genealogy, where connections between Fort McKay First Nation and Métis members remained strong. Furthermore, the close kinship interconnections among the local Indigenous population provided Fort McKay with its cultural identity and helped its members organize their response as a community to governmental and industrial incursions on their traditional territory, especially in the 1960s and later.

The first chapters focus primarily on the community's early history and its network of genealogies. The genealogical analysis shows how the community was organized through interlocking kinship networks and how those networks persisted through time. It builds upon the work used in the Fort McKay Métis Nation's credible assertion package.

While kinship provides one source of evidence to understand the community's identity, their relationship to the environment, their shared land-use practices, and the fur trade economy provide an important second. The third chapter will examine this period, exploring the community's connection to the "bush economy." Those practicing the bush economy were able, over a long period (in the case of Fort McKay from roughly 1850 to 1970), to successfully integrate the trapping of small fur-bearing animals into their traditional way of life. During this time, Fort McKay community members thrived as they wove the fur trade into their pre-contact ways of life on the land, utilizing a decentralized communal system for organizing and managing their land uses.[30] Their way of life remained without serious challenge until the mid-twentieth century, when a series of changes to how the government managed land in northern Alberta began to take hold. Of critical importance was a new provincial policy for trapping, whereby the government implemented a system that forced community members to take individual "traplines," today known as "registered fur management areas." Indigenous people resisted this policy, aided by federal Indian Affairs officials, which allowed Fort McKay families some success. However, the 1960s presented new challenges, when the government sought to "professionalize" trapping and encouraged trappers to focus on the pursuit more as a commercial activity and less as a cultural endeavor or part of a way of life.[31]

At the same time, the waves of industrial activities — all afforded priority over Indigenous bush-based economies — left little room for the community to maneuver. Like many governments in the post–Second World War era, the Alberta government had a vision that "high modernism" would uplift the world into a prosperous new future. As defined by James C. Scott, high modernism was "a strong, one might even say muscle-bound version of the self-confidence about scientific and technical progress, the expansion of production, the growing satisfaction of human needs, the mastery of nature (including human nature), and above all, the rational design of social order commensurate with the scientific understanding of natural laws."[32] In the province of Alberta, high modernism was most directly felt in the northeast, where governments began to see anew the possibilities offered in the Athabasca oil sands region, where billions of barrels of oil lay mixed with sand just below the surface of the forests and wetlands that Fort McKay community members depended upon for their livelihood. The federal and provincial governments invested heavily in the new ventures, providing government subsidies to pioneering companies and developing policies that would clear the way for extractivism, a new form of settler colonialism that focuses on:

> acquiring territory, eliminating (or containing) Indigenous presence, and controlling land and resources. In short, extreme extraction can be a product of and an agent of these settler colonial relations, which are also enmeshed in the dynamics of capitalism.[33]

As the government began to view the region with new eyes, Fort McKay was forced to respond, though they were ill-prepared for the undertaking. Traditional governance structures that had served the community well since the mid-nineteenth century were little match for the big words (and dollars) thrown around by oil company executives and the government that had little desire to imagine the landscape as a "homeland" in opposition to a frontier where extraction should take place.

Unfortunately, as this book will show, the "scales of justice" would rarely tip in Fort McKay's favour from the 1960s onward, though increasingly, the community would find leaders who would learn through a mix of direct actions and litigative process ways to push back against overwhelming odds.[34] In this sense, though it is undeniable that the so-called energy frontier transformed the community, it is also true that it galvanized the community to action and that the leader's responses were rooted in their desire to maintain what they still consider to be essential components of their core Indigenous identity: their connection to the land through their mixed economy and their kinship connections to one other.

These issues will be considered in more detail in the fourth and fifth chapters of this work. The fourth will look at the community's response to governmental policies surrounding land management in Fort McKay, specifically considering the strategies used by the First Nation and Métis to defend the community's needs through the Fort McKay Association. It will also look at how governmental inflexibility eventually forced a clear administrative separation between the Métis and the First Nation.[35]

This context will be important as the fifth chapter looks primarily at how Fort McKay responded to extractivism — the expanding industrial development of oil sands projects — that began in the 1960s. Though the entire community was forced apart in terms of land-tenure discussions, members continued to work together in other important ways, most notably in their response to the continued incursion of new oil sands projects and forestry into their homeland. In the late 1970s, the First Nation and Métis jointly intervened in the regulatory hearings without great effect, forcing the community to consider other strategies, including a road blockade and increasingly mounting legal challenges to defend their rights. Such moves forced the government and industry to commit to working collaboratively with the community as a whole. This commitment ultimately led to the establishment of the only jointly-owned Industrial Relations Corporation in the region. The Fort McKay IRC would go on to negotiate agreements for nearly twenty years to benefit the whole community. These agreements provided the capital necessary to build much of the community infrastructure still used today. These responses forged the modern community of Fort McKay, and its members have both adhered to their traditional land-based livelihoods and simultaneously attempted to influence the shape of new industries that are defining the boundaries of their future.

The study concludes with an epilogue, "From Community to Nation," that analyzes how, in the last decade or so, the Métis community of Fort McKay began explicitly on the path toward nationhood and self-government.

Over that time, the Fort McKay Métis began forcefully asserting its "nationhood" in the hope that external governments and other Indigenous organizations would recognize them like they already recognized the Fort McKay First Nation. In 2021, the Fort McKay Métis issued a "Position Paper on Consultation and Self-Government." The text is included as an appendix in this volume. As they undertake this move, they have tried as much as possible to maintain the fluidity that was a founding feature of the community: for example, by adapting their membership codes to allow community members to move between Métis and First Nations groups based upon what the laws of the day allow; by providing equal support to all community land users who choose to continue using the land for traditional activities; by continuing to work as a whole to defend community land interests; and by working together to develop community infrastructure that will benefit Fort McKay members for generations to come. In these ways, the community of Fort McKay is attempting to re-form the unified Indigenous community that the government originally attempted to divide at the beginning of the twentieth century.

While few studies similarly consider an Indigenous community that includes both First Nations and Métis members at a micro level and carries through from the historic to the modern era, there are several that bear specific mention. Patricia McCormack's important study of Fort Chipewyan provides one key source of comparison when she convincingly argues that, over roughly the same time period, the multiple Indigenous groups in the northern fur trade economy came to form a "complex entity with multiple ancestries and meanings" that were encompassed in several fluid subcommunities in the Athabasca region.[36] The work of Trudy Nicks and Kenneth Morgan is also useful as it considers how the Indigenous community of Grande Cache, which was first developed in the nineteenth century, later adapted and changed when traditional "strategies for dealing with external influences no longer served their needs."[37] Fort McKay community members, like those in Fort Chipewyan or Grande Cache, did not "dwell on the question of their identity, vis-à-vis the outside world."[38] In this sense, this study follows in Nicks's and Morgan's footsteps, tracing another Métis community's history over the *long durée* and demonstrating how it developed and persisted through the twentieth century.

Indigenous voice is crucial, and knowledgeable community members reviewed this project at different stages. While there have been minor disagreements over the community's memory of events and the written record, everyone has enthusiastically supported the work to date. In addition, the project was reviewed and partially financed by the Fort McKay Métis Nation. Although it is an independent study, it has Fort McKay's blessing.

A scholar working closely with a community — particularly one who has also worked in an administrative role for the community — has the distinct advantage of unique lines of sight. For example, the family trees used in the book are those of friends and colleagues who, over a number of years, I've had the pleasure of getting to know on a deeply personal level. I could share maps of historical registered fur management areas I found in the archives with community members. In some cases, those community members then framed those maps to show their children the places where their parents and grandparents trapped before oil sands projects transformed the land. I found letters and newspaper articles that clearly connect today's community with that from earlier generations, which show community members that their ancestors fought like hell for the land where they now live.

Finally, on the topic of sources, readers will quickly be made aware that although this is a community history that had access to community members' knowledge, and I used the oral histories that had been compiled, I depended heavily on newspapers, government records, and other published materials to construct many of my arguments. As will be seen, numerous quality studies have been completed by and on the community's behalf from the 1970s through the 2000s that heavily draw on oral histories.[39] Additionally, in 2005, *Mihkwâkamiwi Sîpîsis: Stories and Pictures from Métis Elders in Fort McKay* was released, which compiled interviews from four Métis Elders in the community.[40] In these studies, community members' knowledge about their land use, land management, and ways industrial incursions were impinging on traditional ways of life were invaluable. While working for and with Fort McKay, it became clear that many of my questions regarding the dynamics and processes that shaped its development were largely outside the community's common knowledge and poorly reflected in local oral histories. Few community members understood the shifting government policies that led to changes in land tenure, trapline management, and industrial expansion. Thus, many of the findings in this history were welcomed by community members who, on more than one occasion, replied upon reading the manuscript: "I always wondered how these things came to be, now I know." By shedding light on bureaucratic histories, I hope that community members will now be in a better position to understand the external pressures that have shaped their circumstances, as well as those of their parents and grandparents, and be better prepared to undertake community histories in the future.

Another advantage of working closely with the community was that it provided easy access to the many studies Fort McKay commissioned over the years in response to oil sands projects. As well, the existence of this collective body of works underscores how the First Nation and Métis populations in Fort McKay have so often worked together to address their many shared concerns. A number of important studies have been completed or directed by the community that provide important local voices. Probably the two most important are "From Where We Stand: Traditional Land Use and Occupancy Study of the Fort McKay First Nation" (1983) and *There Is Still Survival Out There: A Traditional Land Use and Occupancy Study of the Fort McKay First Nations* (1994).[41] In both cases, the community either led or directed the studies and used them to defend local rights. In addition, the community has more recently produced a number of reports that directly consider the impacts of oil sands development. The most definitive work was completed in 2010 as part of a "Fort McKay Specific Assessment," submitted as supplemental information for the Shell Jackpine Mine Expansion and Pierre River Mine project hearings.[42] As a product of the IRC, the assessment was completed on behalf of the whole community and built on earlier community-specific studies. It was an important achievement because it considered all the same scientific and social science disciplines typically found in an environmental impact assessment, though its audience was technical. These community-led studies, importantly, provided a detailed glimpse into Fort McKay's changing way of life, mapping key sites of community land use and attempting to understand the human and economic costs of the changes brought by industrial development. The most recent study was Métis-specific, "Teck Frontier Mine Project: Fort McKay Métis Integrated Cultural Assessment."[43] The Fort McKay Métis Sustainability Centre commissioned it for the hearing on the proposed Teck project. Similar to the Fort McKay Specific Assessment, this work was undertaken in a project-specific context and directed towards a technical audience.[44] While the majority of these works are "public" in the sense that they were submitted to regulatory bodies, they are often difficult to find and are rarely available in university or public libraries. One spin-off of this book project is dissemination: I am working with Fort McKay to make more of these documents publicly available for researchers—these can be accessed via the University of Calgary Press website here: https://ucp.manifoldapp.org/projects/9781773855936. At the same time, I hope researchers and publishers will similarly seek out opportunities to make their work readily available to non-university affiliated researchers, particularly those who live in rural, remote, and Indigenous communities so that everyone can benefit from the knowledge that is often only available to those with formal academic affiliations.[45]

Finally, the community weighed in on some stylistic considerations. Members stated their preference for the term and spelling "Métis" as opposed to "Metis" or "metis" in the document. Similarly, they prefer "Fort McKay," not "Fort MacKay," a spelling often found in government documents. The community is working with the provincial government to standardize this spelling in all official correspondence.[46] In cases where these terms are used in quotations, the spellings used are those of the original documents. Finally, the terms "Indian" and "half-breed" are both common in the historical record for the Indigenous people in the region. In the text, the preferred "First Nations" and "Métis" are used unless "Indian" and "half-breed" is used in a quotation.

1

Early History of the Fort McKay Métis: Origins to 1899

The first French Canadian voyageurs entered the Athabasca region in the late 1700s.[1] This group, as will be described below, included fur trade employees who would establish relationships with the local Indigenous (primarily Dené) women in the region and would lay the groundwork for the establishment of the Fort McKay community.

The employees of the North West Company (NWCo) and, to a lesser extent, the Hudson's Bay Company (HBC) encouraged local community members to reorient their economic efforts to maximize the collection of small fur-bearing animals, which were traded for a range of goods mostly from outside the region.[2] Through the nineteenth century, small hunting groups became specialized in this new "bush economy," and, at what was to become Fort McKay, the Bouché, Piché, and Tourangeau families formed the most important group in the region.

The arrival of Peter Pond's trading party in 1778 and the creation of Fort Chipewyan in 1788 spurred the transformation of Athabasca country into the "Emporium of the North," where the fur trade became a new and key aspect of local Indigenous life.[3] Men, primarily from the St. Lawrence Valley, moved to the region for work and married local women.[4] It would be their children who became the founding members of the Fort McKay Métis community. These men typically aligned themselves through marriages with Indigenous families to encourage trapping and the production of furs and provisions for sale.[5] The first fur trade posts after the establishment of Fort Chipewyan were constructed around 1790 at the confluence of the Athabasca and Clearwater Rivers (Fort on the Forks near present-day Fort McMurray).[6] Around the same time, Vincent St. Germain built a post near present-day Fort McKay, though it only lasted a handful of years.[7] In the early 1800s, the

NWCo built a post named Fort Pierre-au-Calumet approximately twenty-five miles below present-day Fort McKay on the Athabasca River.[8] After Pierre-au-Calumet was built, HBC established Beren's House on the Athabasca River at the mouth of Calumet Creek.[9] In 1819–20, it was reported in the Fort Wedderburn (near present-day Fort Chipewyan) district report that:

> A few years ago there might be reckoned between thirty and forty families of Cree Indians, who in general hunted in the vicinity of Pierre au Calumet (lower Athabasca River), but they could not be considered as particularly belonging to that place, as they were in the habit of going between there and Lesser Slave Lake according as they found game, or it suited their inclination. Of late great numbers of them have died, so that at present there are not about twenty families at most.[10]

While these posts were "abandoned shortly after the coalition" of the Hudson's Bay Company and the North West Company in 1821,[11] many workers who had operated the posts stayed in the country and established their independent trading networks along the Athabasca River.[12]

Partly in response to this increased competition, in 1870, HBC founded Fort McMurray, and a short time after that, the Little Red River Post (sometimes referred to as Old Red River House), which likely began as an outpost of Fort McMurray.[13] Ernest Voorhis, in his monumental *Historic Forts and Trading Posts of the French Regime and of the English Fur Trading Companies*, suggests that the fort at what was to become Fort McKay was founded at the same time as Fort McMurray,[14] though the first post records only begin in the late 1890s.[15] By 1899, the *Edmonton Bulletin* explains that "The Hudson's Bay Co. have almost completed the removal of their post from Fort McMurray on the Athabasca to [Little] Red River, about 30 miles further down. The McMurray post will be abandoned. The change is owing to their being more Indians at [Little] Red River, and the fur trade, in consequence, being better there."[16] The post was renamed Fort McKay in 1911–12.[17]

These new HBC posts were meant to stem competition with the local traders who dominated the trading region. As recorded in the 1885 HBC Fort Chipewyan journal: "In consequence of the presence of opposition in the Athabasca at Red River, 35 miles north of McMurray, we have had to establish an out or winter post, which will have to be kept up as long as they remain

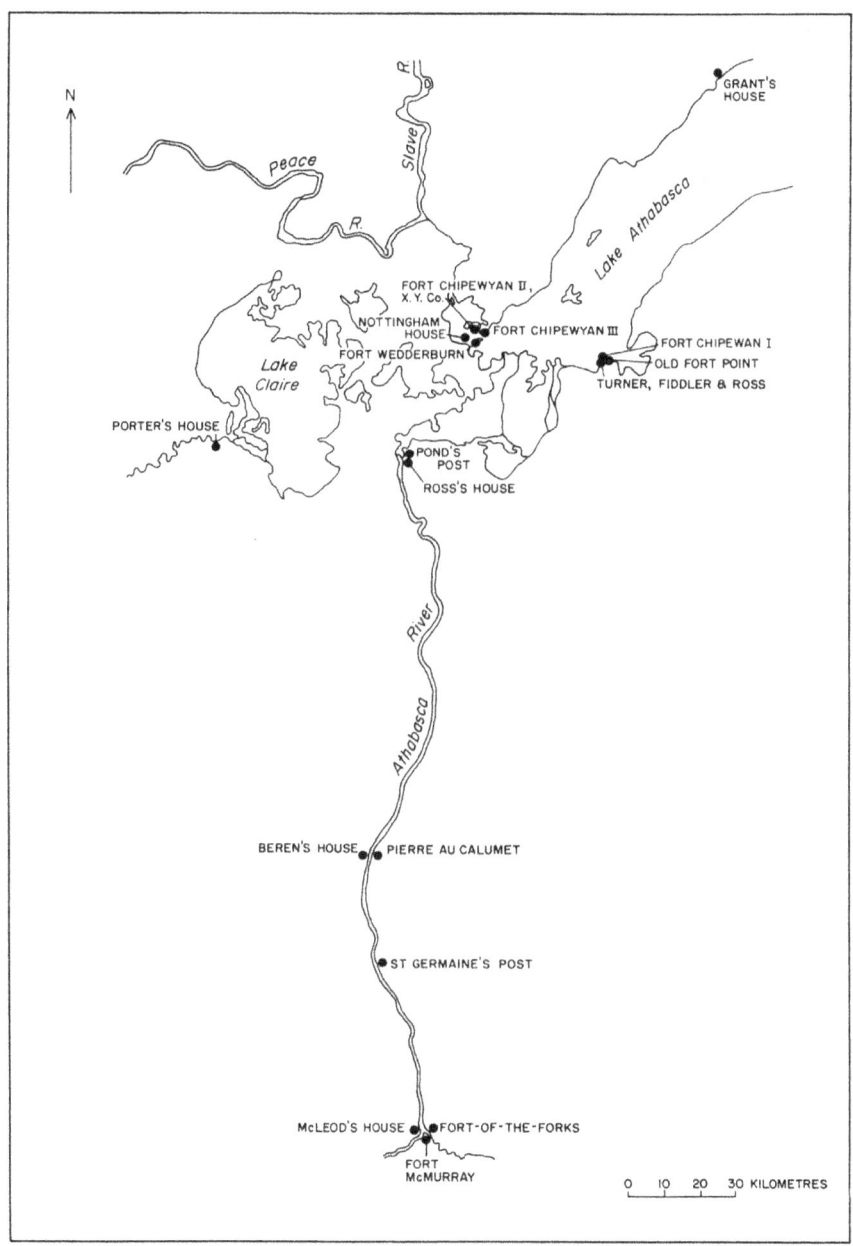

MAP1.1
Early Fur Trade sites in the Athabasca Region. From Forsman, "The Archeology of Fur Trade Sites in the Athabasca Region," 76.

there."[18] As such, the HBC posts at Fort McMurray and Little Red River were reactive, as the company hoped to protect its financial interests in the face of the growing regional competition.[19]

Early Genealogy of the Fort McKay Métis Nation

It is a mistake to understand the Cree, Dené, and Métis families that lived in the region as parts of separate communities. Rather, as Patricia McCormack points out, in the latter half of the nineteenth century traditional divides between "Cree," "Chipewyan," and "Métis" broke down in the Athabasca region, as the developing bush culture "contrasted with the 'settlement culture' of the people living in Fort Chipewyan."[20] In areas along the Athabasca River, most Indigenous families began speaking Cree as the trade language and "marriages between Chipewyans and Crees" became normal, creating a "cultural convergence" that replaced historical "Chipewyan-Cree antagonism."[21] This pattern of social organization follows more generally what was happening in the provincial north, where, as James G.E. Smith describes, the hunting band was the primary means of social organization amongst the Cree and Dené.[22] The hunting bands consisted of several (typically two to five) extended families numbered between ten and thirty. For most of the year (typically through the fall, winter, and spring), these groups lived in relative isolation on traditional lands often used for generations. In the summer, they might gather with other similarly organized groups on the shores of lakes that would sustain large fish camps and local hunting (which in Fort McKay was usually Moose Lake, sixty miles west).[23] The larger bands resulting from this gathering could number from 100 to 300. Membership in both the local and regional hunting bands was adaptable. It allowed individuals to move freely from one group to another and encouraged community members to speak multiple languages and remain open to different ways of thinking. In fact, as late as the mid-twentieth century, members of Fort McKay spoke multiple languages and moved with ease between various cultural configurations.[24] These groups, along with women connected with other traders and trappers in the region, ultimately formed the basis of the historic Fort McKay community.

By the late 1800s and early 1900s, the majority of Fort McKay community members were interrelated through a handful of close-knit families. The first was the Dené–Métis Bouché[er] family of the Little Red River valley, who were leading free traders in the region.[25] The Bouché family at Little Red River were likely descended from one (or more) Bouchés who were engaged in the region's fur trade by the late eighteenth century. François Bouché and Jean-Marie Bouché were two of the earliest voyagers in the region, and both were referenced in *The English River Book* in the 1780s.[26] Additionally, Joseph and Louis Bouché were North West Company employees working in the region in the late eighteenth and early nineteenth century, with Joseph transferring to the Hudson's Bay Company after the HBC–NWCo 1821 merger.[27] It seems likely that Joseph Bouché referenced in NWCo ledgers was Joseph "Wakan" Bouché, who was a mixed-ancestry man who joined HBC in 1816 as an interpreter and worked at Fort Wedderburn (near present-day Fort Chipewyan) under George Simpson from 1820–21.[28]

In 1824, Joseph Bouché "Sr." (most likely Joseph Wakan") signed a contract renewal as a "canoe middle man and fisherman at Fort Chipewyan" with HBC.[29] His probable son Joseph "Jose Grand" Bouché was born in the 1810s, and would eventually rise to become the family patriarch by midcentury. Upon his death in 1882, Jose was recognized in the HBC post journal as "a noted hunter and headman of the Chips," with a "large grown up family which constitutes about half of the hunters" in the Little Red River region.[30] Jose Grand Bouché was married to Madeline Piché, who lived at Little Red River along with her brothers Charlot and Chrysostome Piché.[31]

Much like the Bouchés, the Pichés also had a long history in the region. François Piché was first recorded as being in the Athabasca District in *The English River Book* in May 1786,[32] and may have been responsible for the death of John Ross at Athabasca in 1778, an event which caused him to hide with the "Chipewyans" for three years.[33] Duckworth suggests that François remained at English River as late as 1821 and that "Métis employees named Piché in Athabasca in the 1820s were probably sons of the elder François Piché."[34]

As brothers-in-law, Charlot Piche and Grand Jose Boucher followed the traditional pattern of local organization in the region, forming a small, interrelated hunting group.[35] This is unsurprising, as both the Bouché and Piché families were descended from voyageurs who had married into the local Chipewyan community. McCormack has argued that these families were likely considered "Chipewyans." However, it seems equally probable that their identities were fluid and centred around the growing fur trade in the region rather than distinct "Cree," "Chipeywan," or "Métis" communities. For example, in her scrip application, Charlot's daughter Isabelle would claim halfbreed scrip in 1899, listing her father, "Charles," as a "halfbreed" despite the fact he had chosen to sign onto Treaty 8.[36] Such an act seems to suggest that, in the least, Charlot likely spoke English as well as French, and his daughter at least viewed him as a "halfbreed."

His choice of marriage further demonstrates the complexity of Charlot's identity. His first wife was Josette Martin, the daughter of an important Fort Chipewyan Cree family.[37] Patricia McCormack argues that Josette's father, Job, married "all of his children strategically to both Chipewyan and Cree men and women, thereby gaining access to those lands for all their families and the local bands in which they lived."[38] The marriage of Charlot and Josette proves that by the mid-nineteenth century, traditional ethnic boundaries were breaking down, and communities were organized strategically around extended family units.[39] It also suggests that Charlot had some knowledge of the Cree language, which would have been important as Cree was the preferred trade language in the region.[40] Furthermore, while his lineage undoubtedly had strong Dené roots, he chose to marry the daughter of a regional Cree leader. Charlot's identity should, therefore, be understood as fluid and complex, with his ability to speak multiple languages and claim multiple ethnicities a local strength.

The Piché–Bouché group's focus on the fur trade, cultural plurality, and ability to welcome outsiders would be important to their growing influence along the Athabasca River. Matsui and Ray note that by the 1880s, "the Bouche kinship network extended toward Little Red River," where "members of this family traded extensively with HBC and its competitors for furs, birch bark, and shingles. Some of the Bouchés including Adam, Lowis, and Maurice, were engaged as temporary workers for the fort."[41] The Bouchés and Pichés were both identified as Little Red River Indians on the North West Mounted Police (NWMP) census, which was completed in preparation for the Treaty 8 negotiations, as well as an earlier census completed in 1881.[42]

While the relationship between the Bouché and Piché families was extremely important to their success, they were not the only locally connected families. The Tourangeaus were a key third founding Fort McKay family. Like the Bouchés and Pichés, the Tourangeaus were also partially descended from voyageurs who travelled to the region in the late eighteenth century, with Antoine Tourangeau being identified in *The English River Book* as trading with "the Indians between L'Isle a la Crosse & River au Rapid—May 1786."[43] While it is not perfectly clear, it seems that Antoine had a son of the same name, who married Madeleine Larocque. They had multiple children in Fort

Chipewyan, including Jonas Tourangeau. Both Antoine and Jonas are identified on the 1899 NWMP Census titled "List of Halfbreeds at Chipewyan, 1899,"[44] Though in his squatter's right claim made a few years later, Jonas states he was living on the Athabasca River at what would become Fort McKay with other members of the Piché and Bouché family by at least 1898.[45]

Jonas married Isabelle Piché, the before-mentioned daughter of Charlot Piché and Josette Martin.[46] Jonas's marriage into the Piché family likely helped cement his place in the regional trading network where he "hunted, fished and gardened."[47] In 1899, Jonas claimed Métis scrip for himself and his three underage sons, Isidore, Antoine, and Louis.[48] As already noted, his wife Isabelle also claimed scrip simultaneously.[49] Like his father, Louis Tourangeau settled in Fort McKay, marrying Fort McKay First Nation member Adeline Boucher in 1913. The marriage of Louis Tourangeau to Adeline Boucher provided another intergenerational connection between the Bouché(er), Piché, and Tourangeau families at the Little Red River post. Louis' son Edward Tourangeau would marry Mary Boucher (the great-great-grandchild of Grand Jose Boucher), providing yet another intergenerational marriage in the modern era.[50]

Unsurprisingly, these three families would form a strong connected trading network, as they all grew up in the same geographic location with similar backgrounds. In addition, they all seemed committed to the bush economy, which helped to establish them as key fixtures in the region and the development of the community of Fort McKay.

This complex pattern of pre-treaty relationships carried into the twentieth century and helps to explain why Treaty 8 had such a marginal impact on Fort McKay's way of life, even for people who opted for half-breed scrip. As Heather Devine notes, "because of the continued intermarriage à la façon du pays between aboriginal [i.e., "Indian"] and métis groups living in the remote forests and parkland of Athabasca, the Native population outside of the large settlements was more or less homogenous culturally," with "the arbitrary ascription, and subsequent separation, of these same groups into 'Indian' and 'Métis'" not taking place until after the negotiation and implementation of the treaties.[51] In Fort McKay, it could be argued that this did not happen until at least the mid-twentieth century, as recently designated Métis and First Nations members continued to marry one another and live a similar lifestyle, cooperating despite government attempts to divide them. In his study of the community in 1978, Edward W. Van Dyke noted that "Ft. MacKay, a settlement of 204 persons, allows literally everybody to know everybody else in a relatively intensive manner. Not only that, but virtually every individual has multiple relationships within the kinship system. The entire village is inter-related."[52]

Early Fort McKay Métis Culture and Land Management 1800–1920

The Bouché–Piché–Tourangeau hunting group members were part of a regional fur trade network that maintained relative independence through much of the nineteenth and early twentieth centuries. An important aspect that contributed to the group's success was their commitment to family, which helped to cement alliances. As noted in the genealogy above, the multiple marriages across generations helped to build trust and alliances. Some scholars have suggested that these types of interconnections, at least in Cree and Cree–Métis communities, are best described through the concept of wahkotowin. As explained by Brenda Macdougall, wahkotowin is "'a style of life' that reflected a shared cultural identity." With relation to her study area, Sakitawak (Île-à-la-Crosse), she suggests that wahkotowin allowed the local people to organize all aspects of their lives, from intergenerational knowledge transfer to "Métis cultural and socio-economic activity." For Macdougall, wahkotowin reflects part of a "larger cultural world view that informed the ways in which relationships were formed and resources utilized."[53]

Similarly, the "Dené Laws" in Dené communities defined people's relationship to the land. As described by the Athabasca Chipewyan First Nation, a neighbouring community that shares a similar ancestry to Fort McKay:

> Dene laws depend on sharing, helping, and living in loving relation with the land and water, and with all human and non-human kin. Under Dene law, living in good relations with the land and water is closely interconnected with living in reciprocal and caring relationships with community and kin.[54]

As Fort McKay Métis ancestors shared Cree and Dené lineage, they likely incorporated the two ways of knowing with an emphasis on their connection to their surrounding environment. As explained by the Fort McKay Tribal Council, "since time immemorial we have roamed this land, lived from this land, been a part of this land. To separate us from this land would be to split our very identity in two."⁵⁵ Through the community's relationship with the land and each other, Fort McKay's ancestors maintained their way of life, moving purposefully throughout their traditional territory to sustain their families.⁵⁶

It was, and continues to be, Fort McKay's connection to one another and to the land that centres its community, supported by the traditional (bush) economy, medicine, ceremonies, and kinship connections. As described by the Fort McKay Tribal Council:

> The life of the community and all of its families revolved around the traditional economy. Hunting, trapping, fishing and gathering were a way of life and the people moved over their large area making sure they had food for their families, skins for clothing and pelts for sale. Store bought goods were limited to dry goods, equipment and bulk supplies of flour, sugar, and salt to sustain them in the bush. Game, fish, and berries were plentiful and eaten fresh, dried or smoked. The subsistence lifestyle and the extended kinship network provided secure work for everyone, young or old, food and income, maintenance of the traditional values such as sharing and respect for man and nature as well as ample leisure time to enjoy the environment in which they lived, to have Tea Dances, spiritual ceremonies and to provide the Elders with opportunities to pass on the oral history, the traditions, the culture, the experiences of a life time of learning.⁵⁷

Ceremonies like the Tea Dance connected Fort McKay's long-ago past to the present, providing an opportunity to establish connections and share wealth and knowledge. As a Fort McKay Métis community member explained:

> the tea dance was a spiritual event. Because if they do that, you know some, like long time ago, people used to lose their children, and stuff like that . . . It's for good luck, that they would give a big feast. And it was for good luck for the year, like here. They're paying God for their luck and others, by sharing with people.⁵⁸

As described by community member Francis Orr, "at Tea Dances we invited people six months ahead of time. [At the dances] there was a lot of give away:

Horses, saddles, dogs, guns and everything. Hopefully it'll come back."[59] Johnny Orr added: "Everything was free at the tea dance. There was no drinking. We smoked pipes and offered something on the fire for the spirts" and that the dances were held every year and "they included trading a gun or moosehide jacket for a hundred dollar bill. If you got a gun you had to shoot one shell to thank the person who gave the gift."[60]

The Tea Dance provided an opportunity for the redistribution of wealth that was part of a larger system of kinship reciprocity that helped the community to ensure everyone could live a good life. As described by Edward van Dyke:

> Traditionally, the principles underlying economic transactions for residents of Fort McKay was one of reciprocity. When food, shelter and so on were available to an individual, one had an obligation to distribute these goods in a prescribed manner within one's own kin group. Conversely, when one's kin had goods available, one had a claim to a set portion. The kinship system indicated to the individual those persons to whom one had economic obligations, as well as those from whom one might receive economic privileges. Reciprocity was activated and operated through the kinship system.[61]

At the core of the pre-1960s community culture was the bush economy, which was closely connected to kinship, reciprocity, and use of the land. Community gatherings — whether dances or other special events — flowed into this cultural system, providing opportunities for these cultural exchanges.

In Fort McKay, sharing extended beyond material goods and included the land. Ernest Thompson Seton observed this process when he travelled through the region before treaty, explaining that when community members along the Athabasca River came together,

> by an ancient, unwritten law the whole country is roughly divided among the hunters. Each has his own recognized hunting ground, usually a given river valley, that is his exclusive and hereditary property; another hunter may follow a wounded animal into it, but not begin a hunt there or set a trap upon it.[62]

It is unsurprising that Seton, when viewing the bush economy through the lens of English common law and land tenure, would see a highly structured and divided territory based upon property lines passed down through the generations. In reality, communities like the one that developed around Fort McKay had their own system of land organization that did not include the notion of "land ownership."[63] Rather, community members shared the space and the various animals, plants, and spirits necessary for the community to practice the bush economy.[64]

Since the first trading posts were founded along the Athabasca River, the local Indigenous community was increasingly drawn to participate in the fur trade economy that came to dominate the region. Before 1899, the ancestors of almost all Fort McKay people lived a life on the move within their traditional territory. While it is difficult to determine the specific limits of the territory, particularly in the time before treaty, there are definite clues provided in the historical record. For example, the Hudson's Bay Company Post journals for Fort McMurray (1877–1885) and Fort McKay (1901–1911) make frequent mentions of Little Red River community members travelling throughout a territory that extends from Fort Chipewyan in the north, Moose Lake in the west, Portage La Loche in the east, and Willow Lake/Lac La Biche in the south.[65] While the purpose of these trips (and, more importantly, the recording of the trips) was primarily for company business, they demonstrate the various places that members of the historic Fort McKay Métis community regularly visited and maintained connections. Additionally, as part of the 1983 *From Where We Stand* project, the community completed a series of map biographies, which were combined to create a map of their traditional territory.[66] A second set of territory-wide map biographies was created with community members in 1994 as the main impetus of the *There is Still Survival Out There* project.[67] In both cases, the map biographies primarily interviewed community Elders who actively participated in the local bush economy before the industrialization of the territory in the 1960s. Furthermore, the territories are validated when other pieces of evidence, including federal government requests for "Indian" harvesting areas produced in the 1940s and historic Registered Fur Management Area (RFMA) maps from the 1960s, are compared.[68] The maps, when overlayed, provide a rough estimation of Fort McKay's traditional territory.[69]

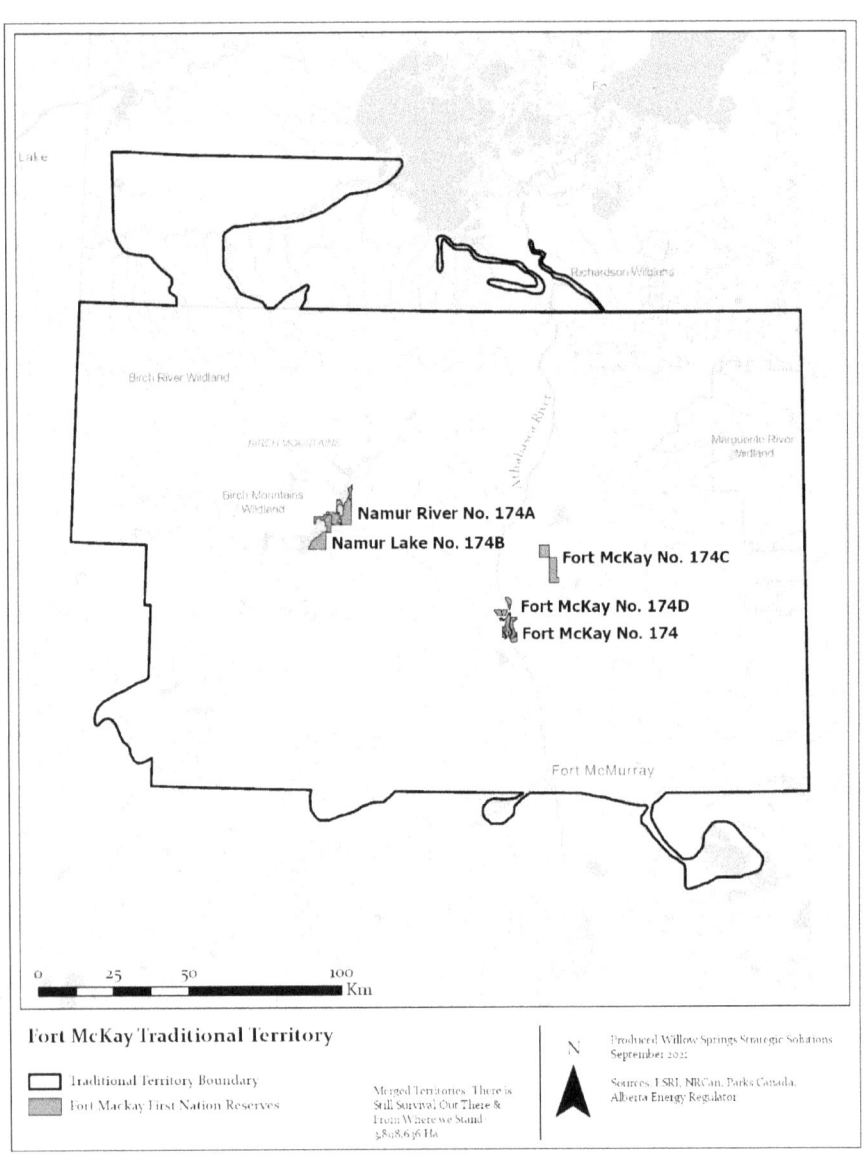

MAP 1.2
Fort McKay Traditional Territory

FIGURE 1.1
Felix Beaver, Mary Ann Beaver, and granddaughter, Mary Beaver. Rod Hyde collection.

Before 1960, Fort McKay had five seasons: "dry meat hunt [fall], early winter hunting and trapping, late winter hunting and trapping, spring beaver hunt and the summer slack," during which men would sometimes take jobs in the shipping industry.[70] Community members managed their hunting and trapping areas through a series of cabins or camping locations along pre-determined routes. The trappers and their families returned to Fort McKay at Christmas, in late winter or early spring, and in the fall before trapping season. Women and children usually travelled with the men, particularly in the winter months, helping with the trapline. In the summer, they picked berries, fished, and processed moose meat and hides to prepare for the coming winter. They lived mainly in small family groupings, or "local bands," which should not be confused with the legal Indian bands created by Treaty 8.[71] The local bands gathered together during special events (most notably Christmas and New Year's) and to fish in the summer at Moose Lake, but then dispersed into smaller groups after that.[72] As described above, before 1900, the family grouping in and around Fort McKay was made up almost exclusively of members of the Bouché, Piché, and Tourangeau families. In the first decades after 1900, they were joined by members of the Shott, Powder, Lacorde/Janvier, and Beaver families who married into the original group (and whose genealogical connections will be described in length below) and together they used a traditional territory that extended roughly from Fort Chipewyan to the Saskatchewan border, to Willow Lake, and to Moose Lake.[73]

They regulated and organized their land uses through kinship patterns and social customs. As James Parker explained, Indigenous people in the oil sands region (including Fort McKay community members) explained that their early "decision making" was "centred on the trapping economy," with an annual meeting of the trappers in the fall used to "decide upon their trapping areas, which in the early days were not zoned or registered."[74]

Land has always been important to the community of Fort McKay. The deep and intertwined family interconnections were responsible for using and governing the lands over a large geographical space, and boundaries to this space were fluid and not easily mapped in a European fashion, though always there.[75] In the twentieth century, external government and industrial pressures forced Fort McKay members to adapt to new policies and procedures that reduced community members' land availability as they strove to maintain their traditional bush-based way of life. The following section will look at how the community of Fort McKay managed land through to the early 1920s.

2

Fort McKay, Treaty, Scrip and the Immediate Aftermath: 1899 to 1920

As the government came face-to-face with the communities in what was to become Treaty 8 territory in the late nineteenth century, it quickly recognized that the Indigenous people were organized in strikingly different ways when compared to the groups they had negotiated with for Treaties 1 through 7. Specifically, government officials explained that these northern groups:

> indulge in neither paint nor feathers and they never clothe themselves in blankets. Their dress is of the ordinary style and many of them were well clothed. In the summer they live in teepees, but many of them have log houses in which they live in the winter. The Cree language is the chief language of trade, and some of the Beavers and Chipewyans speak it in addition to their own tongues. All the Indians we met were with rare exceptions were professing Christians, and showed evidences of the work which missionaries have carried on among them for many years. Few of them have had children available themselves of the advantages afforded by boarding schools established at different missions. None of the tribes appear to have any very definite organization. They are held together mainly by the language bond. The chiefs and headmen are simply the most efficient hunters and trappers.[1]

The description of the people found in the Treaty 8 territory broadly demonstrates that, for the most part, all community members had a certain level of acculturation as they were heavily invested in the "bush economy" and had structured their lives accordingly. Families such as the Bouché–Piché–Tourangeau group, for over 100 years, had engaged in the fur trade to a greater or lesser extent and had chosen to incorporate elements of Euro-Canadian, Dené, and Cree cultures into their own. Increasingly, they were adopting a semi-sedentary lifestyle where they would maintain temporary camps, but also increasingly setting building structures at what was become Fort McKay before 1899, with surveyor Donald Robertson noting that Chief Adam Boucher "had his residence there long previous to Treaty, in fact for 20 or 30 years."[2]

Recognizing this difference, the commissioners were granted broad "discretionary power as to including in the treaty those characterized as Halfbreeds, should they prefer being dealt with as Indians rather than as Metis."[3] Clifford Sifton revealed that it was practically impossible to instruct the commissioners to "draw a hard and fast line" between the Métis and the Indians, as most were closely allied in manner and customs.[4] Ultimately, he recommended that the commissioners be given considerable latitude to allow Métis who so desired to be treated as Indians to be taken into treaty, which "would be more conducive to their own welfare, and more in the public interest . . . than to give them scrip."[5] Opening the negotiation at the Lesser Slave Lake, Sifton reiterated in person that "Half-Breeds living like Indians have the chance to take the treaty instead, if they wish to do so. They have their choice."[6] This option helps to explain why the majority of the Bouché and Piché families, despite their genealogical background and involvement in the fur trade, would have been able to take treaty, while the Tourangeau family were able to take half-breed scrip.[7]

It also seems that Clifford Sifton and the government had ulterior motives for establishing separate Treaty and Scrip commissions. While Sifton recognized the close connections between the "Indians" and "Half-Breeds," he (as well as others in the government) saw Métis people as agitators who were disproportionately involved in the Riel Resistances on the prairies.[8] In 1886, the government had gone to great lengths to expel Métis people from Treaty Bands, and Sifton was concerned that if the "Half-Breeds" were not offered scrip, they would "use their great influence with the Indians as to make it extremely difficult, if not impossible, to negotiate Treaty."[9] As such, the Government of Canada formed the Treaty 8 and Half-breed Commissions to travel to northern communities in the summer of 1899 to offer treaty and half-breed scrip.[10]

Needless to say, the government's process for categorizing Indigenous people through the commissions was less than perfect, and the reasons why people chose either Métis scrip or treaty were complex. Adding to the complexity was the fact that Catholic clergy, who often acted as commission translators, generally encouraged individuals to take treaty for fear that those taking scrip would not be given the ongoing assistance the clergy felt they needed.[11] On the other side were the scrip speculators who travelled with the commission and were quick to profitably convert scrip signatories' paper documents into money. The speculators were motivated to see people sign scrip and sell those scrip applications to them for a fraction of the document's value.[12] While undoubtedly both the clergy and speculators influenced individual decisions with regards to the taking of treaty or scrip, it is also likely that individuals had agency in the decision, some deciding to take the security that was offered through treaty, while others determining that money in hand was preferable to being paid a lesser amount annually (with yet others not understanding the process at all and signing their X where their advisor told them to).[13] It was within this setting that groups such as the Bouché–Piché–Tourangeau chose to take either scrip or treaty, and it remains difficult, if not impossible, to discern the specific motivations for how they came to their final determinations.

Unfortunately, few references describe the specific negotiations with the local "Chipewyan and Cree" at Little Red River or Fort McMurray.[14] Charles Mair's Treaty 8 memoir only makes passing reference to the commission travelling through Little Red River and Fort McMurray, and the official Treaty report explains:

> The Chipewyan and Cree Indians of Fort McMurray and the country thereabouts, having met at Fort McMurray, on this fourth day of August, in this present year 1899, Her Majesty's Commissioner, James Andrew Joseph McKenna, Esquire, and having had explained to them the terms of the Treaty unto which the Chief and Headmen of the Indians of Lesser Slave Lake and adjacent country set their hands on the twenty-first day of June, in the year herein first above written, do join in the cession made by the said Treaty and agree to adhere to the terms thereof in consideration of the undertakings made therein.

FIGURE 2.1
"Paying Treaty at Old Fort McMurray, 1903". C.W. Mathers. PAA B784.

> In witness whereof Her Majesty's said Commissioner and the Headmen of the said Chipewyan and Cree Indians have hereunto set their hands at Fort McMurray, on this fourth day of August, in the year herein first above written.[15]

After the presentation, Adam Boucher signed his X to treaty on behalf of the Dené families in attendance, including the Bouchers and Pichés.[16] It is unclear whether members of the Tourangeau family were at this meeting, but Jonas Tourangeau, along with many of his relatives, would take half-breed scrip three days later in Fort Chipewyan.[17] As will be shown below, the different designations seemed to mean little to the community itself, which continued to remain structured around the bush economy and to one another.

The Genealogy of the Fort McKay Métis After Treaty

In the time shortly after the signing of Treaty 8, Fort McKay saw a significant migration into the community, which notably increased membership, though importantly, all those who came were Indigenous and married into one of the founding families, becoming enmeshed in the local bush economy that held the community together. Neil Reddekopp hypothesizes that the in-migration could be attributed to the fact that it was becoming more difficult to procure furs close to Little Red River at the turn of the century. This, in turn, led Little Red River community members to expand their land use to the north, west, and south, which facilitated additional contact with Indigenous people in those areas.[18] At the same time, it seems as likely that the economic opportunities that came from the end of the Hudson's Bay Company monopoly and the improved regional transportation methods (specifically the shift from scow brigades to steam boats and railway that occurred between 1870 and 1920) led to the movement of Indigenous people to the Fort McKay region.[19] By the 1880s, competition in the region required HBC to establish a permanent post at Little Red River, and in 1899, there were at least three independent trading posts at Fort McKay.[20]

Brothers Narcisse and Emile Shott were two such individuals leaving Lac La Biche to trap and trade in the north. They both moved to Fort McKay in the early 1900s and would marry local women, joining the local kinship network and cementing their trading operations. Narcisse would marry Elizabeth Tourangeau, and they would adopt Henry Quintal (who would change his surname to Shott). Emile first married Alice McDonald, daughter of John McDonald and Josephine Cook of Fort McMurray.[21] Emile later married and had children with Helen Boucher, the daughter of Maurice Boucher and Angelique Kokan (and granddaughter of Jose Grande Boucher) in Fort McKay. Narcisse and Emile were the sons of the Louison (Shott) Fosseneuve, a man from Lac La Biche famous for his work with the Athabasca scow brigades in the late nineteenth century.[22] Emile is recorded in the Fort McKay Hudson's Bay Company Journal as having trapped and traded with Chysatum Piche, Elzear Robillard, and John Cowie up and down the Athabasca River in the early 1900s, having trading posts at Poplar Point, Jackfish Creek, and Point Brule.[23] Elzear Robillard seemed to have been his main partner, which was important as Elzear's stepson, James Robillard, married Rosalie Boucher, the first daughter of Jose Grande Boucher.[24] Emile, after marrying Helen,

FIGURE 2.2
Hudson's Bay Company post at Fort McKay. Photo by Karl Clark (1888-1966). PAA, PR1968.0015.

opened a store at Moose Lake and was remembered as "a travelling salesman; he sold flour, lard and baking powder by dog team."[25] Helen became a community midwife, helping with the birth of many, including Emmy Faichney (née Beaver).[26] One of Emile and Helen's daughters was Lina Gallup (née Shott), who is currently the oldest living Fort McKay First Nation member. Gallup has a number of grandsons and granddaughters who were members of the Fort McKay Métis Nation, including Billie Fortier, a lawyer acting for the Nation on various court cases before she, too, joined the Fort McKay First Nation. Her daughter, Soleil Cree Neufeld is enrolled as a member of the FMMN.[27]

The genealogical connections between root families continued into the twentieth century. For example, Narcisse Shott and Elizabeth Tourangeau's adopted son, Henry Shott, married Clara Boucher (great-granddaughter of Grand Jose Boucher).[28] She lost her status as a Fort McKay First Nation member after marrying Henry. Still, she went on to represent the Métis community in various official and unofficial capacities, most notably joining her good friend FMFN Chief Dorothy McDonald in organizing a community roadblock in 1983 (an event covered in detail below).[29] The three eldest sons of Ronald Quintal, the former president of the FMMN, are descended from the

FIGURE 2.3
Lina Gallup, Billie Fortier, Holly Fortier, and Soleil Cree Neufeld (Fortier).

Narcisse Shott family and include genealogical connections to the original Tourangeau and Boucher root ancestors.[30]

The Shotts were not the only brothers who moved and married into the community. Two other brothers were Alphonse and Modest Powder, who travelled north to Fort McKay in the late 1910s from Lac La Biche. While it is impossible to know the exact reason for their move, their grandparents, St. Pierre Lapoudre and Theresa Cardinal, were members of the Kahquanum Band at Beaver Lake before taking half-breed scrip in 1886.[31] The brothers were born in the 1890s and, therefore, were not able to take scrip.[32] Nonetheless, both were possibly looking to move to an area to avoid the increased scrutiny many in Lac La Biche were experiencing at the time.[33]

Modest and Alphonse Powder married into two key Fort McKay families. Modest married Helene Piché, the daughter of Chrysostome Piché and Louis Lemeg (possibly Lemaigre), and Alphonse Powder married Louise Boucher, the daughter of Maurice Boucher and Angelique Kokan. Like the Shotts, the Powder brothers continued the practice of single Indigenous men moving to different regions, marrying into the local population, and easily joining

FIGURE 2.4
Modest Powder, circa 1980. Bill Jorgensen Collection. https://billjorgensen.zenfolio.com/p994248149

the new community.[34] In fact, both brothers became so important that they feature prominently in the later oral histories of Fort McKay, with Modest in particular being repeatedly mentioned as a key community Knowledge Holder in *There Is Still Survival Out There*.[35] Alphonse and Modest held traplines near Fort McKay (2324 and 1714) in the 1960s, along with Alphonse's son, Zachary Powder, who owned trapline 2155 from the 1960s until he died in 2020, which was then taken over by his daughter Lucy.[36] Zachary was also a founding member of the Red River Point Society (1972) and later the Fort McKay Métis Local 122 in the late 1970s (both organizations are described below).[37] Zachary was also interviewed for *Mihkwâkamiwi Sîpîsis: Stories and Pictures from Métis Elders in Fort McKay* in 2005, where he shared stories as a key Fort McKay Métis Knowledge Holder. Shortly after participating in the book project, Zachary learned that he could qualify for his Fort McKay First Nation status, and for housing, economic, and medical reasons, chose to join the band in the 2010s.[38] Several of his children and grandchildren remain

Fort McKay Métis Nation members with genealogical connections to the Boucher, Piché, and Tourangeau root families.[39]

Isadore "Lacorde" Janvier similarly moved to the region and married Mary Rose Tourangeau, Louis and Elisabeth Tourangeau's sister, in the early 1900s.[40] Isadore's grandfather was Pascal Janvier, a free trader who often travelled to Fort McMurray and Fort McKay before the turn of the nineteenth century.[41] The connection to Fort McKay may help explain why his grandson Isadore moved to the community.[42] Another reason may have been that Isadore's cousin, Catherine Janvier, married François Boucher around the same time.[43] Isadore, who like his father Joseph took the surname "Lacorde," could "speak English, French, Cree and Chipewyan" and worked with "the RCMP in Fort McMurray often serving as an Interpreter." The family divided "their time between their regular Fort MacKay home" and "Moccasin Flats in Fort McMurray," where they "would spend the summer living in a tent" working for the Northern Transportation Company Limited (NTCL), which operated a paddle wheeler on the Athabasca River.[44] By the 1950s, Isadore held trapline 1650, and his sons Ernest (Ernie) and McCauley held traplines 2455 and 2457, just outside of Fort McKay. Ernest played a key leadership role in a number of the early Fort McKay Métis organizations founded in the 1970s, including being a signatory on the community's Red River Point 1972 land lease.[45] He married Maggie "LuLu" Powder, the daughter of Alphonse Powder and Louise Boucher. This marriage genealogically connected the three root families yet again, as Ernest's mother was Mary Rose Tourangeau, and his grandmother was Isabelle Piché, while Louise was the daughter of Maurice Boucher, Joseph Boucher Sr.'s brother.[46] Ernie later passed his trapline down to his son Howard Lacorde, who remains a key member of the Fort McKay community and contributed to various knowledge-sharing projects including the Fort McKay Métis book project *Mihkwâkamiwi Sîpîsis: Stories and Pictures from Métis Elders*.[47] In the mid-2010s, Howard joined Fort McKay First Nation to receive housing and access to medical and dental care.[48] Howard's sister Margie Wood remains a member of the Fort McKay Métis community and was a founding board member of the Fort McKay Métis Nation. A number of the descendants of Isadore Lacorde are members of the Fort McKay Métis Nation.[49]

The Beaver–Faichney family originated from Felix Beaver, who similarly married into the Fort McKay community.[50] Felix was a Cree–Métis person who moved originally from the Chipewyan Lake region.[51] Felix's father, Julian

FIGURE 2.5 Ernie Lacorde with Alex Boucher circa 1980. Bill Jorgensen Collection. https:// billjorgensen. zenfolio.com/ p994248149

Beaver, used to guide scows down the Athabasca River, and it was probable that this experience acquainted him with the Fort McKay community.[52] By moving to Fort McKay, he was likely following the path of other future Fort McKay First Nation members, specifically the Ahyasou and Orr families who joined the Fort McKay First Nation in the 1920s.[53] As the Ahyasou and Orr families were members of the Bigstone Cree First Nation, their transfer to the First Nation was administratively simple. Felix Beaver did not similarly join the Fort McKay First Nation, likely because his parents, Julian Beaver and Augustine (Joustine) Cardinal, were not members of Bigstone Cree First Nation (though there is no evidence that Beaver or Cardinal took Métis scrip).[54] Nonetheless, Felix was welcomed to the community, marrying Marianne Boucher in 1933.[55]

Marianne was the daughter of François Boucher and Catherine Janvier, with François being an original Fort McKay First Nation member and Catherine, as noted above, being Isadore "Lacorde" Janvier's cousin.[56] Felix's marriage into the Boucher family and his language skills (he spoke Cree and understood Chipewyan) helped him easily become a welcomed community member.[57] Marianne and Felix lived at Jackfish Lake north of Fort McKay in the willows, where their first child, Emma, was born.[58] The Beaver family lived there until Emma was about five years old, when they moved closer to Fort McKay, likely so she could attend the recently constructed day school.[59]

FIGURE 2.6
Betty Ducharme, Marianne Beaver, Mary Beaver, and Felix Beaver with a collection of furs circa 1950. Barb Faichney collection.

Emma Beaver went on to marry white fur trader Ian Faichney in 1955, and they raised a ten-person family on trapline 2137.[60] Like Felix, Ian's marriage to Emma was welcomed into the community, and the Faichney family would go on to have a very influential role in Fort McKay's development. Emma became recognized as a key Knowledge Holder, a role she passed onto her daughter Barb.[61] Ian and Emma's son Roger became president of the Fort McKay Métis in the 1990s and 2000s, and their other sons Arnold, Brucie, and Glen took various leadership positions and managed the family trapline at different times.[62] Again, some members of the Faichney family chose to join the Fort McKay First Nation for housing, economic, and medical reasons, though Barb's daughter Janice Richards and Arnold's son Felix Faichney have both served as Fort McKay Métis Nation councillors.[63]

FIGURE 2.7
Marianne Beaver with her "pet wolf" circa 1950. Barb Faichney Collection.

By the turn of the twentieth century, the Bouché, Piché, and Tourangeau families were well established at Little Red River with genealogical roots that extended back over 100 years, including French Canadian voyageur, Dené, and Cree ancestors. It seems likely that through much of the nineteenth century, the majority spoke Dené on a day-to-day basis, though most were increasingly adopting Cree as well, as it was the language of the fur trade.

In the first decades after the signing of Treaty 8 and the offering of scrip, a number of migrants, mostly single Métis working men, moved to the region, married local women, and integrated into the community. It is important to note that there is little evidence that any of these newcomers attempted to change the community in any meaningful ways; instead, they seemed to have adopted the community's languages and cultural norms as their own and, within a single generation, were fully integrated into the Fort McKay community, with their children connecting into the local kinship network and adopting the bush economy.

The community's shared history, kinship network, and reciprocity were key to the development of Fort McKay and the bush economy, which provided for the whole community. By sharing the land and resources with fellow community members, welcoming newcomers who were willing to share, and largely ignoring external identities ascribed by the government (specifically "Treaty" and "Métis" status), the community was able to remain largely intact. By the 1960s, external pressures brought by industrial development and the government's unequal treatment of community members forced the community to "transition" into something new. This process was "frightening and disorienting promoting insecurity within individuals" and forced community members "more and more into a world which is heterogeneous, where emphases upon personal relationships are of lesser importance; where one does not have a personal knowledge of associates and co-workers, bureaucracies, government industry and assorted other impersonal entities."[64]

Before this forced adaptation, the community of Fort McKay remained deeply invested in the bush economy. This, along with close kinship bonds, facilitated reciprocal relations and provided a mechanism for the community to easily welcome newcomers who were willing to adopt the community's practices.

3

The Bush Economy and the Registered Trapline System

As the previous chapter explained, the members of the Fort McKay community have always maintained a close connection to the land, moving with the seasons for sustenance. Since the late eighteenth century, trapping and hunting to produce commodities for sale have been part of their land-based activities. Several scholars have demonstrated that participation in the fur trade was an essential characteristic of many of the communities in Athabasca country beginning around the same time and extending well into the twentieth century, with only the changing fur market and industrial development in the mid-twentieth century placing considerable strain on the fur trade in Indigenous communities in northeastern Alberta.[1] This chapter will explore the history of the fur trade in Fort McKay and how the trade influenced the development of the Fort McKay Métis community. All the key historic families described in the section above actively participated in the fur trade economy before "effective control." Their families continued to trap throughout the twentieth century and even into the twenty-first century. However, that continuity of culture, economy, and land use was badly disrupted in the 1960s due to the expanding oil sands industrial complex.

By the early 1900s, the region was attracting outside white trappers who began disrupting the traditional "Indian trapping economy." The majority of these trappers came north, viewing the region as an untapped resource where profits could be maximized by using poison and other "modern" techniques that were typically avoided by Indigenous trappers, if for no other reason than because they often ate the meat provided by animals they trapped.[2] This intrusion continued to intensify and reached a tipping point in the 1920s and 1930s, as described in "From Where We Stand":

> The next major wave of influence and restriction accompanied the invasion of white trappers during the 1920s and 1930s who were fleeing the Great Depression at a time when fine fur prices were high. They came into our hunting and trapping territories in droves. This inevitably led to competition and/or conflict and considerable amount of racism where the European notion of land and resources collided with ours within our territories.[3]

The creation of the trapline system was partially developed as a response to these disputes.[4] White trappers lobbied the provincial government to be able to control trapping areas directly, and the wildlife department wanted to be able to accommodate them. First Nations lobbied Indian Affairs for the removal of white trappers from their lands, and some, such as the Cree and Chipewyan Bands of Fort Chipewyan, called for the creation of exclusive Indian game-hunting preserves. While the federal government contemplated the establishment of such areas, none were formally implemented. The Métis had little formal voice but presumably made their arguments through their First Nations relatives. From at least the early 1920s, Indigenous people in northern Alberta had been calling for measures to protect their access to game, prompted also by the establishment of the Wood Buffalo National Park in the Northwest Territories and northern Alberta in 1922 and 1926.[5]

The conditions shaping the discussions between Indigenous people and the federal government over game preserves for Indian hunters were affirmed by the transfer of control over natural resources from federal to provincial jurisdiction in 1930. Section 12 of the transfer agreement concerned Indian harvesting rights:

> In order to secure to the Indians of the Province the continuance of the supply of game and fish for their support and subsistence, Canada agrees that the laws respecting game in force in the Provinces from time to time shall apply to the Indians within the boundaries thereof, provided, however, that the said Indians shall have the right, which the Province hereby assures to them, of hunting, fishing and trapping game and fish for food at all seasons of the year on all unoccupied Crown lands and on any other lands to which the said Indians may have a right of access.[6]

As noted by H.W. Theisen, the provincial legislation that followed the transfer of resources to the province included:

> Ch. 43, The Provincial Lands Act, assented to on 28 March, 1931. Section 72(1)(b) allowed for the setting aside of lands for Indians in fulfillment of treaty obligations. Ch. 44, The Alberta Forest Reserves Act, assented to on 28 March, 1931, among other things, provided for the preservation of game. Ch. 71, The Water Resources Act, assented to on 28 March, 1931 transferred authority for the administration of water from the federal statutes to Alberta. It made no mention of Indians.
>
> This was the first time since 1870 that the administration of Crown lands, and the regulation of game was the responsibility of a single government: Alberta.[7]

Regulation and control of the fur trade were initially provided by various licensing arrangements, fur stamps, and closed seasons. As early as 1933, provincial authorities indicated their preference for a registered trapline system similar to the one that had been introduced in neighbouring British Columbia in 1925.[8] Legislation was passed in 1939, and formal implementation began in the 1940s, though it was not fully implemented until the 1950s.[9]

Under the new licensing and registration system, the federal government agreed to pay the province for Indian trapping licenses. Licenses for Métis people did not have a special process, nor were they differentiated in the records, though federal agents themselves often distinguished between "half-breeds" and "whites"; largely, however, Métis and First Nations were lumped together in their discussions and recommendations. For example, on February 9, 1938, Fort Chipewyan Indian Agent Dr. P.W. Head asked for clarity regarding muskrat and beaver laws as conflict between "Treaty Indians, Treaty Halfbreeds, non-treaty Halfbreeds and White trappers" was increasing.[10] By 1939, the concerns had reached a boiling point with the two Fort Chipewyan Indian Bands supported by local Métis community members complaining to a sympathetic reporter about how local game restrictions were contributing to regional suffering and starvation.[11] Presumably, in an attempt to deal with some of these conflicts, N.E. Tanner, the provincial minister of lands and mines, seemed willing to entertain a federal plan to create a "trapping and hunting grounds for Half-Breed and Indian population of Alberta" as a solution for "the difficulties with which they must contend."[12]

Tanner's letter suggests that as late as 1938, the provincial government was considering the idea of creating larger trapping areas for Alberta's "Half-Breeds and Indians," and later, correspondence from the federal government went as far as to propose where such areas could be located.[13] Disagreements over the terms and limits of Indian trapping permits are well documented between federal and provincial agents in and around the Fort McKay traditional territory, just when the provincial trapline system was implemented. Indian Agent Dr. P.W. Head articulated the federal government's position when he stated that "Fort McKay Indians" trap "mainly in the Birch Mountains to the West of Athabaska River (*sic*) and North of the 25th Base Line. This area, like Poplar Point, is uncharted to great extent and should be covered by a blanket permit."[14] The federal Indian agent argued in favour of the province issuing blanket permits to Indians in the area. The provincial response is not included in the record. However, in the federal record, we learn that the Alberta government disregarded the request and stated that it "would not issue blanket permits."[15]

The next series of correspondence begins with a memorandum written by Mr. J.L. Grew in December 1944. Grew discussed the "two most difficult problems that beset the Indian trapping situation in Alberta." These were "the payment of fees by Indians and the removal of white trappers from traditional Indian country." He then suggested ways to "solve" the "difficulties," including a proposal to create set-asides or group areas for Indigenous people in areas that were traditionally used by communities. Accompanying this proposal is a series of maps showing two areas encompassing much of Fort McKay's traditional territory. The first region outlines a "2,650 square mile" area near the Firebag River with "14 Indians registered [. . .] 1 or 2 Indians without lines; about 5 half-breeds and possibility 1 or 2 whites included." The area was described as "badly burned over and overtrapped" but would "present fewer difficulties in organization because of the small number of whites to move," with the "Indians not [being of] a particularly good class morally but [are] good hunters." The second region was described as a "3,750 square mile area" centred around Namur [Moose] Lake and was noted to contain "at least 24 Indians registered [. . .] 11 Indians without lines; 8-10 half-breeds and 2 or 3 whites." Similarly, the report states that these were "not particularly good type of Indian although most of them [are] good trappers and hunters."

MAP 3.1

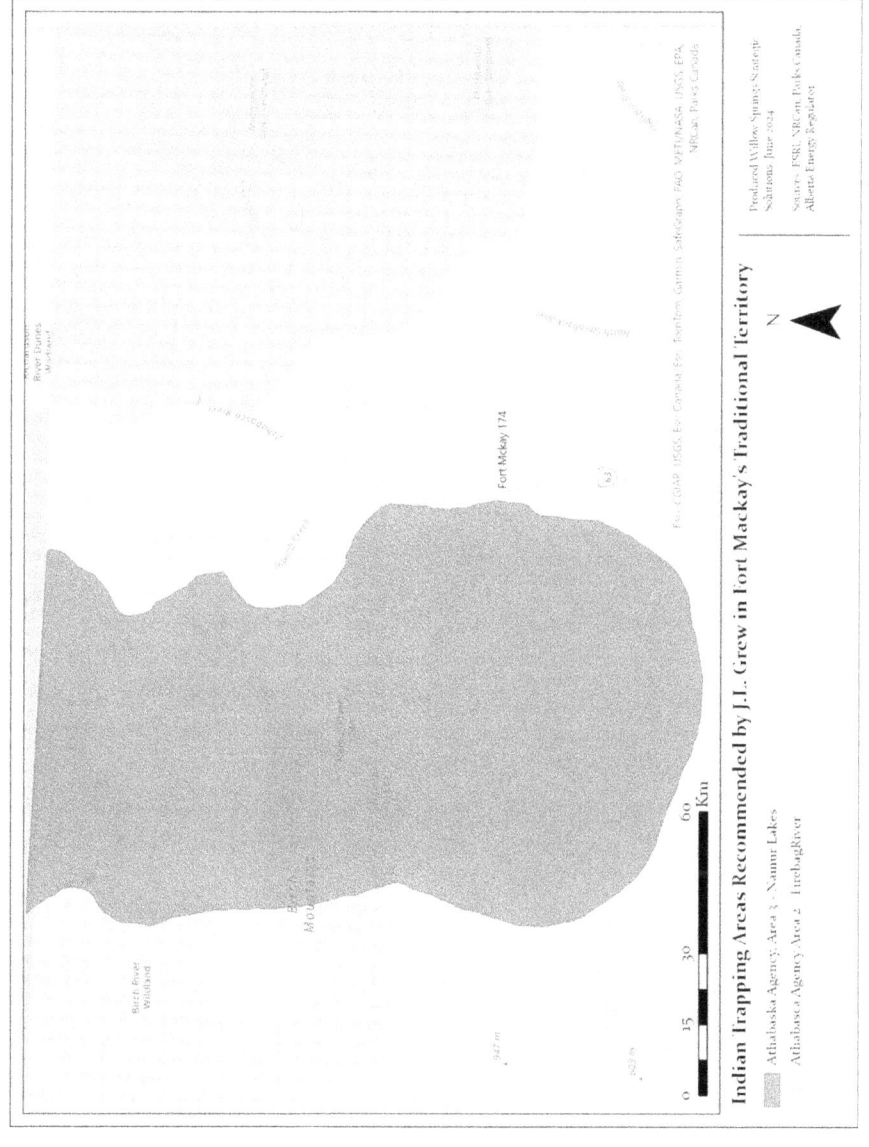

While this statement suggests that the writer held Indigenous people in low esteem, it also demonstrates that the government recognized the importance of these areas to the community of Fort McKay.[16]

It is not particularly surprising that the report understated the number of Métis people in these areas. Mr. Grew was responsible for "Indians" in the region and did not have good census information for Métis people. As later data shows, the number of Métis community members was likely higher than he recorded. Nonetheless, the memorandum underscores the fact that the federal government of the day recognized that areas both east and west of the Athabasca River were traditionally used by Fort McKay Indigenous people and believed they could and should be set aside for the creation of an Indigenous hunting and trapping territory. It also supports the assertion by Fort McKay Métis that the federal government has long recognized these areas for traditional land use by both the Métis and the First Nation.[17]

The provincial government did not support Mr. Grew's recommendation to establish Indian-specific areas. Instead, the province implemented a registered trapline system where individuals controlled specific lines and areas. Despite this direction, J.L. Grew, in a 1945 report, discussed how Indian Affairs continued to push for the establishment of "Indian blocks" through unofficial means, stating that "provincial field men have been very helpful in securing trapping grounds for the Indians." Grew explains that the provincial field men were similarly "anxious to have the Indians grouped as far as possible in areas where they are free from interference with white or non-treaty trappers."[18] Grew, working with provincial "field men," did his best to group Indigenous trappers together, in practice creating de facto Indian blocks, but without official provincial sanction in law or policy. In the Athabasca region in particular, Grew mentions that local Indigenous communities were concerned that white trappers were moving into their traditional land use areas and causing "friction." Within the registered trapline system, Grew preferred to create a "block of Indian lines or areas" where the agents and province might have "better control" over their activities. The report refers to "at least 32 trappers . . . out of a possible 45 to 50" from the Cree–Chipewyan Band who had been able to secure lines, many in the Birch Mountains–Namur Lake area.[19] It does not speak to how many Métis community members also secured lines, but later trapline maps show that a significant proportion of Fort McKay Métis community members were also successful. The fact that federal Indian agents attempted to ensure that Indigenous trappers obtained licenses under Alberta's registered trapline system in blocks within their traditional and customary harvesting areas to avoid potential conflict with non-Indigenous trappers is significant. It indicates that Fort McKay's claims to areas within their traditional territory predate the registered trapline system and are not purely a product of it. The concentration of Fort McKay traplines is evidence of a long history of community land use in the area.

Fort McKay's use of the region is not simply because of the abundance of community members' traplines post-1940. Additionally, the provincial government's refusal to officially adopt a block system suggests a deliberate attempt to downplay the collective character of land use in the province. Since the registered trapline system was based on individual ownership of traplines rather than collective or community use, Indigenous trapline holdings in the region could be jeopardized over time if registered traplines — now Registered Fur Management Areas — become increasingly fragmented and divided between Indigenous and non-Indigenous trapline holders. The Fort McKay Tribal Administration was not far off when it claimed that "the registered trapline system was the first major attack upon and restriction on our way of life and economy within our territories."[20]

Even registered traplines in the Fort McKay traditional territory were organized around interconnected family groups to the extent they could do so within the registered system. That helped limit disputes amongst the trappers and helped community members continue to trap in ways they had always done. As stated by W. B. Skead in his 1948 Alberta fur supervisor's annual report:

> The principal difficulty is encountered in that it is the nature of the Indian trapper to operate in family groups and bands and they do not seem to be inclined to confine themselves to a fixed line or area. This is particularly so in the North. There is difficulty, too, that the Indian does not know the exact location of his line or area and the existing maps being what they are the local Ranger is faced with an almost insolvable [sic] problem in trying to show line or area locations to an Indian in a very inaccurate map.[21]

Skead was obviously wrong in claiming that the Indians did not know where their lines were located; they were hardly lost in the bush. Instead, it speaks to a disconnect between those trappers and attempts to record the lines on official maps.

In the late 1950s and early 1960s, the Forestry Department created maps representing the traplines across the north, with a second group produced roughly ten years later. These maps provide a provincial government record specifying who held or "owned" individual lines over time.[22] The maps were created to enable administrators to identify, on one map for the first time, the location of traplines held by those who had registered leases with the government. At first, specific trapping areas and lines were hand-drawn with coloured pencils on aerial maps. The government created two series of maps, one using the 1957 aerial maps and a second using the 1967 aerial maps. The first set includes names on the maps, whereas the 1967 series only contains numbers that had to be cross-referenced with registration cards. This was likely done because the ownership of the lines and areas could be easily transferred and were, sometimes yearly. It is unclear when exactly the maps were created, though it seems likely that they were produced shortly after the aerial maps were made. Administrators used geographic details about trapping areas and trapline locations to regulate trapping activities and licensing. Another important difference between the two series of maps was the shift to using trapping "areas" nearly exclusively in the second series. What this meant was that the initial registered traplines, which had formalized trappers' customary long "lines" that followed creeks and rivers for upwards of forty miles (and sometimes crossed with other trappers' lines), were redrawn to bounded registered "areas" that were easier for government to administer. The Fort McKay Tribal Administration argued that this policy change had a major detrimental effect on the community: "As a result of this imposition, our people were forced to change the way they did their trapping. They were expected to just move over. Cabins, trails, caches and many improvements were rendered useless as our peoples' registered trapping lines were shifted. There was no compensation whatsoever."[23]

There are approximately twelve 1:50,000–scale maps that detail the area in and around the Fort McKay traditional territory. As discussed in federal government correspondence, Indian Affairs' preference for grouping traplines together according to family or band membership prevailed. The 1957 map series shows an overwhelming majority of Fort McKay First Nation and Fort McKay Métis trappers controlling lines within the traditional territory, with an estimated seventeen of the forty total traplines being connected

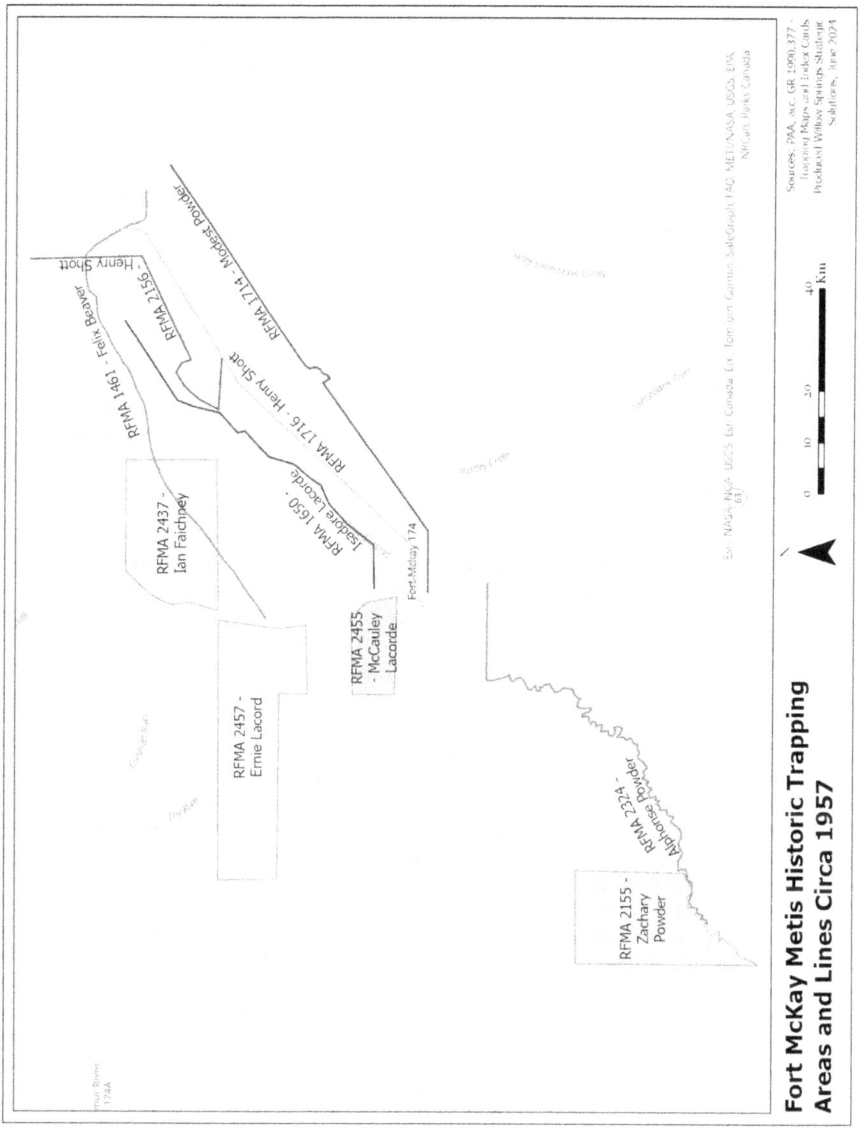
Fort McKay Metis Historic Trapping Areas and Lines Circa 1957
RFMA 1461 - Felix Beaver
RFMA 2156 - Henry Shott
RFMA 1714 - Modest Powder
RFMA 1716 - Henry Shott
RFMA 1650 - Isadore Lacorde
RFMA 2437 - Ian Faichney
RFMA 2455 - McCauley Lacorde
RFMA 2457 - Ernie Lacord
RFMA 2324 - Alphonse Powder
RFMA 2155 - Zachary Powder
Fort McKay 174
0 10 20 40 Km
Sources: PAA, acc. GR 1990.377 - Trapping Maps and Index Cards
Produced Willow Springs Strategic Solutions, June 2024

Map 3.2

with historic Fort McKay Metis members. Those seventeen lines represent the family groups of McDonald, Beaver/Faichney, Lacorde, Powder, Shott, Tourangeau, and others.

It is very likely that there are even more connections between community members and traplines in the region, particularly considering the pervasive interconnectedness among members of the Fort McKay community.[24] However, the Fort McKay Tribal Administration pointed out that the registered trapline/fur management system still caused an overall loss of trapping areas in the community, with approximately "half" of the traplines within the Fort McKay traditional territory in 1983 owned by "non-Fort McKay people."[25] This forced Fort McKay members "to double and triple up on traplines which were in the poorest parts of [their] territory."[26] In 1994, the community again identified the traplines held within the community's traditional territory. This exercise revealed that approximately thirty-five RFMAs belonged to Fort McKay members, and based upon the genealogical analysis, about eleven belonged to Métis community members, with the historic Fort McKay Métis families McDonald, Lacorde, Faichney, Shott, and Tourangeau all being represented.[27] Undoubtedly many First Nations' trapline lease holders had informal Métis connections through marriages and friendships.

While the collective and communitarian nature of Indigenous ties to traditional harvesting areas was not formally recognized through the creation of "Indian blocks," the Alberta government did formalize Fort McKay's ties to its traditional customary harvesting areas. As long as Fort McKay Métis and First Nations members can hold lines in customary trapping areas, the traditional and community character of the area can be assured. However, a clear official policy on how to do this is still lacking. Of course, the traditional character of the area is now in jeopardy as traplines are eliminated by the expanding oil sands industrial footprint.[28] Unfortunately, provincial government records on the creation of the registered trapline system fail to provide detailed information concerning the processes by which Indigenous people obtained lines. This is particularly true when those documents are compared to those from the federal government. This said, the 1933 Alberta legislative debate demonstrates that the issue of traplines was front and centre for the government of the day and that there was a clear understanding at that time that Indigenous people's rights needed to be considered. One of the debaters noted that "the fur trappers" in his northern Alberta "district are 90% Half

Breeds or Indians" who needed to be protected against "migratory trappers" who were increasingly moving into the north.[29]

Provincial documents also outline the erosion of Indigenous ownership of traplines, which accelerated in the late 1960s when a number of Fort McKay traplines were not renewed for various reasons.[30] As detailed by Dawn Balazs, the Government of Alberta wanted to "professionalize" the trapping industry, which conflicted with the view of Indigenous people that trapping was a "way of life" — with community members using their trapping areas to hunt, fish, and gather — rather than a capitalist industry.[31] A comparison of the 1957 and current trapline maps shows that changing provincial policies and increasing industrial encroachment on Fort McKay territory impaired the ability of community members to continue using the land. In 1983, community members stated that "some 25 Fort McKay people who require traplines and who have been unable to get them."[32] This situation has changed little in the modern day, as noted by one participant in the 2016 Fort McKay Métis Nation Integrated Cultural Impact Assessment:

> A long time ago, you have a trap line, that's yours to keep. Yours to make a living on. Nowadays people come in here give ten thousand dollars, here they have already taken over the line, and now companies they got it [the trap line]. Yeah, ten thousand dollars, what the hell is that nowadays? It's ten dollars. Now industry's they come in, they come in to trap line. They tell you, get the hell out I'm taking over and I'll give you this much, don't ever come back. Where the hell is that guy from? But for fifteen thousand, you know, full of baloney, that.[33]

As noted in the above quote, industrial expansion is, today, the most direct source of stress on the local traplines. This pressure began with the Great Canadian Oil Sands mine in the 1960s, and conflict between Indigenous trappers and oil sands development was recognized early on. For example, in 1972, G. A. Kemp, then senior management biologist with the provincial Department of Lands and Forests, Fish, and Wildlife, stated in a memo that it would be "far more difficult" to address the problem of

> the loss of a trapper's right or privilege to trap [for] trapping is a very traditional activity and for many members of this community the fact they can indulge in this type of activity is far more

> important than any financial gains they make from trapping. In short, "the way of life" far out-weighs the financial returns of the activity. Some trappers in the McMurray area have been resident on their traplines for over twenty years. What happens to this individual when he is displaced?[34]

The memo concluded that the Government of Alberta should develop policies regarding the loss of Indigenous hunting and fishing rights in the "Tar Sands," for the "topic" had as of yet been "relatively unexplored."[35]

By October 1974, the issue had reached the desks of Syncrude's Executive Committee, which sought a way to compensate the Indigenous trappers whose traplines would be disrupted by the proposed Syncrude development.[36] A confidential memo spelled out the options for Syncrude regarding three Fort McKay community members who owned traplines in the project vicinity: "Vincent Boucher (Métis), Theodore Boucher (FN), and Francis Orr (FN)." The report noted that all three community members were at least "partially dependent on the lines for income (fur) and food (meat)" and that the Syncrude project would destroy or had already destroyed significant proportions of Vincent and Theodore's lines. While Syncrude's legal department believed the company had no legal reason to compensate the individuals, the public relations department felt it would "be very damaging to Syncrude's public image not to voluntarily agree to a reasonable settlement." The report pointed out that "both men [Vincent Boucher and Theodore Boucher] are natives; both are unskilled and poorly educated; both have families to support; both are in ill health" and that "a voluntary settlement with both men, based on reasonable guidelines, would be a strong demonstration of good corporate citizenship and social responsibility."[37] Syncrude's memo recommended that the company should develop a compensation guideline that would provide each affected trapper the average annual earnings over the pervious three years "times ten or the number of years to retirement." The memo reiterating that this "matter [should] be decided quickly" as "any delay may result in the issue getting into inflammatory headlines."[38]

While it is clear that representatives in Syncrude's public relations department understood the potential ramifications of the company completely obliterating Fort McKay members' traplines, the Alberta government seemed less convinced. At a meeting between J. J. Barr, representing Syncrude, and Gordon Kerr, the Director of Fish and Wildlife, Kerr agreed to "speak to the

Government of Alberta within a week or two as to whether they support" the proposed agreement. Still, Kerr seemed concerned about "the precedents that this settlement might create for other tar sands developers, and other industries, e.g., Forestry." Barr commented that he found it "interesting that the first thought that came to Kerr's mind was that we [Syncrude] should be compensating the Government rather than the trappers" for the trapline's loss. Kerr stated that in the future, Syncrude should seriously consider "having his group represented in any negotiations with the trappers."[39] While the letter was clear that Syncrude felt it was important to inform the provincial government of its plans, it is also clear that they would not change those plans for fear that it may make the government look bad. As such, Syncrude prepared and delivered offers to the trappers approximately a month later.

Before Syncrude made an offer, Vincent Boucher made a request for $10,000, which the public relations department felt was reasonable based on an average take from the trapline of about $1,000 per year.[40] Boucher's lawyer then sent a letter in mid-December 1974 asking why Syncrude had not paid the requested $10,000, to which Syncrude responded that it required evidence from the claimant, such as an income tax return, before it would consider the offer. In early January, Syncrude moved forward with a counteroffer for $6,500, which was accepted once Boucher agreed to sign a release with the company.[41] Syncrude also reached an agreement with Theodore Boucher to provide $1,591.56 in compensation, which seemed to be based on how many furs he had trapped in the three years prior, as outlined in the Syncrude memo above.[42] Given that Syncrude's lease only crossed a small portion of Francis Orr's trapline, no compensation seems to have been given at the time, and, as shown in the section below, was the beginning of a deteriorating relationship between Orr and Syncrude that would boil over in the mid-1980s.[43] No compensation was paid to anyone for the loss of other valued bush products, especially bush foods.

Trapline compensation appears to have been a complicated matter in the mid-1970s, and there seemed to be little, if any, willingness by provincial officials to recognize the potential impacts of industrial development on Indigenous people.[44] Further, it is fair to state that both the companies and the government were concerned that trappers were now viewing their lines as "economic opportunities," something that would "bring them money in the future through compensation by oil companies ready to develop their leases."[45] However, such a view failed to recognize the importance of traplines to

FIGURE 3.1
Francis Orr on his trapline, 1978. Terry Garvin Collection.

the community as a cultural space that allowed for a way of life or as a source of livelihood. As outlined by Fox and Ross:

> If neither the Department of Energy and Natural Resources nor the Fish and Wildlife Department has the power or the inclination to help the trapper, this leaves the trapper in the unenviable position of having to depend on the goodwill of the company for compensation. This is a bad situation, for the trapper lacks an understanding of the legal system, as well as the education and sophistication to deal with large oil companies [with] compensation for loss of livelihood [being left with] the discretion of the company at this time.[46]

A number of other provincial government pieces of correspondence discuss the need to develop a compensation plan for trappers who are negatively impacted by resource development. However, besides the already referenced

Kemp report, there is little recognition of the Aboriginal rights potentially held by trappers. This policy position was questioned by Fox and Ross, who asked "whether it is sufficient for the government to allow enlightened corporate self-interest to be the sole guiding principle for future negotiations" with trapline holders.[47] Fox and Ross go on to question whether any amount of money would compensate the community for their lost income[48] — a point that is emphasized in later Fort McKay reports and publications.[49] A 1986 *Fort McMurray Today* article astutely observed that "modern trappers (are) caught in a squeeze between encroaching civilization, resource hungry timber companies and government indifference."[50] While the exact numbers are unclear, there has been a dramatic decline over the last fifty years from the number of RFMAs owned in the 1960s. This reality has caused a great deal of concern for the Fort McKay Métis community and is still an issue today.[51]

Fort McKay Métis community members, and Fort McKay community members as a whole, still believe that the traplines are essential to the Fort McKay "way of life," not just for trapping but for other bush products as well. There are at least eight traplines still used regularly by Fort McKay Métis community members, and the community would like more traplines for their members, particularly if they could have a greater role in managing the negative impacts of industrial development more effectively.[52] It is important to understand that traplines have *always* been more than commercial leases. As perceptively recorded in *There Is Still Survival Out There*:

> All [community members] remember childhoods in the bush economy, and fondly recall trapline life. The term "trapline" as used in this study means more than just a place to harvest furs for sale on the commercial market. It means the territory where people hunted, fished, picked berries, gathered duck eggs and trapped fur for local domestic consumption and trade. The trapline was the community food supply for the people interviewed in this TLUOS; it was and is synonymous with meat for the table; with stewardship of all natural resources; with extended family sharing; with the socialization of children; with the role of the elders as carriers and teachers of traditional environmental knowledge; and with cultural sustainability.[53]

In short, traplines are areas where Fort McKay people continue to go out and practice their traditional livelihoods, similar to how they did in earlier times. Their continued use demonstrates the Fort McKay Métis's connection to the historic community. The Métis community's response to oil sands encroachment will be analyzed in more detail in chapter 5, but first, I will set the stage with an examination of the uncertain legal title that the Métis of Fort McKay had to the lands on which they had resided for hundreds of years.

4

Land Tenure in Fort McKay: "Split Our Very Identity into Two"

Land has always been important to the community of Fort McKay. The deep and intertwined family interconnections were responsible for using and governing the lands over a large geographical space, and boundaries to this space were fluid and not easily mapped in a European fashion. As noted earlier, the Fort McKay Tribal Council stated: "Since time immemorial we have roamed this land, lived from this land, and been part of this land. To separate us from this land would be to split our very identity in two."[1] In the twentieth century, external government and industrial pressures would force Fort McKay members to adapt to a new land-management regime meant to reduce land availability as they strived to maintain their traditional bush-based way of life. The following two chapters will look at how the community of Fort McKay managed their land over roughly one hundred years. The first will focus on how the community worked with government to secure permanent land tenure to build the community. The next chapter will focus on the community's response to extractivism, which greatly challenged the community's use and management of the land from the 1960s onward. Together, both chapters provide further examples of how the Fort McKay Métis grew in the twentieth century to become a contemporary self-governing Métis community in close partnership with the Fort McKay First Nation. It will also show how the government attempted to split the community "into two" and how the Fort McKay community resisted and adapted to keep their community whole.

The ancestors of the modern Fort McKay community, given the highly mobile nature of their land use, did not have, nor need, a secure form of land tenure prior to 1960. When First Nations members entered treaty in 1899, they were worried that they might be forced to live on reserves, which had become places of impoverishment for other First Nations in the Treaty 6 area. The treaty commissioners assured the signatories that would not be the case, and it seems doubtful the treaty would have been signed had access to "their traditional economy and freedom of movement" not been guaranteed.[2] As treaty commissioner James Ross stated at the time of the Lesser Slave Lake Treaty 8 negotiation: "As all the rights you now have will not be interfered with, therefore anything you get in addition must be a clear gain."[3] Thus, community members in 1899 believed their lands would remain open and managed locally so everyone could hunt, fish, and trap, as they always had, in a "collective title" or local Indigenous commons. This desire to keep managing the land communally also helps to explain why community members who chose scrip most often chose money scrip over land scrip.[4] Those who chose scrip lived a similar (if not identical) lifestyle to those who chose treaty, and a promised land allotment in the agricultural frontier far south of the community would have little if any value. Rather, a money scrip would provide a valuable asset they could easily sell to improve their trapping outfit, even if scrip buyers never paid full value for their purchases.[5]

Despite the signing of treaty and taking of scrip, little changed for the community until well into the twentieth century regarding land uses and land-use management. As described by the Fort McKay Tribal Administration, at the beginning of the trapping season: "There would be a meeting of the trappers to decide upon their trapping areas and in that context any other issues of importance would be brought forward and discussed."[6] People built log houses where they were needed, and with the land being plentiful and land-use conflicts being few, there was very little that the community could not work out amongst themselves at these meetings. The first pressure on this lifestyle came approximately a decade after the treaty and scrip commissions. This resulted from white settlers moving into the district (primarily south near Fort McMurray) in hopes of taking advantage of oil and mineral exploration to the north around present-day Fort McKay.[7]

Land speculators moved to Fort McMurray around this time and attempted to assert various claims to land in the region, but without a proper survey, such claims could only be guarded through squatter's rights and evidence of land "improvements."[8] For example, by 1909, Charles Gordon had fenced off two thousand acres south of Fort McMurray, attempting to evict people from the area based on his unsubstantiated claim.[9] Stories of such conflict undoubtedly reached Frank Oliver in Edmonton by 1910. Oliver, the owner of the *Edmonton Bulletin* and the Canadian minister of the interior, was no stranger to the use of land speculation as a land settlement tool. He understood how such activities could increase immigration into previously sparsely settled regions like Fort McMurray.[10] As such, he took a personal interest in the region and, in 1910, directed surveyor Henry Selby to inspect the occupied lots for those wishing to settle while also surveying adjoining lands "for which a demand may be seen in the future."[11] Selby began the difficult task of sorting through the competing claims in July of that year. He completed initial surveys in both Fort McMurray and Fort McKay but unfortunately died in a river accident. However, the government would use his draft records to settle the majority of the claims.[12] The work seems to have been completed and approved in late 1911, and Fort McMurray lots were advertised for sale in the *Edmonton Journal* by June 1912.[13] Dominion Land surveys to the north of Fort McMurray would be completed a few years later in 1914–15.[14]

At around the same time as the surveys were moving north of Fort McMurray, the Department of Interior was applying pressure to the Department of Indian Affairs to begin assigning reserves in the region. The Department of the Interior informed Indian Affairs about its plans to begin a formal survey of the Fort McMurray area, which would include lots just five kilometres south of Fort McKay. Even though a preliminary survey of lots was completed in 1898 (by the Hudson's Bay Company) and drafts completed in 1911 by Selby, members of the Cree–Chipewyan Band (the precursor to the Fort McKay First Nation) had "refrained" from choosing their treaty land, only asking to keep the land where they had already built houses along the Athabasca River near the present-day community.[15] By 1914, the status quo would evidently no longer stand. The Department of the Interior planned to initiate another survey in the region to open it up for settlement, petroleum exploration, and potentially a new railroad. It informed Indian Affairs, which prompted the latter to survey the reserve lands for the Cree–Chipewyan Band provided for by Treaty 8.

Donald F. Robinson undertook this survey in 1915. Robinson had already completed several Indian reserve surveys throughout the west and was well situated to complete the work.[16] Unfortunately for Robinson, the details of earlier surveys completed in the region were not shared with him, and he was quite surprised to learn that the people at Fort McKay already had what they thought was a survey in place to organize the whole of the community. As Robertson reported:

> The work [in Fort McKay] was considerably increased by my finding that the Indians desired land on the river at this point and that they had a number of houses in what is now known as McKay Settlement. This was at variance with the information I received before leaving Ottawa, and as a consequence I had not with me any information regarding the Department of Interior settlement survey at that point and lands adjoining same, as information on our files showed all lands desired by Indians in this district a considerable distance from the river.[17]

Robinson described some of the "variances" he had to sort through:

> In laying out this settlement and taking declarations from squatters, the rights of these Indians appeared to have been disregarded by the surveyor for the Department of the Interior, nor am I able to find in his report published in the Topographical Surveys Report for the year, any mention of the conditions there. Even an old Indian graveyard is included in Lot No. 4 on which Elzear Robillard made declaration.
>
> <u>Re Lot 5:</u> This lot is on the settlement plan as belonging to the Hudson's Bay Co. On this lot are two Indian houses and gardens, which have existed there even previous to the first Hudson's Bay post at that point. One of these belongs to Chief Adam Boucher, who has had his residence there long previous to Treaty, in fact for 20 to 30 years. This information I consider authentic, since I obtained it not only from Boucher himself but also from Jno. MacDonald who was one of the first, if not the first man in charge of a trading post at Ft. McKay for the Hudson's Bay co., and he stated that Adam Boucher was in possession of his location before the Hudson's Bay Co., first traded there.[18]

Robertson recommended that Lots 5, 6, 7, 9, and 10 be provided for First Nations people, although that would not provide the local Indian band with legal title to those lots. The other lots remained with the other claimants, most of whom were Fort McKay community members who had taken scrip in 1899–1900. Neil Reddekopp concluded that the land recommended for the Band "fell well short of the full reserve status promised to the Cree–Chipewyan

Band in 1912"[19] with the only substantial reserve land available to the First Nation being 257 acres surveyed on the east side of the Athabasca River, with that land "not being considered suitable for settlement" and 7,715 acres at Namur (Moose) Lake, which the government believed "would not invite settlement for some time." [20]

It seems doubtful that the surveys meaningfully changed the organization of the Fort McKay community for some time. Most Indigenous families were not full-time residents at Fort McKay, making only temporary visits to the community to sell furs and acquire supplies, meet with family and friends, and sometimes take summer employment, usually with Northern Transportation Company Limited (NTCL), which operated the paddle wheeler on the Athabasca River.[21] However, over time, these visits to Fort McKay lasted longer, and community members began to build more permanently in the community, even though they did not have title to the land on which they were building. The federal government recognized this fact and asked the Dominion Land Surveyors in 1922 to reserve Lots 7, 9, and 10 "for individual treaty or non-treaty Indians by which it is sufficient that the lands claimed be reserved for them during their occupancy thereof". However, it seems only Lot 10 was actually set aside for settlement.[22]

After the Second World War, a number of significant changes were on the horizon that would affect Fort McKay. The first concerned education. While some Fort McKay children attended residential school, mostly in Fort Chipewyan,[23] there was no formal education for other children until the first Indian day school opened in 1949. As Rod Hyde explained:

> In 1949 the Department of Indian Affairs wanted to start an Indian Day School in Fort McKay in order to meet their Treaty 8 obligations. They didn't have a teacher or a building, so they asked Father Begin to teach for one year (which became two) using the Church as the school classroom.[24]

The Department of Indian Affairs took over operation of the school in 1951, constructing a new school that same year on the Hudson's Bay Company lease. Although the Department of Indian Affairs managed it as an Indian day school, it actually served the whole of the community, with both First Nations and Métis children in attendance.[25] By the late 1950s, the federal government made school attendance compulsory, and more and more families began to

FIGURE 4.1
Paddle wheeler on the Athabasca River. Fort McKay is in the background. Ca. 1922. Fred Jackson, NWT Archives, N-1979-004: 0116.

FIGURE 4.2
Fort McKay's first school. The church altar is hidden by a screen at the back of the classroom. At this time, Father Begin held daily mass twice a day, and the desks were replaced by pews for each service. Rod Hyde Collection.

establish permanent residence in the community.[26] As one community member explained: "We lived off the land in the past. We had no formal school. [It was not until] the Indian agent said that everybody had to move into Fort McKay to bring kids to school, or they would be charged."[27]

By the mid-1950s, it seems more Fort McKay families were heeding the call of the Indian agent and moving to the west side of the river so they could easily access the recently built school. Unfortunately for them, the land on the west side of the river had not been included in the Robertson survey. Although the federal government had reserved Lot 10 for "Indians," it was unclear who actually "owned" the land, with the Alberta government claiming it had been transferred to them as part of the 1930 Natural Resources Transfer Act.[28]

Additional residents meant that the Department of Indian Affairs needed a larger school. The land ownership situation came to a head when the federal government attempted to build a school on Lot 10, which Alberta claimed it owned. Alberta refused the request and threatened to remove First Nation members from Lot 10 for trespassing if the federal government did not pay for the lease.[29] In response, R. F. Battle, regional supervisor of Indian Agencies, wrote to the Alberta Department of Lands and Forests, describing the existing situation and searching for a solution:

> Briefly, though the Indians reside on Lot 10 on the west bank of the Athabasca River, they have a reserve No. 174 on the east bank, comprising 256.8 acres. We constructed a school several years ago on property owned by the Hudson's Bay Company, and we are now considering the provision of additional facilities to include a second classroom and teacher's quarters. It may be of interest to you to know that a number of non-Indians attend this school; in fact if we were not operating a school there, these non-Indians would be without education facilities.
>
> Naturally, it would be rather unwise for us to enter into a sizable expenditure for a new school if the security of tenure of the Indian residents of the settlement is threatened. I believe we could agree to surrender part or all of the present small reserve in exchange of the lands they occupy on the east bank. This would have to be discussed with them and their approval obtained, but we are anxious to be advised of your Department's attitude

> before embarking on our school construction program planned for this year.
>
> If you do not consider an exchange feasible, I wonder if there is any other basis on which the land occupied by the Indians could be made available. Apparently, the Indians were of the opinion that they occupied land set aside for Indian settlement. There seems to be some basis for this because you will note they all live on Lot 10.[30]

Understandably, the Department of Indian Affairs believed that setting aside Lot 10 would help address the First Nations land situation by providing "more permanent tenure."[31] However, the ownership of the land was still in question. Even though it had been "administratively set aside" in 1922, the Fort McKay lots had not been confirmed by the Department of Indians Affairs through an order-in-council. The provincial government believed it owned the land thanks to the 1930 Natural Resource Transfer Act. In a series of letters exchanged in February and March 1958, both sides agreed that the provincial government would sell the land to the federal government for $3 per acre. However, some federal officials felt this was unnecessary as "lands in use or reserved by Canada for the purpose of the Federal Administration were not transferred to the Province."[32] Or, as put by W. C. Bethune: "Arranging of the purchase of the 32.7 acres [in Fort McKay] should not present any difficulty as the amount involved is less than $100.00. On the other hand, it is somewhat embarrassing to ask for the approval for payment for something that is already possessed."[33] Ultimately, the land in the community was sold to the federal government for the purpose of building a new school and housing for Fort McKay First Nation members, but it was not made a reserve. As Neil Reddekopp explained, before 1960, "very little action was taken by the government to recognize the [Fort McKay First Nation's] territory."[34] The example also provides further evidence that the people of Fort McKay were largely left to manage their land on their own affairs without serious oversight. There was no official recognition of Métis land ownership (individually or collectively) until the early 1970s, with community members continuing to build houses when and where needed, though still mainly on a temporary basis.[35] To sum up, by 1960, few community members had what would be considered permanent residences, and even fewer (if any) could claim ownership of the land to which they lived even though nearly everyone had lived there their whole lives, many for generations.

The ambiguous land tenure situation was also problematic as the Great Canadian Oil Sands Project (GCOS) began its operations in the region in 1967. While there had been exploratory and test oil sands facilities near Fort McKay since the turn of the century, this project was different; its massive scale outpaced anything the community had ever seen. The development would be the beginning of the transformation of Fort McKay and its surrounding lands from a "fur and forest area, to an energy resource frontier."[36] Fort McKay would find itself at the epicentre of the new economy.

❦❦❦

The mid-1960s brought, almost overnight, a massive influx of outside workers who moved to Fort McMurray, creating a "Boomtown in the Bush."[37] The *Fort McMurray Today* and *Edmonton Journal* are filled with stories describing the issues facing Indigenous people in the region, including but not limited to workplace racism, violence, and, in Fort McMurray, the forced relocation of Indigenous people.[38] In Fort McMurray, community members were asking local leaders to "do something" about squatters in "Indian shacks." In response, one anonymous author wrote:

> After reading your article on the Oil Sands Boom in Fort McMurray (Sept. 3) I find myself wondering whether there is really freedom from racial prejudice in this "democratic" land of ours.
>
> Referring to the article, it must be assumed that the Indian and Metis people living in and around Fort McMurray, perhaps longer than the white people, have been disregarded for years as the town lay dormant. Now the white land owners realized the value of these people's property and have come to the dire conclusion: the "Injuns must go!" This problem now confronts the provincial government.
>
> It seems the Indians are "free" to live in any part of this "free" country of ours until we whites have placed a value on their land surpassing their own. If we are to assume that the Indians are Canadian citizens this must be truly a breach of Confederation.

> The Indians having been ousted, the next problem will be, to quote *The Journal*, "finding some place to put them." Perhaps the Alberta Game Farm would serve, as the reference made to these people hardly differs from references to animals.
>
> I am sure if the Indians were given half a chance, the so-called native shacks in the middle of the right-of-way on the proposed bypass highway to the south of town would be replaced by decent, respectable houses in town, not on the fringe, and the Indian citizens would contribute to the growth and development of this new community. This would be a much better solution to the problem than restraining these people from their rightful place in our society.[39]

Fort McKay residents began to face their own challenges around the same time. By 1962, the GCOS project had received approval, and shortly thereafter construction began. Around 1966, the bridge to Fort McKay was completed across the McKay River, officially connecting Fort McKay year-round to Fort McMurray.[40] As described by the Fort McKay Tribal Council:

> Until the mid-1960s, Fort McKay's communication with the south was by winter road in the cold winter months and by the Athabasca River during the summer months. Then in 1963 came the Great Canadian Oil Sands Company plant and thousands of new people flocked into Fort McMurray. Then came the permanent road linking Fort McKay to Fort McMurray and points south. Then came the loss of berry grounds and traplines and the depletion of fish. Then came the increased competition for the animal and fish resources, and wage jobs, and more cash and less time in the bush, easy access to alcohol and drugs and very little time to adjust and cope with the changes, and no special programs to help them cope with family and community problems, mental and physical stress.[41]

While exploratory roads and cutlines had existed from the 1930s onward, the new permanent road fully connected the community to the outside world. It opened the Fort McKay lands to outsiders with competing land use interests. It also opened Fort McKay to a capitalist economy and ethos that directly

FIGURE 4.3
Bridge leading to Fort McKay crossing the McKay River, ca. 1966. Rod Hyde Collection.

challenged the traditional "Indian economy."[42] The region's expanding industrialization drastically impacted how community members could operate in the bush and harvest their traditional resources. A number of traplines were destroyed without compensation, and hunting, fishing, and berry and medicinal plant harvesting were all negatively affected without any recognition by the provincial or federal governments.[43] These developments built upon the earlier move to town by families who wanted to send their children to school. More and more, residence veered toward the sedentary, with the community of Fort McKay becoming the equivalent of a "single base camp," a location from which people went to the bush for hunting, trapping, fishing, and gathering.⁴⁴

The pressure brought by the coming extractivism forced the community to respond on multiple fronts. First and foremost, they needed to secure land where they could build a permanent community. Second, they needed to protect, as best they could, their lands in the region that were now being transformed by industry and government into a new kind of space for a new type of economy. By exploring these two post-1960s developments, we are provided yet another window into the development of the Fort McKay Métis community and how they continued to chart their path forward to becoming their own unique entity.

❧ ❧ ❧

While not documented, there is a picture of Premier Manning meeting with the leadership of Fort McKay, likely in the summer of 1966, in the leadup to the opening of the GCOS' mine. Given the evidence of this meeting, it seems likely that the premier encouraged the community's leadership to begin organizing. This spurred the creation of the Fort McKay Community Association, which wrote its first letters to the government in the winter of 1967. While the matters discussed at this meeting are unknown, they likely included a wide range of issues facing the community dealing with large-scale industrial development for the first time. It also seems likely that in response, Manning and his team encouraged Fort McKay to organize themselves and engage with the appropriate mechanisms of government to begin dealing with these concerns.

The first official letter from the Association came from Theresa Grandjambe in February 1967 concerning the water quality in the community. Water was being contaminated when Bechtel, the primary contractor for GCOS, emptied its lagoon downstream from Fort McKay into the Athabasca River, making it "not very healthy for us people to drink."⁴⁵ The tone of Grandjambe's letter is mild when compared to what was actually happening. A number of health studies were completed from 1968 onward. By 1973, Dr. C. L. Pearson, the Northern Alberta Health Services medical officer, described a situation in Fort McKay where "for several years gastroenteritis has been prevalent among those enduring the first decade of life, most the result

FIGURE 4.4
Ernest Manning meeting with leaders from the Fort McKay First Nation and Métis community. Date unknown. The picture was shared by Fort McKay community members on a local Facebook page.

of contaminated water supply. Deaths have ensued ascribable to diarrhea of dysenteric origin and frequently water borne."[46]

Grandjambe's letter was sent to the Alberta Rural Development Administration, which was responsible for encouraging "local communities to initiate self-improvement programs."[47] The community development officer assigned to the file, L. Gareau, described Fort McKay as a settlement of "224 people, of native blood; 138 being Treaty Indians and 86 non-treaty" with some of the "Treaty Indians being "located on Crown land leased by Indian Affairs Department, most of the residents are squatters without any control of the land on which they are built."[48] The officer went on at length to explain why he felt the community of Fort McKay was incapable of taking advantage of the Rural Development Program, concluding that:

> While a few of the local people seemed interested in the immediate welfare of the community, and some of the natives have been motivated to go out and undergo training for further employment, there is an apparent attitude of apathy, a lack of foresight, and a complete absence of able leadership at the local level. Therefore, for the present, talking of rural development or of programs of self help is the height of futility. To them, their need is one of outside help, without contribution of their own.[49]

Gareau's conclusion was perhaps not surprising considering the general misunderstanding — or lack of interest — about the impacts that resource development might have on rural Indigenous communities. Given that the water situation in the community was one of many logistical challenges facing Fort McKay, significant attention and investment from government *was* required.

Around the same time (and possibly as a result of the same Fort McKay Association meeting), Ernie Lacorde wrote to the Community Development Branch to request a meeting regarding a number of other issues. The request was granted, and the department agreed to pay for "transportation and food and lodging for a short trip [to Edmonton] if you were well prepared before you came."[50] While minutes were not recorded from the first meeting, a follow-up was held in Fort McKay about a month and a half later, when approximately twenty people attended. The second meeting was organized by S. J. Sinclair, a provincial economic development officer. A wide range of topics were discussed (from trapping to firefighting), but two key community concerns were highlighted: lack of local economic development and land tenure. Specifically, the community wanted the government to help kickstart a community-operated sawmill to provide local employment and address the land-tenure situation for all residents. As Mr. Sinclair reported:

> One other problem that seemed to concern them, is their location of residence which is outside the reserve. Both Metis and Treaty are in the same situation. They were told by the Chief that they had a long term lease, but nothing has ever been shown in writing. What mainly concerns them is, if a new [industrial] development moved in, what would happen in such a case?[51]

The situation, as described by Sinclair, was neither new nor surprising. As shown, community members knew that settlement land had been surveyed earlier (in 1911 and again in 1915). However, they probably did not know that those surveys were never confirmed through an order in council. Furthermore, once the day school was established, and the area's Indian agent told the First Nations members to move across the river so that their kids could attend school, they may have rightly assumed that the federal government would have secured land and housing for them in the settlement. But, although land at Lot 10 was purchased and leased to the Fort McKay First Nation, it was not set aside as reserve land and local people did not seem to fully understand the terms of their residence and why no services were provided on the land.[52] Finally, nothing was done for the Métis community members, who were never provided with secure leases for land on which they could build permanent houses.[53] Despite the building of the school, Métis were in no better situation in 1967 than they were in 1899 in terms of a secure land base.

By 1967, the community of Fort McKay was frustrated and wanted to take ownership (literally and figuratively) of the situation. Representatives of both the Métis and First Nation travelled to Edmonton to meet with the provincial and federal governments to begin what they felt should be a relatively simple process leading to the ideal solution: providing the community with control and ownership over their land so that they could build modern houses. Unfortunately, as they would soon learn, this dream was far from reality and would require years of negotiations that ultimately would not be resolved, at least for the Métis, until 2018.[54]

In October 1968, J. Audibert from the Department of Indian Affairs, Clive Linkletter, a community development officer based in Fort McMurray, and G. W. Fyfe, the chief housing advisor with the Alberta Commercial Corporation, met with the "treaty and non-treaty residents with respect to their submission of September 11th, for housing assistance in the form of materials for repair for a number of their families." There were nine Fort McKay members, two representatives from the federal Department of Indian Affairs, and twelve from the provincial Departments of Municipal Affairs, Lands, and Forests, Human Resources, Welfare, and Community Development.

The meeting was productive. The community members were given the opportunity to express their concerns about land, water, and the lack of economic development. In particular, they "appeared determined to live [in Fort

McKay], so planning of the town site would continue."[55] As the discussion proceeded, the Government of Alberta agreed to continue with a plot survey that would allow community members to continue living together in the settlement. The Department of Indian Affairs committed to providing "$7,000–$8,000" for homes to Indians "as soon as the plans were ready." The Alberta government stated that Métis community members' homes would "have to be purchased and would be subject to assessment and taxes," although who would pay for the houses and lots had yet to be determined. This became a point of contention, with the Métis delegates stating they would prefer the government to provide them with just the land and lumber, which "they could use to build their own home[s]."[56] This last point seemed to raise the question "for further discussion both [by] Fort McKay and by government officials" as to what "was the differences between the policies of the two governments and thereby the kinds of problems being created at the local level." While the details of the conversation remain unclear, the reality was that the people of Fort McKay — a community made up of First Nations and Métis people, which had come together to meet with the government to discuss their common interests — were now being treated in two different ways, according to the different legal statuses of its members.[57] The meeting continued with the group agreeing to work on solutions regarding bus transportation to GCOS, water quality, and derelict homes in the community. The provincial government agreed to send representatives from the Community Development Branch to Fort McKay during the last week of October to continue work on these issues.

Fyfe went on to inform the participants from Fort McKay that "should Government decide to assist them," they would require the community to form "an association or an organized group who would agree to handle the purchasing and distribution of materials." The families in Fort McKay discussed the situation and decided to form a "housing committee" headed by "Mr. Francis Orr (treaty) and Mr. and Mrs. E. Tourangeau (non-treaty)." Based upon his initial appraisal, Fyfe recommended that resources be made available to Fort McKay community members for housing repairs and that the provincial government provide the funds at the meeting that was scheduled for October 23 between Fort McKay and "senior members of the government" so community members could begin making emergency repairs to their houses. At the same time, Indian Affairs stated that it had already processed an order on behalf of the "treaty Indian families" for $2,600 to begin making repairs.[58]

Though the meeting left a number of unresolved issues on the table, it guided a flurry of activities over the next year. On November 4, 1968, Fort McKay forwarded the Fort McKay "committee" names to the Community Development Branch, which included both Métis and First Nations representatives.[59] The committee worked with the provincial Community Development Branch to try to resolve several issues facing the community. On the same day, R. H. Botham from the provincial Planning Branch came to Fort McKay to "check out tentative subdivision designs, and ground conditions." Upon his initial survey, he asked his supervisor a series of logistical questions to help determine how best to subdivide the land, such as where infrastructure like schools would be located, what type of water system would be installed, how many people the settlement should be sized for, how future developments such as Syncrude would affect the townsite, what types of houses were expected, and finally, what was the community's future economic plan.[60]

The provincially funded building materials arrived on November 15. The housing committee then commissioned repairs on community houses, including those belonging to Ernie Lacorde, Richard Loutit, Henry Shott, Alex McDonald, Ian Faichney, Alex Boucher, Zachary Powder, Alphonse Powder, Basil McDonald, Edward Tourangeau, and Freddie Boucher—all Métis community members at the time.[61] Additionally, the committee successfully resolved the busing problem in the community. At that point, Roy L. Piepenburg, the regional superintendent of Vocational Training and Special Services, commented that he "certainly appreciated the co-operation we had from your branch in resolving this problems which effects both Treaty and non-Treaty Indians."[62]

These early meetings demonstrate the community's willingness to work together to address issues of common interest. On November 26, 1969, Provincial Planning Director Noel Dant started "to prepare a basic subdivision design at Fort McKay," which would create about sixty new lots. However, he had to interrupt his work to obtain answers to a number of questions, many of which reiterated points made by Botham in 1968. Specifically: What have the people of Fort McKay been informed or promised? Would the establishment of an "Indian settlement attract other Métis or Indians who may want to locate there? [and] What type of housing will be provided [and] will services such as sewer and water be installed?" Finally, he asserted that "the needs and wishes of the people should be heard and interpreted before any plan is prepared so that the first approximation may be closer to the final plan, without causing unnecessary friction."[63] Unfortunately, this last idea was more wishful thinking than direction, for as time passed, the community's needs and interests increasingly took a backseat to bureaucratic stasis.

On March 10, 1969, J. E. Oberholtzer, the director of Human Resources Development, explained to his manager, G. J. Armstrong, that Indian Affairs had placed "a freeze on all Indian housing for the coming year" and that "consequently, the Indian Affairs Department will apparently not be pursuing the town building plans for Fort MacKay in the immediate future."[64] Though it is not clear, the decision of the federal government to delay their portion of the development seems to have caused the provincial government to also slow their work on the new Fort McKay subdivision that had previously been approved. This episode suggests many of the challenges facing those in government who attempted to kickstart development in the community. The event demonstrates how difficult it was for government departments, particularly between the federal and provincial levels, to work together, especially when there was an overall lack of political will and funding to move forward.

The file remained cold for over a year, until May 1970 when C. J. McAndrews of the provincial Joint Specialist Group requested that a plan for a "permanent settlement at Fort McKay" be presented to the minister of human resources development. McAndrews went on to state that government employee Jim Ducharme should "compile a report and plans with a consensus of recommendations from those most vitally concerned" and that a broad range of provincial government departments (with representatives cc'd on the correspondence) should be consulted to provide input. He added that the opinions of Fort McKay's residents would be "considered" and that contact with the Department of Indian Affairs "may also be necessary."[65]

Ducharme quickly got to work, completing a preliminary report by early July. Ducharme seemed to have a relatively strong understanding of the community and its desire to build consensus.[66] His July 1970 report was based primarily on interviews with key government individuals and internal correspondence generated around the Fort McKay "situation." Additionally, Ducharme drew from his experience as a member of the Northlands School Board and a trip he had made to Fort McKay in 1967. Ducharme planned to present the findings to the community later in the summer.

The first key finding in the report was that "the people of Fort McKay almost totally want to remain in [the same] location" — an assertion they had maintained since their first meetings in 1967. Ducharme wrote that there was no "economic base right at or near the community at this time to justify full scale plans of any real permanent nature." He explained that previous governments had been reluctant to invest in the community, which helped explain some of the long-term problems around health services, food supply, and economic development. He identified the community's problems as follows:

1. Health, apathy – causes – alcohol – susceptibility to disease – little or no education of adults. Lack of proper health services.
2. Taking advantage of lack of sophistication – captive trade – prices exorbitant.
3. Lack of economic base – lack of game from influx of Industrial activity in the general area.
4. Water supply due to oil pollution etc.
5. Métis – Indian. Indian problems in working or co-operating together – Cree – Chipewyan – Metis.
6. Cannot compete in work situation with white and more sophisticated Natives in existing projects at GCOS, etc.[67]

While he did not elaborate on these issues, it is not a leap to correlate them with the stark realities facing Fort McKay, as they were forced to adapt to the changes brought by the extractivism that was undermining the fur trade economy. The population in Fort McKay was largely isolated, and few members had received even a basic education, let alone the technical training that would prepare them to work at GCOS. Further, they were living in homes without basic services and a water supply that was tainted by the region's industrial developers. But perhaps most importantly, they remained without land security.

Ducharme proposed several solutions, including improving housing and providing education (especially for adults), preventive health, and recreational programs in the community. He also recommended that a permanent fix was needed for the water supply and that the government provide the community with some form of land tenure:

> Land plotting for housing so that residents can at least lease their property. The guideline I would recommend here is that the present location of each resident should be considered in a flexible plan to take care of expansion in the same manner.[68]

It is unclear when Ducharme presented the report to the community, but it is known that Fort McKay was beginning to agitate elsewhere. On July 8, 1970, recently appointed Premier Harry Strom drafted a response to Stan Daniels, president of the Métis Association of Alberta, about the lack of progress that was seen in Fort McKay, specifically around water quality in the community, the lack of jobs with GCOS, and the land situation. The premier's response noted the work Jim Ducharme and his supervisor, G. J. Armstrong, were doing on the file and anticipated that Ducharme's report would provide a path forward for the Provincial Executive Council to consider and implement.[69] Unfortunately, it does not seem that the provincial government officials either appreciated the depth of the problems facing Fort McKay or were willing to commit the required resources, or both, beyond planning future meetings. Fort McKay needed action, and they were given bureaucratic stalling.

In October 1970, Ducharme and his colleagues were ready to present their report to the minister responsible for Human Resource Development, R. A. "Ray" Speaker, for a decision. The report was short — only three pages — and focused on key issues. First, it recommended that water be taken from the Athabasca River and treated using a new water treatment plant, which would have to be built. This recommendation was elaborated upon in a separate Government of Alberta report that outlined the possible solutions and found this, though costly, to be the best option given the community's desire to remain in Fort McKay.

Second, the report recommended that the

> Human Resources Development Authority be permitted to co-ordinate negotiations between the "Land Tenure Committee" appointed by Dr. J. D. Ross, Minister of Lands and Forests and the residents of Fort McKay as soon as possible so that housing and community plans can be put into motion.[70]

Third, they recommended that a housing program be initiated once the land-tenure situation was finalized, with the Human Resource Development Authority being permitted to

> co-ordinate negotiations between A.H.U.R.C.[71] and Fort McKay residents; Indian Affairs and Fort McKay residents; and other interested groups such as Indian and Métis Associations and government departments as necessary, to bring the community all available resources toward an effective housing program.[72]

The authors concluded that they were aware of the "many other problems that the community has and is experiencing, such as illiteracy, health, etc., as a result of disruptive outside influences, i.e., oil exploration and the oil sands operations, as well as the general exposure to a growing urban community nearby and all that means to the ecology of the area." Despite this, the report concluded that the "above recommendations, when implemented, will in our minds help immeasurably toward alleviating the basic problems and other necessary services will then have a firm basis for improvement."[73]

Once it was accepted by the Speaker, Assistant Human Resources Officer George Sanderson presented the report to Fort McKay. He stated that the Fort McKay report "was met with favourable acceptance by the Committee," with "general agreement that the report is representative of the true conditions and needs of Fort McKay."[74]

On January 13, 1971, G. J. Armstrong followed up with Fort McKay, sending two nearly identical letters to Phillip McDonald, Chief of the First Nation, and to Ed Tourangeau, who was representing Métis interests. The letters were a response to a petition Fort McKay had sent the government asking for the implementation of the Fort McKay report. The community had apparently (and justifiably) grown impatient with the government's dithering. In response, the government proposed another meeting with the community in late January 1971 to begin more formal discussions about the land and moving toward a land lease agreement like that implemented in other isolated communities.[75]

Unfortunately, by January 1971, frustration had overtaken the Fort McKay First Nation, and Chief Phillip McDonald removed the First Nation from the community's negotiations with the Government of Alberta. Around this time, Indian Affairs agreed to independently start building housing for

First Nations members on Lot 10, which the federal government had purchased from the provincial government. However, it was still not designated as reserve land. In Armstrong's eyes, this move "had the effect [of] encouraging the Treaty Indians to consider that it is not necessary to work with Metis residents to obtain desired benefits [of community land tenure] as they are being looked after."[76] The move also prompted the local Métis to turn to the Métis Association of Alberta (MAA) for support. In the summer of 1971, the MAA sent at least four different representatives, including President Harry Daniels, to Fort McKay in the hope of better understanding and advocating on behalf of the Fort McKay Métis to the government.[77] T. F. Roach of the Government of Alberta's Métis Study Task Force described the situation, appreciating why the Fort McKay Métis

> tried to "go it alone," because the Metis people have the most to lose if the problem remains suspended in mid-air. The Treaty Indians are able to get off-reserve housing. The Metis are not because of the foul up in land. It strikes me as paradoxical that Metis people (the responsibility of the Province of Alberta) are unable to acquire land or housing on Crown Lands vested in the right of the Province yet Treaty Indians seem to have little problem in this area.[78]

Roach recommended that the government attempt to establish a "local Government Authority" to begin selling or leasing lots to those community members without secure land tenure in Fort McKay. Roach noted that he

> could hear the screams from Lands and Forests but possibly it is time to take the issue to them on a specific area, not necessarily on a philosophical level. Saskatchewan is able to accommodate people ahead of Green Zone policies, and I see no <u>valid</u> reason why it can't be done in Alberta.[79]

As alluded to in Roach's letter, since 1948, the Department of Lands and Forests had implemented a policy whereby no new lands in the Green Zone could be easily sold or transferred to a third party, particularly for a "non-productive use" like Indigenous housing. The "Green Zone" was reserved for "forest management planning and protection of important watershed areas" while the "White Zone" was "set aside as land primarily suited for agriculture

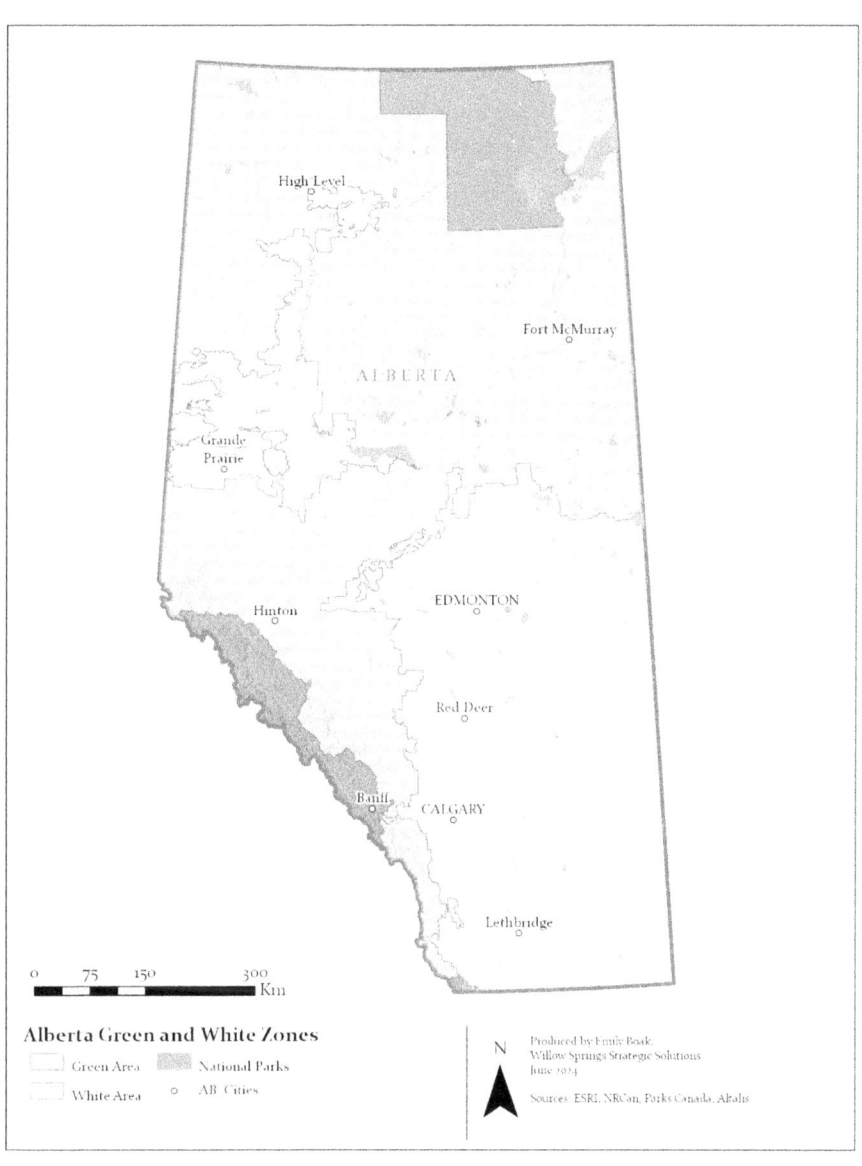

MAP 4.1

4 | Land Tenure in Fort McKay: "Split Our Very Identity into Two"

and settlement." [80] As described by Van Dyke and Loberg, through this policy, the government was "now applying southern land use rules with a pronounced effect on native people in the North" making it virtually impossible for northern Indigenous people to secure free and clear title to land in the "Green Zone."[81]

A week later, Armstrong forwarded Roach's letter to his director, J. E. Oberholtzer, stating he was "particularly interested in the proposal" to establish a "local Government Authority to set out the townsite, sell lots or have direct leases to individuals." He reiterated that the community of Fort McKay had been "in a state of uncertainty for some 4–5 years" and that "it was extremely difficult trying to get the whole of the community to work together, when a portion of the community was being treated differently than the other."[82] He also wrote that he felt it would be difficult "to have the Metis Association or Indian Association representatives work out a proposal without considerable input from outside." In reply, Oberholtzer asked Armstrong to develop a Fort McKay–specific proposal that he could present to the minister with respect to community development and housing, concluding that "although the Community is very slow, the potential via the oil sands is great."[83]

The next day, Armstrong redrafted the recommendations from the Fort McKay report made initially in fall 1970. In this latest letter, he asked the provincial government to establish a Fort McKay task force with the responsibility to allot the land in the townsite, devise a housing program, determine what was required to create a safe water supply, and create a training program so workers "may participate in the Tar Sand Development proposals." Additionally, he recommended that a human resource officer be placed in Fort McKay to support the new local government and that consultation with the whole of the community should continue, but that such consultation "not be confused with consultation with the respective [provincial Indian and Métis] associations." He concluded:

> The Fort McKay situation is serious and of long duration. They have not been able to achieve a co-operative approach in dealing with their problems. Government action has followed the departmental structures in dealing with proposals, but there has been a lack of co-ordination of effort. Decisions have been postponed waiting for firm proposals representing all residents of Fort McKay.

> I recommend that the Government go ahead with a Task Force, representing Departments concerned, with instructions to work out a proposal for Fort McKay, present it to them, and be prepared to negotiate with them for changes in the proposal.[84]

It is unclear what happened with this proposal, but it does not seem that the government ever acted upon it. In 1971, the upstart Progressive Conservative party unseated the Social Credit government, causing a major political change that the province had not experienced for generations. The election of the Progressive Conservative government in Alberta initiated a new era in Alberta politics, and this shift affected northern First Nations and Métis communities, just as it did all Albertans.

One key shift was that the new government showed a preference for working with umbrella organizations rather than with local groups. This is evidenced in the fact that the Métis Association of Alberta got an audience with the premier to present a briefing report titled "The Metis People and the Land Question in Alberta."[85] The brief provides a detailed background of the land-tenure situation for Métis people in the province, as well as a discussion about the current situation and a proposal for future land management.

The new provincial government seemed to believe that the Métis Association of Alberta could be a key part of the solution to the northern land-tenure issue and that long-term leases would sufficiently work around the Department of Land and Forests' long-standing policy of not readily giving land to anyone in the Green Zone. At around the same time that Armstrong was making that suggestion, another Fort McKay committee was established to work with the community as a whole to negotiate a broader land-tenure agreement — a proposal to establish a lease with the "Red River Point Society" on behalf of Fort McKay was sent to the government that would secure land for Fort McKay Métis. The agreement was lambasted by T. F. Roach, who was responsible for heading up a provincial task force examining Métis land tenure throughout the province. He vented that the Red River Point Society lease can be seen as a

> typical example of [Government] working in isolation and, the faults are many. The Métis Association [of Alberta] knows of the efforts made to create a community in Fort McKay. This lease will dispel any immediate prospects of reaching any agreement

in the area. How much consultation took place between Lands and Forests, Municipal Affairs and our office. We are not suggesting a community approach for the mere sake of unity, the Syncrude development could lead to a fairly steady increase in the Native population in Fort McKay. We will find services and/or homes spread around that area if some reasonable controls are not developed real soon. I suppose the Métis people got fed up with the stalling tactics of the Treaty Indians. Nonetheless, we could find ourselves faced with a request from the Treaty Indians for a small tract of land to be set aside as a reserve at Fort McKay Settlement.[86]

Roach was undoubtedly frustrated that years of negotiations and meetings meant to work with the community had failed to secure a land-tenure system. He would likely not have been surprised that the various factions within Fort McKay were looking to take any advantage they could to better their own situations. It should not be forgotten that the Fort McKay Métis and First Nations went together to the government to request various solutions to the community's problems, but there had been very little substantive change that resulted from the five years of meetings.

The establishment of the Red River Point Society and the building of houses by the Department of Indian Affairs on the land it had bought from the provincial government seemed to have addressed the community's immediate need to secure housing and land. However, it also opened a series of new issues. The Red River Point lease did not include the existing houses in the community. Métis members had to move or rebuild between fifteen to twenty houses without funding nor a final community land survey.[87] In 1973, concerns about the continued lack of Métis housing remained. In April 1973, Zachary Powder wrote to Métis Association of Alberta's president Stan Daniels, asking about housing in the community. To this request, Daniels replied that "Hon. A. Adair, Minister without Portfolio, Responsible for Northern Development and Native Affairs is presently preparing Policy regarding the Housing Program," and he had no new information, but that Fort McKay should "remain patient."[88] It seems little information was provided to Fort McKay over the months that followed, and by July, Ed Tourangeau, acting as president of the Métis Association Local, wrote to MAA president Stan Daniels:

Dear Stan,

I'm writing about housing. Our Local had [a] meeting last nite [sic], and I was asked to write.

First:

How soon is the housing going to start here in McKay?

We would like to know if we are going to get those houses or not?

If we're getting those houses would you speed it up and let us know just where we stand?

Didn't Alberta housing start at Fort Chip all ready? I would like to get a reply back soon as possible, as I really need a house badly myself. If I don't get a house, I have to build a shack for the winter and build it at the lease. Also I'll take a picture of it and send it to premier Lougheed. I'll be waiting your answer.

Yours Truly
Edward Tourangeau
President[89]

This letter was followed up with a second, more forceful letter in late August:

Dear Stan Daniels,

We Local #122 would like to see some action this week coming. If we do not hear from you in the next few days all the metis people from Ft MacKay are coming to Edmonton to your office. These promises be[en] going on to [sic] long, always different people and promises, no action.

We will put all these promises and minutes of the meeting in all the proper journals etc. If you can not build right away, how about some trailers or something. We also need a field worker in our area who speaks Cree.

Yours Truly
Ed Tourangeau
President Local #122[90]

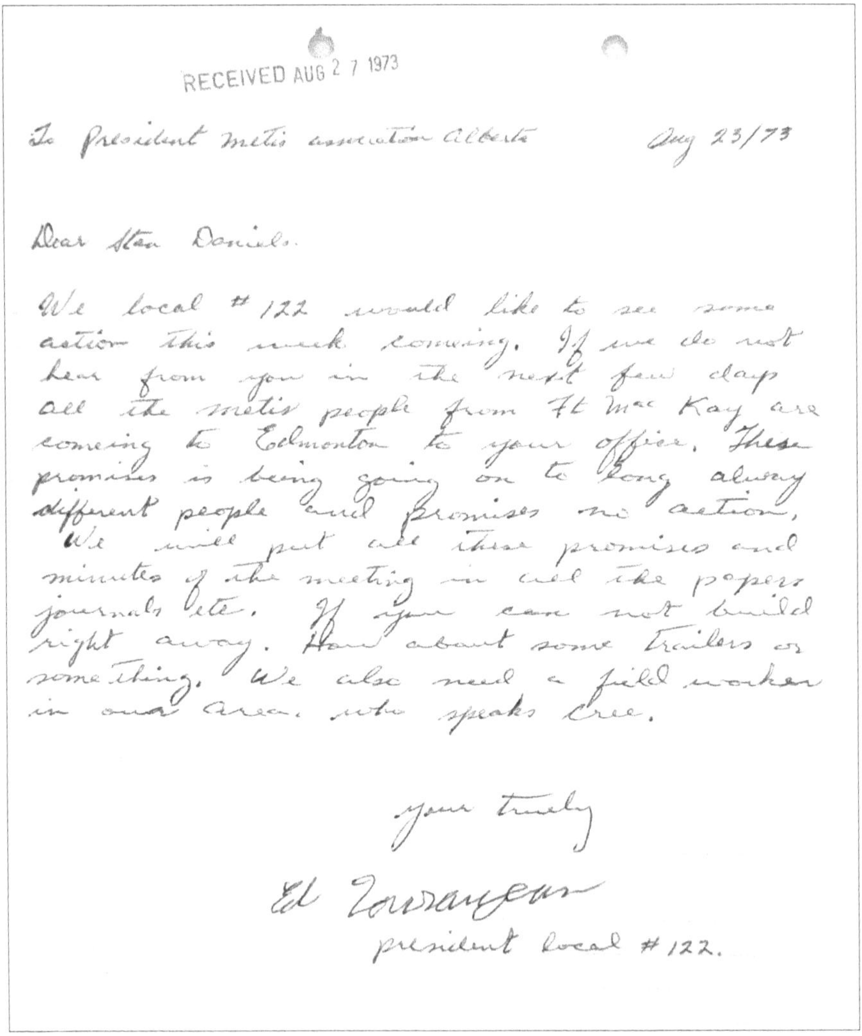

> RECEIVED AUG 2 7 1973
>
> To President Métis association Alberta   Aug 23/73
>
> Dear Stan Daniels.
>
> We local #122 would like to see some action this week coming. If we do not hear from you in the next few days all the metis people from Ft Mac Kay are coming to Edmonton to your office. These promises is being going on to long always different people and promises no action. We will put all these promises and minutes of the meeting in all the papers journals etc. If you can not build right away. How about some trailers or something. We also need a field worker in our area. who speaks cree.
>
> your truely
>
> Ed Tourangeau
> president local #122.

Figure 4.5
Edward Tourangeau to Stan Daniels, July 27, 1973. Glenbow Museum and Archives, M4755, file 470.

Clearly, the Métis in Fort McKay were growing increasingly tired of promises made by outside agencies while being told to "be patient" and wait for the next policy to be unveiled.

It seems that the provincial Métis Association was also growing frustrated. In January 1973, it presented another brief to Premier Peter Lougheed that described the situation facing northern Métis communities. The briefing seems to have moved Lougheed to action. Lougheed initially "made $1,000,000 available through the office of Northern Development to develop a housing program in response to the Métis Association," with the Alberta Housing Corporation to act as the delivery agent, and with a goal to build fifty houses through a partnership with Kainai Industries Ltd.[91] In 1974, the plan was expanded to provide an additional $3,000,000 of funding through the Alberta Housing Corporation in Grand Prairie, Fort McMurray, Edson, Slave Lake, and Fort Chipewyan.[92] The overall objective of the Métis Housing Program was to

> provide adequate housing for those natives who do not have or are unable to provide their own housing at an acceptable standard. In sponsoring a Metis Housing Program, the Alberta Housing Corporation, in cooperation with the Office of Northern Development, will attempt to satisfy the following goals:
>
> (a) Establish a provincial responsibility for providing housing assistance to Metis people.
>
> (b) Assist in upgrading the housing standards of Native peoples.
>
> (c) To encourage a sense of personal responsibility and a pride in ownership through planned maintenance savings and an option to purchase.
>
> (d) To provide not only housing, but a counselling service which will attempt to encourage Native peoples to respond in a positive manner to a new environment.
>
> (e) To provide opportunities for local Native labour to be involved in construction of the units.[93]

While the program was a move in the right direction, it was little more than a drop in the bucket, as the department estimated that there were "approximately 3,800 living on Alberta Crown Land in the Green Zone without satisfactory land tenure agreements".[94] An estimate by the Métis Association of Alberta suggested that just under eighty million dollars would be necessary to build 5,000 homes and effectively address the provincial-scale crisis in the province's north.[95] By March 1974, Alberta Housing built the first three houses in Fort McKay with the program's funds. These dwellings were for Ed Tourangeau, Teckla [sic] Powder, and Clara Shott.[96]

By 1978, little had actually changed for the community. While some Métis members had obtained houses from the Alberta Housing Corporation, the majority were still without houses or were living in substandard houses, temporary houses (tents), or doubling or tripling up with those who did have houses on the 610 acres leased through the Red River Point Society.[97] The community lease did not include provisions for individual lease agreements, a housing authority, or the policies and procedures necessary to manage a community-housing program. Instead, the traditional land-management practices used for generations prior were employed, with the community deciding internally how land would be allotted and housing managed. While this process worked historically, the lease created a new government-mediated relationship with the Red River Point Society obliged to pay rent for the land that most community members could not afford. Furthermore, there was only a limited understanding of the difference between land ownership and land leasing in the community.[98] This meant that while many community members believed that their position had improved because "nobody bothers you if you have your own land," in reality, their position was just as precarious, if not more so, because the lease had confirmed that the government owned the land and they, as a community, were falling further and further into debt every year they failed to pay their rent and taxes.[99]

Van Dyke, in his 1978 report, also noted that the status of the leased land faced the inherent risk of the government ripping up the lease and providing each community member title to his or her own land and then having that land sold to community outsiders. He further stated that if "patent land is acquired, it may also be sold" and that if the economically deprived community of Fort McKay were allowed to sell land for "appreciably large quantities of cash" many would likely take that opportunity and would suddenly become landless, with the purchasers most likely being "whites looking for acreages."

This would likely mean the Métis community members would be forced to revert to "squatting on Crown land," a situation that would play out in other Métis communities in the region in the not-so-distant future.[100] Van Dyke went on to question whether the government would be willing to accept the ramifications of such a "long-term consolidation" that would likely transform Fort McKay from an Indigenous community to a non-Indigenous community and whether this desire for individual control would work against the community's larger goal of maintaining its current demographic makeup and character.[101] This desire to preserve Fort McKay's Indigenous character may help explain why the government did not move to individualized land ownership, which would have likely led to the loss of much of the land base that the Red River Point lease agreement established. One also cannot help but wonder whether the government was concerned about how a "white" community might react to living in the same situation with massive water, land, and service problems that many Fort McKay community members were forced to accept.

❊ ❊ ❊

In 1975, a number of First Nations in the province's northwest attempted to place a caveat over 33,000 square miles of land "between the Peace and Athabasca rivers 'by virtue of unextinguished Aboriginal Rights.'"[102] The Alberta government took the matter to court and was successful in 1977 in passing Bill 29, which rewrote the law governing caveats and made it retroactive to a time before the group attempted to file the caveat, ultimately leading the case to be dismissed.[103] While the case was dismissed, the caveat forced the government to pay closer attention to the land issue in the north and recalibrate their direction. It was not simply an issue of balancing the poverty caused by landlessness against the cost of implementing a land tenure solution; it was also now necessary to consider the potential of future Aboriginal land claims made by landless northern communities against the government's desire to push through an ambitious northern development program centred on the development of oil and gas projects. The government, therefore, moved aggressively on a number of fronts, attempting to limit Indigenous groups' collective power and, at the same time, minimize the risks associated with land entitlement issues. As such, between 1978 and 1981, the government curtailed the ability of northern Indigenous groups to organize while also offering individuals in the north title to the lands they occupied.

The new program delivered by the "Land Tenure Secretariat" agreed to waive fees associated with surveying individual lots, granting individuals 2.5 acres for a nominal $1 fee. The catch was that the program would only be made available when 75 percent of the community agreed to implement it.[104]

In many ways, the new program seemed to provide an opportunity for the community of Fort McKay, which was still struggling with land issues. In addition to the problems facing the Red River Point Society described above, the First Nation was running out of land on Lot 10. For Fort McKay, it was believed that this program might kill two birds with one stone, allowing the community as a whole to manage the land on behalf of the communal interests.

As such, the Fort McKay Community Association, which continued to represent both the Métis and First Nations in the community and was led by twenty-three-year-old administrator (and future Chief) Jim Boucher, made a proposal to the Land Tenure Secretariat that would see all the land in the community combined "into a municipal organization with everyone getting title to the land in the community."[105] Unfortunately, I have not yet been able to locate the proposal, and it is unclear how exactly the land would be managed once transferred. However, it is clear that the goal was for the Fort McKay Community Association to lead the process. It was also reported that Fort McKay met the 75 percent community threshold required by the Land Tenure Secretariat for communities to request land tenure. Unfortunately, the Fort McKay proposal was not welcomed by the government, with Minister Marvin Moore at Municipal Affairs responding that:

> I have now had an opportunity to fully review the matter of land tenure and the development of Fort McKay.
>
> Review of the future development of Fort McKay must be done in consideration of the potential for oil sands development and inconsideration of overall development in the area.
>
> As you are aware, the community is located on, and surrounded by mineable oil sands.

> Our view of the long term development in the area is that growth should occur in the two major centres, Fort McMurray and the proposed New Town which would service the Alsands Project. The current plans for development do not include any growth or change in status for the Fort McKay community. Only additional services and facilities of an emergency nature will be provided in Fort McKay.
>
> Consequently, we will not be approving or proceeding on any Land Tenure projects in the community of Fort McKay. Although this position will be reviewed from time to time we do not anticipate any major changes in policy in the foreseeable future.
>
> The existing Red River Point Society leases and existing Federal Government leases will remain unchanged, although no expansion or modification of any leases will be approved. No additional provisions other than those available to existing Fort McKay residents will be entertained for status Indians [sic] resident in the community.
>
> For the time being the Fort McKay Community Committee will be the avenue through which we and all authorities external to the community will deal with the community. However, we would like you to consider having elected representation on a new Improvement District Advisory Council for your area, effective the fall of 1980.[106]

As seen in the letter, the government was unwilling to prioritize the Fort McKay community over potential future northern resource development. Furthermore, they seemingly did not support a scenario where Métis and First Nations people worked together to manage a community in the community's best interests, which would likely require the cooperation of the federal and provincial governments and potentially impact future conversations about collective Aboriginal rights.[107]

In later correspondence with Chief Dorothy McDonald of the Fort McKay First Nation, Moore suggested that if the First Nation needed land, they should consider leasing it from the Red River Point Society, which he felt had more than they needed. This was because Moore (and the Alberta government) was committed to limiting the community's footprint and ensuring the continued separation of the First Nation and Métis in the community. To this request, McDonald stated that the First Nation outright rejected

> the provincial proposal that we negotiate with the Red River Point Society to lease some of their leased land for Fort McKay Band housing. This alternative does not provide our people with the long-term security that they have a right to. As well, it is our understanding that the Red River Point Society does not view 625 acres as excessive to their needs as suggested by the provincial government.

Chief McDonald went on to express concern with the government's interpretation of the "Fort McKay Community Plan," arguing:

> The Fort McKay Community Plan was developed to promote and introduce a land tenure system of individual ownership to our community. The Fort McKay Band rejects such a [provincial] land tenure system. The Band wishes to continue to have its lands reserved by the Federal government for the benefit of its people as a whole.

> The Band is in the process of developing its own plans as they relate to the interests of our Band members. We wish to assure the Minister of Municipal Affairs that our plans can and will complement the plans of the whole community. We have always lived in co-operation with our Metis neighbours.

> The provincial government has opposed our Band Council Resolution requesting reserve status for the 40 acres of Federal Crown land we now occupy. The reason for this opposition is that the province's developmental planning for the area is not yet complete. This position is completely unacceptable to us. The Band has never had any meaningful involvement in the provincial planning process. As a responsible Indian government, we have and will continue to plan a type and style of development which best benefits our own people. Provincial planning, to date, has left both the Indian and Metis people of Fort McKay without

> proper or adequate housing, running water sewage or sanitation facilities or adequate health care services.[108]

The government's refusal to develop a system that would acknowledge Fort McKay's right to self-government demonstrates how the land tenure program was designed to limit Indigenous people's rights in the north, particularly around areas where there were competing resource developments.

McDonald's response confirms the First Nation and Métis were committed to working together as a "responsible Indian government" to meet the community's needs, even as provincial and federal planning continued to fail. Additionally, this letter likely stopped the government from implementing its broader land-tenure plan in Fort McKay, which would have transformed the Métis lease into individual freehold lots and, as described by van Dyke, led to community members selling lots on the open market and ultimately creating a new generation of landless community members similar to what happened in other Métis communities in the region, such as Conklin and Chard/Janvier.[109] In the end, the Red River Point Society lease was maintained for the entire term, leaving the community under-resourced, and many of the problems, such as "adequate housing, running water sewage or sanitation facilities or adequate health care services" originally identified as issues in the late 1960s, still waiting to be properly addressed.

In 1987, the twenty-five-year Red River Point lease expired, and suddenly, the Métis community members, who had at least some level of security, were faced with possible expulsion. Further complicating matters was that the Red River Point Society was defunct, and Métis Local 122 had taken over as the community's governance body.[110] The Department of Municipal Affairs, hoping to avoid a situation where Métis community members would once again become squatters on their own land, signed an updated five-year lease with Métis Local 122 for one dollar per year, with terms similar to those originally given to the Red River Point Society — namely, the local would agree to pay and was responsible for "(a) all taxes, rates and assessments, including local improvement charges levied against the lands and premises during the term of the lease; and (b) all utility rates and charges incurred in respect of the lands during the term of the lease." While it is unclear, it seems that the government decided to waive any outstanding debts held by the Red River Point Society when it was folded.

The new lease set out that Local 122 could only use the land for the construction of a community-housing development, must keep the land clean and free of refuse, and also included the language that "any right the Lessee may grant to individuals to occupy the community housing development, the Lessee shall not sublet, assign, encumber, or charge the lands in any way without written consent of the Lessor."[111] Interestingly, the Local, at least under the 2001 version of the lease, was given the option to purchase the land in the final year, provided that all taxes, charges, and assessments had been paid, that the terms of the lease were still valid, and that the land had been developed to the satisfaction of the ministry. The purchase price of the land was to be one dollar more than the rent paid during the lease.

While the Métis Local 122 lease maintained the status quo in the community, the land-tenure situation remained tenuous. The five-year lease term made it virtually impossible for those living on the lease to make permanent improvements through mortgages or other lending agreements. Fort McKay residents who lived on the leased land had uncertain legal entitlement. Additionally, the informal management structure first utilized by the Red River Point Society remained, and the Métis president routinely "gave" houses and land to community members, as had been the custom. The new "owners" of the houses believed they were theirs to manage, similar to personal property, without the responsibilities or commitments due to modern landowners. Yet none of these "owners" had formalized sublease agreements with either the Red River Point Society or the Métis Local. The lack of a formal agreement with members made it nearly impossible for either the Society or the Métis Local to collect rents from members or monitor improvements made on the land. As noted by a community member in 1978: "We have been in trouble for a number of years trying to pay taxes in common for the Red River Point Lease," a situation that would get worse, not better, as the yearly rents increased when the land was transferred to the Métis Local.[112]

The situation became even more complex when the federal government began to change its rules over who qualified for treaty status. Bill C-31 was the first of these measures, passed in 1985. These bills meant that many of the Fort McKay Métis population could now qualify for First Nation status (or requalify, for those who had lost it due to marriage to a non-First Nations person). With Fort McKay First Nation's settlement of their treaty land entitlement and the growth of their community-owned businesses in the early 2000s, they could suddenly offer members per capita distributions, new houses, and other related services on newly incorporated reserve land.[113] While these developments provided a number of former Métis community members the opportunity to reclaim their "status," it also led to questions about "their" houses that were given to them by the Métis president on the leased land. The Métis Local, without a proper sublease agreement, had very little authority to control the houses, and a number of recently enfranchised First Nations members chose to keep and rent out the property they "owned" on the Métis side of the community, sometimes to non-community members, even though this explicitly contravened the Métis Local 122 lease agreement with the government.[114]

By the early 2000s, Métis Local 122 was in financial trouble, having failed to pay the required taxes on the lease for a number of years, and in 2003, the local was struck from the corporate registry.[115] In 2002, the Métis Nation of Alberta[116] declared Métis Local 63 to be the legitimate representative of the Métis people of Fort McKay, replacing Métis Local 122.[117] In March 2006, Calvin Kennedy, then president of Fort McKay Métis Local 63, sent letters to the president of the Métis Nation of Alberta and MLAs Bill Bonko and Pearl Calahasen advising them of the imminent expiry of Local 122's lease on Crown lands and the transfer of Métis political representation from Local 122 to Local 63.[118] They also sent a letter to Alberta Municipal Affairs Assistant Deputy Minister Brian Quickfall, offering to purchase the land leased by Local 122 to construct a housing project in Fort McKay for Métis members. Under the existing terms of the 2001 lease, the Fort McKay Métis seemed to be within their rights; however, the lease terms had been violated by Local 122's failure to pay its taxes. Assistant Deputy Minister Quickfall wrote, in response to the request of the new president of Fort McKay Métis Nation Local 63, Ron Quintal, that

> Honourable Rob Renner, Minister of Municipal Affairs, has asked Municipal Affairs staff and their counterparts in Alberta Seniors and Community Supports and in Aboriginal Affairs and Northern Development, to assess options for securing Métis land tenure in the Hamlet of Fort MacKay. This includes assessing the impact on all of the Métis residents in the Hamlet of Fort MacKay, including those who are members of Fort McKay Métis Local 63 and any who are members of Fort McKay Métis Local 122. The Minister will then make a decision about what course

of action to take, including how to respond to Local 63's offer to purchase. In the meantime, please be assured that the current residents can continue to live on the land in Fort MacKay.[119]

After several drafts and revisions, and after the Métis Local 63 cleared up the unpaid taxes,[120] the new lease agreement between Fort McKay Métis Local 63 and the Ministry of Municipal Affairs and Housing was signed on September 21, 2007, for a period of fifty years for the fee of one dollar per year.[121] The lease included provisions for non-residential/commercial use by the Fort McKay Métis members, as requested by the Métis community in earlier drafts of the agreement, while emphasizing the use of the land for affordable housing. The agreement specified that Fort McKay Métis was responsible for all taxes, rates, and assessments charged against the lands and all utility rates and charges incurred in the use of the lands during the term of the lease. Clause 6 stated that "the land shall be used by the lessee for the purpose of constructing and maintaining an affordable housing development and such other residential and commercial uses as may be authorized from time to time in writing by the Lessor." This represented a shift from the strictly residential provision of the 2001 lease of five years granted to Local 122 and opened the possibility of limited commercial use by Fort McKay Métis members. In developing the lands, the Métis community needed to comply with all laws and obtain necessary licenses, permits, and approvals. The 2007 lease did not contain the option for the Fort McKay Métis community to purchase the land upon successful fulfilment of the terms of the lease, but again, it was now for fifty years as opposed to the five-year lease granted to Local 122 in 2001.

Métis Local 63 President Ron Quintal continued to seek clarity on the relationship between the Fort McKay Métis and occupants of houses on the settlement that existed before the 2007 lease. In response, in a June 2009 email, Wayne Jackson of Municipal Affairs asked that the Métis move toward a formal land and tenure management framework to clarify the relationship between tenants and existing and new occupants. Jackson also wanted further information, wishing to clarify the number of dwellings, whether they were being rented or leased to third parties, who had title to them, and the state of new homes constructed with funds from Alberta Housing.[122]

On January 10, 2010, Jackson additionally asked that Quintal provide the "Fort McKay Métis policies and procedures manual used to govern landlord-tenant relations, rights, and obligations between the Fort McKay

FIGURE 4.6
Fort McKay Métis Nation Council at McLean Lake, circa 2018. Felix Faichney, Janice Richards, Loretta Waquan, Ron Quintal, Glen Faichney. Barb Faichney Collection.

Métis and members residing on leased lands, including details about new home allocation, payment of property taxes, insurance requirements, and so on."[123] He also asked for a business plan for the future commercial use of leased lands and a community plan with a focus on land planning and development. He encouraged Quintal to strengthen ties with the Regional Municipality of Wood Buffalo (RMWB), which Jackson stated had "planning responsibilities for Fort McKay (outside of First Nations lands) as a hamlet within the RMWB," under the Municipal Government Act. Finally, Quintal was asked to provide Municipal Affairs with plans for the subdivision design that would designate commercial versus residential land within the lease area and to point out how the plans would benefit the community as a whole. Quintal and the Fort McKay Métis did not have these policies and procedures at the time. However, the request demonstrated that the Alberta government was seriously considering the Fort McKay Métis as a self-governing group expected to manage its own land. The lack of procedures also demonstrates that Fort McKay's traditional management practices for the land would no longer suffice, as the impacts of industrial projects nearly completely transformed the community. New or "modern" policies and procedures would be necessary to govern the community effectively going forward.

In 2011, the Fort McKay Métis were able to secure funding to begin construction of a new community office and housing on the leased land, but they came to face new obstacles. Specifically, banks were unwilling to provide Fort McKay Métis with a mortgage unless they offered the land lease as collateral. Due to the size of the lease (over 600 acres in the centre of the oil sands region), it made no sense to offer the whole lease as collateral on a single building or even a few buildings, so the Fort McKay Métis requested that the lease be divided into smaller leases or parcelled up to facilitate the acquisition of mortgages for new homes on the part of members.

An email dated March 8, 2012, from Thomas Droege, executive director of Métis Relations for Alberta's Intergovernmental, International, and Aboriginal Relations Ministry, raised a number of issues regarding land transfer to the Fort McKay Métis. First, it was clarified that Municipal Affairs wished to dispose of the land since it was the only land it held, and it did not have the capacity to administer it effectively. However, Droege brought up concerns that the land could not be transferred to a Métis political organization considering the organization's political and cultural character. As a political organization, community divisions such as those that occurred in the past between Métis Local 122 and 63 could potentially happen in the future, for the MNA required only twenty-five local members of the MNA in good standing to form a separate Métis Local, leading to potential conflict over ownership of the leased lands if a new group in Fort McKay emerged. Further, he argued that the Constitution Act, 1982, and the Charter of Rights and Freedoms required the need for governmental neutrality regarding culture, race, and religion; he, therefore, stated that the government would prefer to transfer land to a new "community" organization or a municipal housing authority rather than a particular cultural community such as the "Métis." Such a statement by a government official again failed to recognize the realities of Fort McKay, notably that they had been managing their land since the 1800s and, although they were now forced to take on various names by colonial governments, they were, in essence, the same community, who were by and large descendants of the original Fort McKay community.[124] It was also a direct strike against the rights of a community such as the Fort McKay Métis to self-govern, which is their right under the constitution and, more recently, the United Declaration on the Rights of Indigenous Peoples.[125]

Despite the possible legal arguments that could have been made to the government, the Fort McKay Métis took a more pragmatic approach, establishing the Fort McKay Métis Community Association, the precursor to the Fort McKay Métis Nation. While the details of the last few years of negotiations remain confidential, the Fort McKay Métis Community Association worked diligently to address the concerns outlined in Jackson, 2010 and Droege, 2012 to develop a governance structure that enshrined the community as a self-governing Métis Nation, maintaining linkages to their historic past, but developing new policies, procedures, and a constitution that would allow them to move towards self-government in the future.[126] That work included building the administrative capacity of the organization to manage their leased lands, growing the community business to generate funds for the new houses and social programs that had been requested since the 1960s, and ultimately negotiating the purchase of the land originally leased by the Red River Point Society in 1972 in 2018.[127]

❖ ❖ ❖

A few key points stick out when considering the story of land tenure in Fort McKay in relation to the evidence for a continued community from the historic period to the present. First, there was always a commitment to manage the land through community consensus and historical processes. Before 1972, the local people had a clear commitment to secure their land and maintain it for themselves and future generations by working together as one community. The Fort McKay Métis and First Nation did this by approaching the government together as the "Fort McKay Community Association" and later the Fort McKay Housing Society. However, after years of meetings and a failure by governments to overcome their own silos, the First Nation and Métis were "split into two."

After the formation of the Red River Point Society, Fort McKay common law structured the relationships and organization in the community and organized how houses were built. While this would lead to growing pains in the future as the community learned how to function within the new colonial relationship, paying rent, and managing the housing program, those practices would contribute to the community's establishment of a modern Métis Nation that has passed a constitution and is prepared for self-government.

Finally, it is also worth noting that after the Métis received the Red River Point lease and the First Nation secured housing on Lot 10, the groups stopped officially working together on land-related issues. However, they continued to work together to protect their interests against industrial incursion. The next chapter will look at community cohesion, particularly in reference to Fort McKay's response to industrial development in the region.

5

A Community Turned "Upside Down": Fort McKay's Response to Extractivism

Extractivism challenged land tenure in Fort McKay and changed the land that the community used to support the bush economy that sustained their way of life. This resulted from the government's decision to allow companies to lease significant portions of the land surrounding Fort McKay and transform it to the point that it became unrecognizable to local community members. The First Nation and Métis attempted to coordinate their responses to the industrial incursion, quickly learning that the traditional governance structures they had used to manage the community for generations were no match against the liberal order framework introduced by the government that made the transformation of the land "legal" despite their repeated opposition. This chapter will explore Fort McKay's response to regional industrialization and population growth, and throughout, I will argue that this experience prepared the community to become the self-governing First Nation and Métis Nation we know today.

After the Second World War, and especially in the 1950s and 1960s, change accelerated for northern people. As noted above, the cratering of fur prices likely had the largest single impact on communities that were structured around the bush economy. In addition, the provincial and federal government's attention shifted away from agricultural development toward industrialization, which led them to explore developing "underutilized" land so it might be better "utilized" to benefit a wider society. In Alberta, government officials seriously considered how they might harness the energy potential of the oil sands in the provincial northeast, traditional oil and gas in the province's north-central area, and coal in the province's northwest.[1] These plans would resemble the "high-modernist" strategies used throughout Canada in the 1950s and 1960s that centred on the belief that improved access to science and technology could positively reorder the natural and social world to benefit the majority of Canadians.[2] Unfortunately, many, if not most, of these projects would place the potential benefits of settler-Canadians above those of people (in Canada, most usually Indigenous or otherwise marginalized people) who were in the development or extraction zones, leaving those deemed to be "in the way" to suffer the brunt of the impacts, either by being moved or left to deal with the poisoned land.[3]

In northeastern Alberta, Fort McKay would find itself in the centre of the Alberta government's efforts to modernize and would soon learn what it would mean to be deemed to be "in the way" of progress. This point was made explicit in 1979 in Fort McKay's oil sands intervention to the provincial Energy Resources Conservation Board [ERCB]:

> Before 1960, Fort MacKay was a relatively isolated settlement having little contact with the "outside world." The building of the Great Canadian Oil Sands plant in the 1960s marked the beginning of the encroachment of major resource development upon the settlement. The plant was constructed on the site of traditional hunting and trapping grounds — an area which also provided summer residence for many families from Fort MacKay. The construction of the plant provided the first major conflict between the traditional lifestyle of the community and an industrialized way of life.
>
> In such a conflict, the "old way" can not win. A giant like GCOS has not changed its way because of Fort MacKay. But certainly our community has had to turn "upside down" for GCOS and other specific resource developments . . .
>
> When the present plant was first proposed, we did not know what to expect. But now we have had several years of experience living closer to the plant than any other community. As GCOS has appeared consistently to ignore any ongoing liaison with us to help us adapt to the new way of life, we are prepared now to initiate this cooperation ourselves. As a result, this intervention briefly outlines a number of our concerns pertaining to the

GCOS application for expansion. We request an opportunity at the scheduled hearings to expand upon these issues in the context of questioning and cross-examination of the application.[4]

Before the major oil sands development, the kinship system and bush economy provided the primary organizing principles at Fort McKay and led to community cohesion. Decisions were rarely made formally, and it was meetings between the family heads that sorted out questions or disagreements. Marriages linked families together, and community members easily flowed from being First Nations to Métis to First Nations — if they recognized the distinction at all. People were most likely to identify with their local families rather than endorsing a larger pan-Indigeneity, whether that involved regional, provincial, or national Métis or First Nations organizations. Hunting, trapping, fishing, and collecting during the proper seasons organized their time and activities. Their interactions with external political bodies were limited, and beyond the treaty and scrip negotiations and the accompanying land surveys in the early twentieth century, there was very little need for a common "Fort McKay" voice to respond to colonial incursion.[5]

After the invasion by oil sands industries, those traditional governance structures were disrupted and community members were forced to develop a more unified identity and voice.[6] The first pressures on Fort McKay came when the government began to challenge the community's traditional patterns of land use and land tenure, as detailed in the previous chapter.

The early impacts of GCOS must have felt like a tidal wave crashing down the Athabasca River. Within the first year of the plant's operation, community members began to experience environmental, health, social, and psychological impacts. Community members were becoming sick with water-borne illnesses never experienced before, and wildlife and fish were starting to show signs of distress and disease or disappear completely. The wide range of societal problems that often appear in boomtowns, including alcoholism and familial breakdowns, also began to appear, thanks in large measure to the new bridge and all-weather road.[7]

By the late 1970s, community members had attempted to engage with the provincial and federal bureaucracies to help with land tenure, water quality, trapping regulation, and employment concerns. As described in the previous chapter, at best, these interactions were met with mixed results and, at worst, the requests were ignored entirely. The actions of the provincial government were far from conciliatory, and officials constantly chose to exploit the economic potential of the oil sands, which were considered to be "in the public interest," over the concerns of Fort McKay residents. Fort McKay followed the recommendations by Van Dyke, who in 1978 called for the "community committee" to take on an even more important role in the community, allowing Fort McKay "strong input into their own future," displacing an "absent" provincial government that he criticized for its "lack of concern or commitment" to the community.[8] Around the same time, the committee hired Jim Boucher to "co-ordinate the community effort in making an intervention at the ERCB hearings." Boucher, like many people of his generation, had experienced first-hand the changes that the first industrial projects had brought to Fort McKay and had the basic education that the Indian day school built in the 1950s provided. Unlike many residents, he completed high school at the Blue Quills Indian Residential School in St. Paul, Alberta. The twenty-three-year-old employee recognized that the community's challenges were complex and tied up in the lack of secure land tenure, the shift in the community's economy and land-based way of life, and the increasing pollution brought by the new industries.

The community's first intervention came as GCOS sought to expand its operation from 65,000 barrels per calendar day to 77,500 barrels per calendar day.[9] It was signed by the "Fort McKay Community Committee," which included Marcel Ahyasou, Dorothy McDonald, Ernie Lacorde, Clara Shott, and Rod Hyde.[10] The signatories represented the whole of the community: Dorothy and Marcel represented the Fort McKay First Nation; Ernie and Clara represented the Métis Red River Point Society; and Rod Hyde, the school principal, represented non-Indigenous community members. The signatories also had experience working within the community and with various levels of government. Marcel Ahyasou was the relatively new Chief of the First Nation, and Dorothy was a First Nations councillor and the daughter of Phillip McDonald, who was Fort McKay's last hereditary Chief. Rod Hyde was a teacher in the community; he later became Dorothy's common-law husband. Clara Shott was the president of the Red River Point Society, and Dorothy McDonald's friend; she was originally a Boucher and lost her First Nations status after marrying a Métis man, Henry Shott. Ernie Lacorde had penned some of the first letters on behalf of the Fort McKay Community Association to the government in the 1960s and, by this time, was a well-respected Elder. The fact that all parties worked together on a single intervention demonstrates the community's desire to work as a unified entity in dealings with industrial incursion on their lands.

The goal of the intervention, Boucher told the reporter in 1979, was to "make sure we [Fort McKay] don't go under and get lost. We want the community to stay here for the people."[11] The committee members had learned from the frustrating experiences of the 1960s and 1970s, when they had attempted to work proactively with various levels of government and GCOS. Most of those strategies had failed or, at least, had not outmatched the negative impacts the community were now experiencing daily. For Boucher, these experiences were "a complete learning process for people [in Fort McKay]." He argued that the community needed to actively participate in local development and make its concerns known.[12] By intervening with the ERCB, community members believed they would have an opportunity to outline their concerns publicly, and they hoped to have their issues addressed in future project approvals.

The intervention highlighted the negative "environmental, social, and economic effects that GCOS had had on the community."[13] The Fort McKay Community Committee, in their submission, asked for four things from the company: first, it wanted assurances that the expansion would not "lead to increased detrimental effects upon the natural environment"; second, that GCOS sponsor a program for the "recruitment, training and employment of residents of Fort MacKay"; third, that GCOS cooperate and liaise with the "Fort MacKay Community Committee regarding all matters of mutual concern"; and fourth, that GCOS would "assume responsibility for providing company employees from Fort MacKay with transportation to and from the job site at no cost to the employees."[14]

In response, GCOS argued that its corporate hands were tied as:

> the board's authority was limited to recommendations to the Lieutenant-Governor in Council. If the ERCB decides the socio-economic concerns expressed by groups at hearings warrant further attention, recommendations may be made to appropriate government departments, but the board would not have the authority to attach them as a condition for approval of an application.[15]

Jim Boucher publicly rebutted this point, stating:

> We are surprised by the public statement made by GCOS that the company sees no need to assume any responsibility for the social and economic impacts which it has had, or which it will have, upon Fort MacKay.
>
> We now understand that nothing can be done legally at the present time to make industry accept responsibility for the social and economic impacts upon communities like Fort MacKay. And as we have seen, friendly persuasion only works as long as the company chooses to cooperate.[16]

At the hearing, GCOS attempted to address the concerns raised by Fort McKay, committing that there "would be no adverse environmental effects from the expansion," and that it would "resume a job recruitment and training program for Fort MacKay," a program that had been suspended about a year prior due to complaints from local unions.[17] Given the close ties that the ERCB had to GCOS, it is not surprising that it ignored the Fort McKay Community Committee's intervention and approved the project on March 29, 1979. Similarly, it is not surprising that Fort McKay continued to experience negative environmental, social, and economic impacts due to the industrial development.[18]

Boucher's comment about how "friendly persuasion only works as long as the company chooses to cooperate" could also be applied to the provincial and federal governments, which were often willing to meet but far less willing to take action. Whether regarding land tenure, trapping policies, health, or other socioeconomic issues, the community of Fort McKay was constantly promised that help was coming, though rarely, if ever, did support materialize.

In 1979, Fort McKay also intervened at a hearing for the proposed Alsands project, a $14 million development located on the east side of the Athabasca River just north of the Fort McKay First Nations' original reserve land; a project that would have rivalled GCOS and Syncrude in terms of magnitude. This intervention made it clear that Fort McKay was no longer willing to be left on the sidelines. However, neither the opposition to the GCOS expansion nor the Alsand project seemed to materially impact their approval. This led Chief Dorothy McDonald, who was elected early in 1980, to conclude that the ERCB would not act upon community evidence until the community "rolled in with a wheel barrow with someone dead in it." She added that "the province is so intent on resource development that they don't care what impact it has on the people. They don't care what the public health cost is."[19] This realization forced Fort McKay to take a different approach to dealing with the direct industrial impacts felt in the community, most notably through legal and direct action.

❁ ❁ ❁

Shortly after the two hearings, in the winter of 1981–82, the negative impacts of the new industries were directly felt by the people in Fort McKay, this time in the form of polluted water. While the provincial government failed to act upon recommendations made throughout the 1970s to establish a water treatment plant in the community, in 1976, it finally installed two water towers, one erected on the First Nation's leased land to the north and the second on the Red River Point Society land in the south. The two "holding tanks" were meant to be temporary stopgap measures, and from the time of their installation, "confusion arose as to who was responsible within the government to maintain the tanks. This lack of action resulted in dirty, rusty tanks and poor-quality water" that often froze or malfunctioned in winter.[20] This remained the status quo into the early 1980s, leading community members to occasionally obtain their water from other sources, most often the Athabasca River, particularly when the water tanks froze or were otherwise unavailable due to some other malfunction.

The winter of 1981–82 was exceptionally cold, providing challenges for communities and companies alike. In December of that year, the propane heater on the south tank caught the tower on fire, burning it to the ground. At about the same time, the heater for the north tank also failed. The water froze, the tank cracked, and Fort McKay lost its second water source in the dead of winter. The harsh winter was also hard on the oil sands developers, and equipment failures at GCOS — renamed Suncor in 1981 — began in late December 1981 and resulted in "a massive spill, pouring large quantities of toxic substances into the Athabasca River. On at least one day forty (40) tons of waste and toxic chemicals had spilled into the river."[21] The company failed to inform the Fort McKay community about the discharge, which continued into January 1982, even though community members — who were now forced to get their water from the river due to the failure of their "temporary" water towers — were beginning to become sick with headaches, flu-like symptoms, and sores in their mouths.[22] In February, at an unrelated community meeting with Suncor, Fort McKay brought these health concerns up to company officials, who then told them the "Athabasca river water was 'dangerous' to drink" and that they should stop taking water from the river immediately.[23]

Publicly, Suncor initially downplayed the impacts of their spill. While admitting on February 26, 1982, that it had dumped "oil and grease" into the Athabasca River, company vice president Bill Oliver explained that it was only "a very small amount of oil in a huge flow of river that is used to oil," adding that "the Athabasca River has a fantastic capacity for absorbing oil." This position was contradicted by Fort McKay First Nation Chief Dorothy McDonald, who said that "about 20 to 30 people have reported problems with stomach ailments, vomiting and mouth sores." She added that "all the Indian communities on the river, as well as the trappers in the bush could be using this water, but Suncor cares so little for people that they didn't warn anybody."[24] In an article published a few days later in the *Edmonton Journal*, Suncor's environmental manager, Bill Cary, explained that he had no excuses for not warning Fort McKay of the dumping but that they "were tied up with their own problems" and, therefore, did not get around to letting the community know of the mishap. The article confirmed that Fort McKay First Nation had laid charges "against Suncor, Cary, and M. A. Supple, plant general manager" in provincial court, stating that the company was polluting the river in contravention of the federal Fisheries Act.[25] At the same time, the provincial government issued a control order against Suncor, demanding that the company clean up the pollution and explain to the province what happened by the end of March.

By June 1982, Suncor had spent ten million dollars upgrading its wastewater treatment facilities and testing the results, although Fort McKay remained unconvinced that the company was taking the necessary measures to reduce the community's impacts.[26] The case proceeded through the courts, with the First Nation charging the company with seven violations of the federal Fisheries Act and two violations of the Alberta Clean Water Act.[27] The trial concluded in 1983. Suncor's legal counsel had cross-examined the Chief, pressing her for evidence that Fort McKay residents had been made sick specifically because of the breach at the plant, evidence that Fort McKay (nor anyone else, given the lack of environmental monitoring on the river) simply did not have. Bill Cary took the stand shortly thereafter, and "McDonald reacted to one of [his] statements by yelling at him and running out of the courtroom."²⁸ The Alberta Court of Appeal ultimately acquitted Suncor on the majority of the serious charges, dismissing the appeals because neither Fort McKay nor the Crown could demonstrate beyond a doubt that Suncor had been negligent. An editorial in the *Edmonton Journal* commented that the government had pursued the Suncor pollution trial "in an amazingly lackadaisical way. Because there are indications the oil sands company is not facing the full power of the law, some explanations are needed to remove big question marks hovering over the case."²⁹ The *Fort McMurray Today*'s editorialist, Ken Nelson, blamed the government's lacklustre reporting requirements. Nelson wrote:

> It's not obvious at first, but the real culprit in this case may be the provincial government. Alberta Environment's anti-pollution regulations are out-dated, difficult, if not impossible to enforce and do not put sufficient onus on the industry in question.³⁰

The failure of this court case to find Suncor guilty dramatically impacted the downstream communities, as they realized that their abilities to defend their communities against the impacts brought by industrial development were severely outmatched.³¹

While the regulatory interventions and court proceedings failed to bring about the result hoped for by the community, they did have the effect of raising awareness about industrial impacts with the broader public. The events also taught the community that any future intervention in a regulatory hearing would require expert evidence to counter material provided by the companies. Finally, it showed the community that it could not depend on the government to be a neutral observer. Fort McKay residents came to understand that the government was so heavily invested in the success of the development that it would not actively seek judgments against the developers even when they were "too busy to report pollution" to the communities to which the pollution would have a disastrous impact.³² In response, Fort McKay warned that companies could "expect the most serious scrutiny of their applications that they've ever had, the easy days for Suncor are over."³³

❈ ❈ ❈

In the late 1970s and early 1980s, as Fort McKay was beginning its interventionist strategy, other changes were beginning to affect the community. First, the economic divide between the Métis and First Nation was growing, as the First Nation was beginning to obtain increased support from the Department of Indian Affairs, while the Métis, represented by the Red River Point Society and the Métis Local, received little if any support from the provincial government.[34] Indian Affairs support allowed the First Nation to fund its first staff position, and Jim Boucher moved from Fort McKay Community Committee coordinator to become the Fort McKay First Nation's band administrator.[35] While leaders still wanted the community to work as a whole, the Band administration led the court cases, interventions, and later reports. Additionally, over this time, Chief Dorothy McDonald's profile increased. She proved to be a fearless advocate for Fort McKay, and as the community increasingly found itself in the news, Chief McDonald was often quoted —speaking truth to power — becoming the public voice of the community.

Federal legislative changes began to alter the demographic makeup of the community as well. A series of court cases forced the federal government to grapple with Section 12(1)(b) of the Indian Act, a sexist provision by which First Nations women who married non-First Nations men automatically lost their "Indian" status and assumed the legal status of their husbands.[36] This law had already had a major legal impact in communities such as Fort McKay, which had a long history of intra-community marriage and where the legal status of its Indigenous members was largely irrelevant before 1960. That changed when the federal government started to invest in First Nations housing programs, medical care, and other social services (however inadequate those services were) specifically for First Nations people. Thus, from the 1960s forward, Fort McKay members were increasingly incentivized to maintain a legal Indian status. It affected how community members structured their relationships, in particular forcing First Nations women to consider the legal ramifications of marriage to non-status men, which included Métis.

The existing law affected Dorothy McDonald and other community members in several different ways. First and foremost, if McDonald had chosen to officially marry her common-law husband, she would have become ineligible to be Chief of Fort McKay First Nation, the exact situation three of her sisters, Clara Shott, and many other members of the First Nation found themselves in.[37] While it is telling that Clara easily took a position as president of Red River Point Society, the law added an additional level of stress to those who found marrying the person they loved could mean losing their First Nation status.

Second, in early 1982, the Fort McKay First Nation changed its membership code to ensure that "all Fort McKay Indians, male or female, married after Jan. 12, 1982 will retain their status for life and pass on that status to children in mixed-blood marriages."[38] Fort McKay was the first Indian Band in Alberta to make such a move and one of forty-eight (out of a possible 576) to do so in 1982. This event is often cited as a demonstration of Chief McDonald's leadership ability in the face of seemingly insurmountable odds, though it also had a pragmatic element.[39] As McDonald noted at the time: "My greatest concern is that we are losing all our members."[40] She was rightly concerned that Fort McKay First Nation would eventually disappear if the law remained unchecked. First Nations marriages with non-status people were increasing, meaning each generation, fewer and fewer people could qualify for their First Nation status. This provision of the Indian Act had been part of the federal government's strategy to do exactly that: reduce and eventually eliminate all distinctive Indian persons through "legislative extinction."[41] The move also had an economic dimension, for if members were "lost" from the First Nation (though those "lost" members often stayed in the community), the Band would not be able to access the same level of funding, which was generally tied to population numbers and used, in part, to fund industrial interventions.[42]

The revised membership code, along with Indian Affairs support, were factors that heightened the influence of the First Nation and inadvertently diminished the influence of the Red River Point Society and the role it would officially play in the community's development. From the early 1980s to the late 2000s, the "Ft. McKay Band, formally or informally," undertook "many administrative, program and service responsibilities for the community as a whole, including the Red River Point Society."[43] However, the leadership in the community ensured that the new First Nation administration worked on behalf of the community as a whole and that although administrators were formally paid through by the band, they also represented the needs of the Métis. It seems to have been an informal commitment that ensured the Métis continued to have input in community decisions and access to community programs. It would also help to maintain cohesion in the community and resist new pressures from government and industry.

❋ ❋ ❋

By the early 1980s, the community of Fort McKay became increasingly frustrated with the lack of action taken by the government in the prosecution of the court case against Suncor and with the results of the regulatory hearings for GCOS and Alsands. The final straw occurred in late 1982 when Northland Forestry received a contract to harvest burned logs just north of Fort McKay. The project would require at least ten logging trucks to drive through the community daily. Residents were greatly worried about this new development, which they saw as a direct threat to the community's well-being. Dorothy McDonald's father, former Chief Phillip McDonald, had died in a vehicle accident, and community members, including children, regularly walked along the road to visit friends and go to school.[44] The First Nation and the Red River Point Society sent a petition with eighty-five signatures expressing their concern about the project to the provincial government. As Jim Boucher told a Fort McMurray Today reporter, "the entire community is united in this position," and "we don't want either our children or the peace of the community jeopardized for the sake of economic expediency." Neither the logging company nor the government seemed to appreciate the concern. The owner of Northland Forestry, Roy Ewashko, stated, "I don't know what the problem is, it's a public road," and the government failed to respond.[45]

By January 14, 1983, the concerns had escalated to the point where Fort McKay set up a blockade. In a news release sent from the "Fort McKay Indian Band and Red River Point Métis Society," the community explained that it was protesting the plan to allow logging trucks through the community and that it wished "to start negotiations on environmental issues affecting [Fort McKay]." The release stated that the "federal and provincial governments must recognize their actions for what they are — genocide. An ugly word but unfortunately for us, true." It concluded that "our graveyard is our proof. You are killing us." Dorothy McDonald and Red River Point Métis Society president Clara Shott signed the release. It was not well received by local MLA Norm Weiss, who called the protest "unreasonable" and asserted that spending 3 million dollars to build an alternative road "would not be a good use of the taxpayers' money."[46] It was an indirect statement about the so-called public interest.

If people in the community hoped to raise awareness about what was happening in northeastern Alberta, they quickly gained success. Within a few days, the story was front-page news in the majority of Alberta publications and was also picked up by the *Globe and Mail* and *Maclean's Magazine*, as well as by national TV and radio programs.[47] The protest caught the attention of other politicians, who, like Weiss, were perturbed by the blockade at first. Local MP Jack Shields said: "The area is not a reserve. It's a provincial highway and it's not fair to ask the company to incur such an expense" of building an alternative road. Shields also asserted that "it's a fact of life, large trucks go through small communities," and that while he agreed that community members "have some very legitimate concerns, but to tie it all in with this issue is not too realistic. I don't think she's gaining any sympathy from it."[48] The provincial minister of Native Affairs, Milt Pahl, added that he thought the community's use of children who were pulled out of school to participate in the blockade was a "a callous exploitation" of the situation.[49] But Chief McDonald explained that the blockade was "like a last stand for us, we're fighting the same old battle that Indians everywhere have fought. We're struggling to survive as a people." The idea for the blockade reportedly came from Métis Elder Ernie Lacorde, who said at a community meeting, "Let's setup a roadblock. They won't throw me in jail."[50] This sentiment was reflected by the majority of participants who were prepared to "go to jail" if that was what it would take to have Fort McKay's concerns heard.[51] Eventually, Minister Pahl and provincial Attorney General Neil Crawford agreed to meet with McDonald and Clara Shott. Charles Wood, president of the Alberta Indian Association, attended as a mediator. Though the details remained confidential, the parties discussed long-standing community grievances, including "environment[al] concerns, compensation for trappers and the lack of medical facilities in Fort MacKay."[52] Eventually, they reached an agreement.

McDonald and Shott took the proposed agreement to their respective organizations on January 20, 1983, and the First Nation and Red River Point Society ratified the agreement the next day, ending the blockade. Chief McDonald was ecstatic. "You can't believe how good I feel now that this is over," she said. "I didn't want any of my people to go to jail and I didn't want anybody to get hurt. But we were determined to see this thing through. We would have stayed out there forever if we had to."[53] The two sides agreed to allow the forestry trucks to be escorted through the community, but more importantly for McDonald and Shott, the government agreed to meet with

FIGURE 5.1
"At the barricades in Fort MacKay: fighting the same old battle," photo from Gordon Legge and Peter O'Neil, "The Band That Pushed Back," *Maclean's,* January 31, 1983.

the community and a mediator to discuss the local concerns. However, it is unclear how productive those new meetings were.

The blockade galvanized Fort McKay, demonstrating that the community had the ability to influence government decisions. It also showed that Chief McDonald valued and wanted to continue to work with the community as a whole. Together, McDonald and Clara Shott were able to put up a formidable front toward both industry and government. The protest helped the community recognize the value of publicity and the pressure that just telling their story could place on company executives and politicians who, for years, had chosen to ignore the community's concerns. Numerous editorials criticized the provincial government's ineffective monitoring of environmental impacts, and some framed Chief McDonald as "a fierce fighter of right," battling an overpowering industry and government, who they wished "would stop making news headlines" as a "nuisance and troublemaker."[54] The blockade also helped the community recognize that their only power in the earliest days was to delay development, much to the consternation of local and provincial politicians as well as local industry leaders. Although the community would not erect another physical blockade, it increasingly relied on strategic interventions to delay projects and, over time, increase its influence in the regulatory process. As McDonald had said, "the easy days" for industry applications were over.

❊ ❊ ❊

In the same week that Fort McKay was blockading the road, Syncrude was applying to the ERCB to create a 170-hectare waste dump near its Mildred Lake Plant.[55] The dump was going to directly impact First Nations trapper Francis Orr, who had travelled to the site and taken pictures of Syncrude's current operations, submitting the images to the ERCB as evidence against the project. Syncrude had an extremely negative reaction to the intervention, writing to Orr to tell him that if he continued with his intervention, they might use a "different approach in their dealings with" him and his trapping partners. Chief McDonald did not take kindly to the veiled threat, rhetorically asking the local reporter: "What would Syncrude have done if they had found Francis taking pictures — shoot him or beat him up?"[56] While Fort McKay was successful in delaying the project,[57] it would eventually be approved when the ERCB found that the dump posed "no health risk."[58] The episode demonstrated the growing tensions in the region and strengthened Fort McKay's commitment to challenging every application submitted by the major companies in the region until something began to change.

Approximately a year later, Syncrude put forward a much larger application to expand its Mildred Lake project. The expansion would cost 1.2 billion dollars and be completed in three phases over five years. While it was not a new project, it would significantly increase the company's capacity to process bitumen and produce oil, increasing revenue. Thus, it was seen as a boon by the provincial government, which was facing decreased revenues and job losses due to the prospect of another downturn. Fort McKay remained concerned about the impact of the existing Suncor and Syncrude projects on the community. The First Nation, acting on behalf of the community as a whole, made extensive information requests to the ERCB, asking for more material about both existing operations. They argued that the community would be unable to make a decision as to whether to intervene without such information. The move by Fort McKay put additional pressure on both the company and the

FIGURE 5.2
Editorial Cartoon, *AMMSA*, 22 June 1984 from Rod Hyde Newspaper Collection.

government, which had an agreement that promised the company substantial tax relief if the project was completed within five years — tax relief that was required to make the project economic in the eyes of Syncrude. According to Syncrude spokesman John Barr: "Any delay beyond this summer will cost us money and endanger our completion schedule." He added that "it's not in anyone's interests for anyone to slow this project down." In short, he equated the company's interest with the public interest. It is not surprising that Chief McDonald disagreed with Barr, stating: "millions of dollars doesn't mean anything to me when it comes [to] the health of my people."[59]

The two parties met at a pre-hearing a week later, where Fort McKay presented evidence from two consultants regarding how the expansion would harm the community. The consultants showed multiple gaps within Syncrude's application, although Syncrude countered by claiming that such concerns were "irrelevant to the specific application before the board."[60] Syncrude suggested that the government should undertake a more substantial inquiry into Fort McKay's social and economic concerns but that such an assessment should take place outside the ERCB hearing rather than holding "the application's existing application for ransom to achieve the same objective."[61] At the hearing itself in August, Fort McKay requested and was granted a fifteen-week adjournment so it might review the 431-page submission provided by Syncrude at the start of the hearing. The additional delay forced the company to postpone work on the project for nearly a year, leading Syncrude spokesman Barr to state that "ultimately the people who put the money on the table will evaluate the effects of the delay, and they'll tell us" whether the project should proceed or not.[62]

In the end, the extension was approved by both the ERCB and the Syncrude shareholders. The ERCB provided its approval shortly after the hearing reconvened in October 1984. In its approval, the ERCB stated that many of the concerns brought by Fort McKay were beyond its scope, though it sympathized with the community and was "concerned about the wide difference in views between some of the local residents and the operators (Syncrude) respecting environmental impact," noting that there was a major deficiency relating to the "lack of communication between those conducting impact studies in the area and local citizens."[63]

While Syncrude's expansion was approved without major revisions, Fort McKay had demonstrated its ability to exert pressure on both the government and companies through the ERCB hearing process. If the press releases are to be believed, the pressure was substantial, as both the government and company had expected that the approval process was a foregone conclusion and that work would be able to begin almost immediately. It helped all parties realize that the status quo would no longer suffice and that the government and industry had to do more to include Fort McKay and other local

Indigenous groups in the decision-making process or risk the community finding additional ways to interfere with "development" in the region.

Shortly after the Syncrude hearing, and at the request of and funded by the ERCB, Fort McKay established the "Fort McKay Interface Committee,"[64] to advise ERCB, Syncrude, and the government about community concerns. While the government aimed to avoid future interventions, Fort McKay reserved the right to trigger a hearing with the ERCB if community concerns were not being properly addressed.[65] Additionally, the committee began to receive funding from the ERCB to undertake their own studies and reviews of proposed new industrial projects. Although these funds seemed to have been collected and distributed by the First Nation, leaders from the First Nation and Métis Nation were thanked for their contributions to reports completed on behalf of "the residents of Fort MacKay."[66] While it would be a stretch to suggest that Syncrude and Fort McKay's relationship after the hearing was perfect, the commitment to work together meant that the community's concerns were at least being heard. All sides realized that progress would only happen if they were sitting at the same table.

Fort McKay's relationship with the surrounding oil sands companies was bolstered by the creation of the Fort McKay First Nation Group of Companies in 1986, which was initiated by Chief McDonald to create new job opportunities and revenue for the community. In her vision, a "parallel development" would occur that would see the community prosper simultaneously with the surrounding industrial developers and government.[67]

This new, non-confrontational approach aligned with that of Jim Boucher, who was elected Chief in 1986. In his first post-election interview with the *Fort McMurray Today*, Boucher stated that "Dorothy had her own style, and I think my style is going to be more low key. I'm very interested in sorting out the problems through dialogue rather than through confrontation." He spoke about the "community's" priorities: running water, new office and commercial spaces, employment opportunities, and community-owned businesses, with a long-term goal to "train and employ people in administrative capacity so that the affairs of the community can be done by community members."[68] Though McDonald's adversarial approach had been necessary to get the attention of government and industry, Boucher was able to build on that and begin negotiations involving trusted advisors and technical experts to ensure the community's interests were protected. By choosing to work within the system, Fort McKay was able to procure funding to pay for the community's priorities and gain favour with Syncrude, expanding its newly founded companies, which would eventually fund the community's economic transformation from 1986 to 2005, building new homes, a new Band hall, and providing other related community services.[69]

Fort McKay also began engaging in a number of regional initiatives with the hope of spurring economic development. In 1986, both the Fort McKay Métis and First Nation joined the Athabasca Native Development Corporation, which included all the Indigenous groups in the region and was created to "enhance" the economic development of "Indian and Métis people living in northeastern Alberta."[70] Fort McKay also helped to form the first regional environmental monitoring and policy organizations, such as the Cumulative Environmental Management Association, the Wood Buffalo Environmental Association, and the Regional Aquatics Monitoring Program, which would help to shape how resource development and pollution would be managed in the future.[71]

Fort McKay also strengthened its relationship with regional developers, particularly Syncrude, forming the "Syncrude Expansion Review Group" to work directly with the company and address any community-specific concerns regarding the second Mildred Lake Expansion early in the process. Though the agreement details remain confidential, the review group ultimately concluded that the Syncrude expansion should be approved, as the community's "many concerns" were resolved "outside the context of a public hearing."[72] It is also worth noting that, over this time, the Fort McKay Group of Companies grew exponentially, in no small part due to Syncrude's support by seconding employees and providing sole-source contracts to community-owned or partnered companies.[73]

❊ ❊ ❊

The turn of the twenty-first century proved to be the start of another era of significant change for oil sands development, as the price of oil finally reached a place where multiple companies believed they could profitably build mega-projects in the region. Those same companies were concerned about the adversarial experiences that Syncrude and Suncor had in the early 1980s, particularly in contrast to the relationship Syncrude had developed with Fort McKay through the Syncrude Expansion Review Group. As a result, the Athabasca Regional Issues Working Group (later renamed the Oil

Sands Developer Group or OSDG) — which included the majority of industrial developers in the region (including Suncor, Syncrude, Canadian Natural Resources LTD [CNRL], Albian Sands, Shell, Petro-Canada, and others) — "began to discuss the need for First Nations to build capacity in order to deal with the anticipated blitzkrieg of resource development in the Athabasca oil sands."[74] In 1999, OSDG signed a three-year capacity-building agreement with the support of the federal and provincial governments. With the funding, each First Nation established an Industrial Relations Corporation (IRC) responsible for creating "the capacity for each community to deal with Industry and the impacts of industrial development."[75]

At its core, creating IRCs was how industrial developers hoped to meet the evolving law around "the duty to consult" and the requirement to provide First Nations capacity funding to understand potential impacts on communities' traditional territories. Unfortunately, the duty to consult legal precedence in the late 1990s and early 2000s did not consider Métis groups. As such, governments did not feel the need to require companies to provide consultation funding to them.[76] Capacity agreements such as the one introduced above were only meant for First Nations and not for the Métis. The vision did not align with Fort McKay's history. As a result, Fort McKay chose to establish an Industrial Relations Corporation (IRC) owned and directed by both the First Nation and Métis, tasking it with the following:

1. Preparing and otherwise facilitating agreements between Fort McKay and the Oil Companies for activities related to the application review process not included in the IRC scope of activities, including but not limited to, establishing the principles and method of community consultation, identifying potential project-related environmental, technical, social, and economic issues arising from each Application in consultation with the community members.

2. Working with the community and the Oil Companies to resolve issues within time frames agreed to with the Oil Companies and/or regulatory agencies.

3. As required, retaining third party technical, environmental, social, and economic experts to assess environmental, social, economic, cultural, and legal impacts of the Oil Companies'

activities as well as technical or scientific reports prepared (and?) commissioned by the Oil Companies or regulatory bodies and communicate their assessment to the Fort McKay members.

  4. Summarizing and communicating the findings made by third party experts to lay persons within the community.

  5. Developing and facilitating in-community consultation processes to facilitate effective communication of technical, environmental, social, and economic issues potentially effecting the community and obtaining the community members' input, advice, and if possible, consensus with respect to acceptable and non-acceptable impacts, project plans, and preferred mitigation-measures.[77]

An important aspect of the Fort McKay agreement was that it bound the companies to work with both the Fort McKay First Nation and Métis.[78] This choice was significant as no other First Nation in the region explicitly partnered with its neighbouring Métis organization. Furthermore, every agreement signed by the IRC on behalf of Fort McKay between its founding in 1999 and 2010, when the IRC was formally dissolved, was done on behalf of the undivided community and most included both the First Nation and Métis as signatories. This commitment ensured that all community members would benefit from agreements made with oil sands developers, as they would benefit from all studies, engagements, facilities, and services funded through such agreements. It is ironic that the oil sands companies were willing to work with the community as a whole when the Governments of Alberta and Canada failed to develop a Métis consultation policy and actively discouraged resource developers from considering the concerns of Métis communities in their impact assessments.[79]

The creation of the Fort McKay IRC helped the community negotiate improved agreements with regional developers. The leadership used some of the funding and the leverage it provided to bring much-needed infrastructure to Fort McKay. Additionally, Fort McKay's average per capita income in 1996 was $16,325, notably higher than "any other northern Alberta First Nations community reporting to Statistics Canada," though still "38 percent lower than Alberta's average per capita income."[80]

While the IRC was instrumental in transforming the community, it was also limited in the scope of its negotiations. "Economic development," for example, was to be left to be negotiated with oil companies independently by the First Nation and Métis.[81] With the legal landscape and provincial government requiring "First Nations consultation" and presumably accommodation, companies attempted to stay in the good graces of the area First Nations by typically offering them sole-source contracts guaranteeing significant financial benefits.[82] Since the early 2000s, the Fort McKay First Nation's Group of Companies was able to leverage this position, growing exponentially, reaching over $150 million in annual sales by 2004[83] and a yearly income of $240 million at the end of 2018.[84] While the achievement of the First Nation's Group of Companies is an obvious success story for the community, it also raises the question of why the Fort McKay Métis Corporation (locally called Métis Corp.) did not experience similar success. This story, perhaps better than any other, helps to explain the birth of the modern Fort McKay Métis Nation.

The Fort McKay Métis Corp, like the First Nation's Group of Companies, was primarily engaged in labour and general contracting activities and obtained some of their first contracts from Syncrude in the 1980s. By the late 1990s, industrial developers, recognizing the government's preference to legally recognize First Nations' rights, led most of the companies to seek partnerships with local First Nations. As a result, while Fort McKay First Nation (and many of the other First Nations in the region) were able to successfully negotiate sole-source contracts with members of the Oil Sands Developers Group, the Fort McKay Métis were largely left on the outside looking in. This helps to explain why the Fort McKay Métis were eager to sign an agreement to become the prime contractor for Solv-Ex, a company that had secured a lease and a provincial loan to build a new multi-million-dollar project just north of Fort McKay.

Solv-Ex was founded by John S. Rendall, who claimed to have a new technique using solvents to extract and refine low-grade oil from New Mexican shale or Canadian bitumen. In 1995, the company was able to secure financing (nearly $70 million) and an oil sands lease from the Government of Alberta, and shortly thereafter began building a pilot plant at the Fort Hills site. In July 1996, Solv-Ex hired the Fort McKay Métis Corp. as a general contractor. Roger Faichney, who was president of Métis Corp (as well as Métis Local 122), explained that while they had "a few new contracts," the Solv-Ex agreement would be transformational as their "first major agreement."[85] Despite this optimism, Solv-Ex was already under investigation by the FBI for "alleged stock manipulation, negative media stories, and fund-raising problems." This perhaps explains why the Fort McKay First Nation limited its participation in the project, leaving the Fort McKay Métis Corp. to take on the majority of the risk.[86]

As described by Manuel P. Asensio and Jack Barth, Solv-Ex was "a convoluted, international scam of epic proportions,"[87] By November 1996, the company had burned through the Government of Alberta's investment and began defaulting on its other international loans. As a result, it failed to pay its contractors, including the Fort McKay Métis Corp., which sued Solv-Ex for $3 million.[88] The loss was crippling for the Métis Corp, which had to lay off 250 workers (including many community members) explicitly hired for the Solv-Ex contract. By August 1997, the Métis Corp. was having "a tough time keeping [the] telephones [and] lights on."[89] At the same time, Solv-Ex was delisted by NASDAQ and placed under investigation by the US Securities and Exchange Commission in 1998.

The impact on the Fort McKay Métis community was catastrophic. The Fort McKay Métis Corp. was not only the main source of revenue for the community (as meagre as it was) but also the Métis community's main employer. As reported by Ron Quintal, after the Solv-Ex bankruptcy, community members would literally "race to the bank to see who would cash their cheque first to make sure your cheque didn't bounce."[90] Adding to the challenge was the fact that the Métis Local 122 and Métis Corp.'s finances were closely tied together. This meant that its financial obligations, such as paying the yearly fees associated with the Red River Point lease,[91] were also falling behind, as were its commitments to repair homes on the lease (perhaps contributing to community members' belief that the houses on the lease were individually as opposed to communally owned) and make improvements to the community more generally.

Métis Local 122 remained operational under Roger Faichney's leadership until 2002 when it was finally struck by corporate registries and replaced by Métis Local 63, a new organization with new leadership.[92] The years 2002 to 2007 were politically difficult times for the Fort McKay Métis, exacerbated by the fact that it no longer had a robust social enterprise to take advantage of the economic opportunities available as industrial development in the region grew exponentially. Ron Quintal remembers that "these were the dark days of Métis politics in Fort McKay. Because it was at that time that people were absolutely galvanized and polarized against each other. Like it was scary to walk down the road because you're afraid someone's gonna swear at you or, you know, flip you off because of the political infighting."[93]

Over the same period, the Fort McKay First Nation negotiated a series of economic development agreements that drastically improved its fiscal well-being and dramatically increased its yearly income.[94] The economic benefits belonging to the First Nation were real (including yearly per capita distributions of $10,000 or more),[95] and more and more community members whose ancestry included both First Nations and Métis heritage rejoined the First Nation through Bill C-31 (and after 2011, Bill C-3).[96]

❆ ❆ ❆

In 2007, in recognition of the growing economic disparity between the Fort McKay First Nation and Métis, the two groups signed the "Moose Lake Accord," a memorandum of understanding that provided base support for the Métis to begin building their administrative capacity, restart their social enterprise, and secure their land lease.[97]

Shortly after, the Fort McKay Métis undertook a series of community planning initiatives, charting a path toward recognized modern Métis nationhood. In the summer of 2008, the organization participated in the Fort McKay Specific Assessment, providing input into the community's indicators of cultural change.[98] Through this process, the community confirmed the uniqueness of the Fort McKay Métis experience and its desire for self-determination.[99] The following year, the Fort McKay Métis initiated a comprehensive community strategic plan in which community members were clear that they wanted to "transform the Fort McKay Métis Community through the pursuit of self-reliance, self-determination and self-management."[100] At these sessions, the community's leaders began openly calling for the establishment of the modern "Fort McKay Métis Nation," a move to confirm the will of the community that had been developing this unique identity for generations.[101]

Initially, it was believed that the shift to "self-reliance, self-determination and self-management" could be accomplished through the structure of the Métis Nation of Alberta, whose bylaws confirmed Métis communities had "the inherent right of Métis governance which may be expressed and implemented by its members at the local, regional, provincial/territorial and national levels."[102] After all, the Fort McKay Métis Local 63 was incorporated as a separate entity with its own directors and assets. As such, it seemed perfectly reasonable that the Fort McKay Métis would be able to assert its autonomy, much like First Nations groups assert their autonomy within other provincial and/or national organizations (the Fort McKay First Nation, for example, is a member of the Treaty 8 First Nations of Alberta as well as the National Assembly of First Nations). However, it was becoming clear that the Métis Nation of Alberta was moving away from this commitment to individual community autonomy. Most specifically, a series of court cases and announcements made by the MNA around this time signalled the MNA's intention to remove local authority and enter into negotiations with the provincial and federal governments for "Métis collective rights."[103] As explained by Ron Quintal, this shift was recognized by outside organizations including the Government of Alberta, Fort McKay First Nation, and resource developers who were concerned about the potential for the "MNA to put their hands in the cookie jar" and take resources away from Fort McKay Métis community members.[104]

As the MNA charted this new path, the Fort McKay Métis community was forced to reconsider its options, as there was legitimate fear that "everything" it had built through the generations could now be colonized by the MNA, a provincial-scale collective with little history or connection to the local community of Fort McKay.[105] Continuing the work that had begun through the strategic plan, the Fort McKay Métis began a deep community engagement to create bylaws that reflected the community's commitment to self-determination. Those engagements began in 2010, with the first draft of the bylaws presented to the board of directors in spring 2011. A second draft was reviewed by the board and community members in August 2011, and a final draft was reviewed and approved by the community in late 2011. The Fort McKay Métis Community Association (FMMCA) was officially incorporated in early 2012.[106]

As explained by the Fort McKay Métis Nation, it hoped that the creation of the FMMCA might spark a revitalization of the MNA, encouraging the provincial organization to refocus its attention on issues of provincial importance and to support local communities in a federated governance model, where the majority of decision-making power stayed local. It was their view that Fort McKay should continue to be one of the Otipemisiwak, "the people who own themselves," and not beholden to rules designed by people who did not understand the unique history and culture of the Fort McKay Métis.[107]

As such, Fort McKay maintained its membership within the MNA but with the "local governance functions of the community — including the management of leased land and financial agreements" being transferred to the FMMCA.[108] It continued to participate in the provincial organization in hopes that it might be able to advocate "with other likeminded Métis organizations" for a provincial governance model that allowed for individual members' independence and sovereignty.[109]

Unfortunately for the Fort McKay Métis, over the next number of years, the MNA continued on its path towards creating a centralized Métis government. This forced the Fort McKay Métis to seek out new ways to protect its nationhood, as the FMMN writes:

> Between 2017 and 2018, and after consultation with their members, the FMMCA board took steps to formalize its governance structure so that it could become a self-governing nation. That included developing a Fort McKay Métis Nation constitution. It also ramped up negotiations with the Alberta government to secure its land base and entered into a conversation with Alberta to determine the process by which the Nation could submit its own credible assertion claim. Through these actions the FMMCA hoped to actualize what their research and members were telling them: that they were their own people, capable of governing themselves, and that they were unwilling to relinquish their personal and community autonomy to the MNA or anyone else.[110]

As the Fort McKay Métis undertook these initiatives and began to assert their independence, they realized that their vision was incompatible with that of MNA, which continued in its attempt to centralize governance structures in the province. By late November 2018, the community collectively decided to sever their relationship with the MNA.[111] Subsequently, the FMMCA's bylaws clarified that they were the only group that could represent Fort McKay Métis community members' rights.[112]

In March 2018, the FMMCA purchased much of the land set aside as part of the original Red River Point lease for the community.[113] On May 24,

2019, the Fort McKay Métis community ratified a community constitution establishing the "Fort McKay Métis Nation" as the representative body for the community.[114] On February 13, 2020, the Government of Alberta approved the Fort McKay Métis' credible assertion application, recognizing that "government and industry" need to consult with the Fort McKay Métis when "natural resource development may adversely affect their credibly asserted Aboriginal harvesting rights and traditional use practices."[115] Together, these actions and decisions demonstrate the complete actualization of the Fort McKay Métis Nation and its shift to becoming a fully formed Métis Nation in northeastern Alberta.

❊ ❊ ❊

Fort McKay's commitment to working together throughout the history of the community has helped both the Métis and First Nation prosper and laid the groundwork for creating self-governing nations. The IRC helped ensure that the community as a whole would benefit when agreements with industrial developers were signed. The Fort McKay Métis business ventures have been generating much-needed revenue for the community for key services such as housing, education, and basic group health benefits to all community members[116] It also ensures that benefits are measured against the concerns of the community as a whole, by utilizing expert reports and Indigenous land-use studies that themselves recognize the interconnectedness of Fort McKay. The fact that the community was able to continue working together, nearly 120 years after the federal government first imposed First Nations and Métis distinctions, is a testament to the strength of the community's kinship network and an ideological commitment that seems to be lacking in other settlements in the region where Métis, Cree, and Dene peoples did not integrate, particularly after the 1960s. It is also unsurprising that outside interests would take notice of this success and attempt to insert themselves into the conversation in more recent history.

Epilogue: From Community to Nation — The Evolving Relationship between the Métis Nation of Alberta and the Fort McKay Métis Nation

On March 28, 2019, the Métis Nation of Alberta (MNA) took out paid advertisements in the *Fort McMurray Today* and other Post Media news outlets announcing that Ron Quintal was no longer the president of the Fort McKay Métis Local 63 and that governments, industry, and Métis "Citizens" should engage directly with the MNA Region 1 president James (Jimmy) Cardinal and the provincial president Audrey Poitras if they wish to consult with the Fort McKay Métis.[1] MNA President Poitras explained that consultation in northeastern Alberta needed to occur at a regional scale as this is what was "ethically, legally and politically" the only way "governments, industry players," could discharge their "duty to consult" with the Métis Nation.[2] To this, President Quintal responded that: "Everything [the Fort McKay Métis] did was under the community association . . . We still negotiate directly with government and industry on projects and our rights associated with the land. From our perspective, not a lot has changed."[3] The MNA's assertions came after the Fort McKay Métis had decided to sever their relationship with the MNA and assert their own authority as a self-governing Métis Nation.

For the next year, Fort McKay and the MNA sought clarity on the issue of representative authority and the right to self-representation through the courts.[4] In February 2020, the Alberta government announced that the Fort McKay Métis had achieved "credible assertion," providing them with the authority to represent members "when Crown decisions have the potential to impact their member's credibly asserted Métis Aboriginal harvesting rights."[5] As described in the introduction, the process was not a short one, with the Fort McKay Métis submitting material (including an early version of this community history) in 2017 for the government to review. After careful consideration, the government agreed that the Fort McKay Métis held Métis Aboriginal rights.

In reaction, the Métis Nation of Alberta stated that they vehemently opposed Alberta's decision, claiming, without substantiation, that the government's decision to grant the Fort McKay Métis' leadership the authority to represent their community was rooted in "oil sands money, greed and a desire to not be accountable to the Métis people."[6] In a second release on the same day, President Audrey Poitras explained that the MNA would not "allow the Alberta Government to unilaterally divide the Métis Nation for its own agenda. The MNA is the government for the Métis Nation within Alberta. We will not let governments divide and conquer our Nation." The second release also quoted MNA lawyer Jason Madden, who stated:

> Alberta's decision to recognize the FMMCA as the representative of a rights-bearing Métis community for the purposes of consultation highlights just how broken Alberta's system is. This decision cannot be reconciled with repeated Supreme Court of Canada and Alberta court decisions on Métis rights or Alberta's constitutional duties owing to the Métis. It will not discharge the Crown's duty to consult, and it will not provide regulatory certainty. Alberta has just opened a can of worms for short term gain, but it will have long-term negative consequences for Métis rights.[7]

Core to Poitras and Madden's argument is the idea that the Métis Nation of Alberta had been singularly representing the Métis people of the province since at least the 1930s. For them, the MNA

> is the government of the Métis Nation within Alberta. For over 90 years, our government has been built by our people, for our people. The MNA has the only objectively verifiable registry of Métis Nation citizens and legitimate Métis rights-holders in Alberta. We have over 42,000 registered MNA citizens, including over 3,000 living in northeastern Alberta. Every four years, we

hold province-wide democratic elections. Annually, our citizens gather at an assembly to give their leadership direction. This is how the MNA ensure it is accountable to the Métis citizens from across the province.[8]

What is important in this statement is the notion of the Métis Nation "within" Alberta, which points to the idea that Métis people are part of a singular nation represented by provincial organizations in the west. As further explained on the MNA's website:

> We, the Métis Nation, are *Otipemisiwak*—the people who own ourselves. We have an inherent right to self-determination and self-government. For too long, Canada's colonial policies denied this right. We were pushed to the margins in our own homeland. Now, by governing ourselves, we can determine our own future and build a strong Métis Nation based on Métis rights.[9]

This idea of a singular Métis Nation has gained momentum in recent years, as both provincial bodies and a supporting group of academics and lawyers have increasingly championed the notion, articulating it in a series of books and articles.[10] Most recently, the idea has been placed in juxtaposition against other Indigenous groups who are attempting to claim a new "Métis" identity in British Columbia, Quebec, Ontario, and eastern Canada, many of which have questionable claims of having "Métis" or even Indigenous roots.[11] In reaction, the definition of "Métis-ness" has been increasingly narrowed. Some argue that only those with clear "Red River" genealogical lineage are members of a true Métis Nation.[12]

This narrowing has not only limited in theory who can claim to belong to the "Métis Nation," it has also constricted conversations about how the Nation should be governed. In this sense, this same group has argued that the "Métis Nation" has always been self-governing through a series of laws and customary norms that extend through history and over a vast territory. Unfortunately, this line of argumentation disregards the fact that many communities like Fort McKay have unique local and regional identities and governance structures of various sizes and types. Much like their First Nation relatives, these Métis groups (Nations?) are better understood as a quilted patchwork across the west, stitched together though language, culture, and economy, but usually maintaining their own unique traits and attributes. This point is well articulated by Robert Alexander Innes when he writes:

> emphasis on the racial difference of the Métis people from First Nations and the tension between them belies the fact that these groups in the prereserve period, and into the postreserve period, shared many cultural characteristics, such as kinship practices. What becomes clear is that the Métis people are Indigenous not only because of the inherited ancestral lineages from First Nations but also because of their shared cultural practices.[13]

In particular, Innes argues that the study of the Métis, like the study of First Nations more generally, is best completed at the "band" or local level, as studies completed at the "tribal" or national level tend to gloss over the "autonomous natures of band societies."[14] Furthermore, as pointed out by Ens and Sawchuk, "there seems to be a gap between the way the Métis organizations are defining identity and the way many Métis actually feel about their identity,"[15] with those organizations, backed by Métis nationalist scholars seeking to construct a national myth that, by and large, excludes the possibility of local-level differences that may exist between Métis (and possibly other closely related) communities.[16] Therefore, the question of Métisness has become less a question of historical reality and more a question of political expedience, which helps explain the MNA's attack on the Fort McKay Métis Nation's right to exist.

❧ ❧ ❧

To fully understand the MNA's desire to challenge the Fort McKay credible assertion decision, one needs to look back at the 2015 federal election, when the Liberal Party of Canada, led by Justin Trudeau, committed his government to a new era of reconciliation that would redefine the country's relationships with all Indigenous people. In his first mandate letter to Carolyn Bennett, Trudeau asked the new minister of Indigenous and Northern Affairs, to "work, on a nation-to-nation basis, with *the Métis Nation* to advance reconciliation and renew the relationship, based on cooperation, respect for rights, our international obligations, and a commitment to end the status quo."[17] On the surface, this move seemed extraordinary and positive, acknowledging the need to establish a new relationship with Métis people in the country, something the federal government had failed to do previously for practically its whole existence. However, this move was also opportunistic, as it asked the minister to negotiate an agreement between the federal government and the *Métis Nation* as represented by the provincial members of the Métis National Council. Such a move would work to the government's benefit, as it would limit the number of potential groups seeking self-government agreements to which the federal government would be required to negotiate, sign, and administer.[18] In short, the interests of both the federal government and the members of the Métis National Council were aligned — the federal government, through recognizing the Métis single government, would provide the group with authority, while the existence of the Métis National Council would limit the number of organizations with which the federal government would potentially have to negotiate the existence of Métis rights.

Perhaps unsurprisingly, the provincial organizations and the federal government moved quickly to take advantage of the opportunity. In 2017 and 2018, the federal government signed framework agreements with the Métis Nation of Alberta, the Métis Nation of Ontario, and the Métis Nation–Saskatchewan, along with an MOU with the Métis Nation of British Columbia.[19] In 2021, the government ratified a Self-Government Recognition and Implementation Agreement with the Manitoba Métis Federation, which will build on a separate $154 million dollar funding agreement signed with the MMF in 2018.[20]

It is beyond the scope of this work to analyze these agreements individually. Still, it is worth investigating the Alberta agreement within the context of the government's conflicts with Fort McKay. Specifically, the framework agreement with the Métis Nation of Alberta was rooted in the idea that the MNA would become a self-governing nation with a working constitution that recognized the organization as the sole representative of the "Métis" in the province. It was, therefore, vital for the MNA to develop a constitution that clearly and unequivocally (at least in the eyes of the federal government) demonstrated that it represents all Métis people in the province. As a result, in December 2019, the Métis Nation of Alberta established a Constitution Commission with a mandate to draft a new constitution, engage with citizens, and then negotiate the federal Métis Government Recognition and Self-Government Agreement similar to the one recently signed with the MMF. This work would continue over the next three years and culminate in the ratification of the Otipemisiwak Métis Government Constitution in November 2022.[21]

Throughout the constitution drafting process, the MNA has described itself as "the representative voice of the Métis people in Alberta"[22] and the "only representative of Métis in Alberta with which Canada has signed a Self-Government Agreement."[23] These statements ignore the existence of communities such as Fort McKay (and others), who have a long history of self-governance and wish to speak for themselves rather than cede representation to a provincial governing body.[24] Regarding communities like Fort McKay, the MNA argues:

> By signing the MGRSA, Canada recognized that the MNA is mandated by the Métis Nation within Alberta to implement our inherent right to self-government. The Supreme Court of Canada has recognized that Canada is the level of government with constitutional responsibility for the Métis. After a long process of negotiation, Canada and the MNA have established a nation-to-nation, government-to-government relationship leading to full recognition of our right to self-government in Canadian law.
>
> No other group claiming to speak for the "Métis" in Alberta has been recognized by Canada as representing Métis Nation citizens with a right to self-government, and no such group has signed an agreement that will lead Canada to recognize it as a Métis government. Only the MNA is on track to deliver genuine self-government for the Métis Nation within Alberta.[25]

This position, though, clearly does not align with the historical reality in Fort McKay, where the community has been self-governing and protecting their own rights for generations. Based upon this history, I argue that the Fort McKay Métis Nation has a right to exist and continue governing itself. Recently, the courts agreed with this interpretation, definitively stating that the Métis Nation "within" Alberta do not have the authority to represent all Métis people in the province without their express authorized consent.[26]

This position is supported not only by the history of the community. As the federal court noted, it is also supported by national and international jurisprudence, which has, without exception, found that individual Indigenous communities hold the authority to represent and govern themselves. In what follows, the international and national legal frameworks for Indigenous governments are briefly examined, as well as relevant court decisions on Indigenous self-governance and existing Métis governance structures in Alberta and Canada. My purpose is to provide a detailed account of the legal parameters and criteria for Indigenous governments.[27]

On a foundational level, the United Nations Declaration on the Rights of Indigenous Peoples (UNDRIP) states repeatedly that Indigenous peoples hold the right to self-government at the local level. UNDRIP affirms the right of Indigenous peoples to "self-determination," "self-government," and the right to a "nationality."[28] Notably, Article 3 enshrines the right to "self-determination," Article 4 recognizes that in "exercising" that right, Indigenous peoples have the right to "autonomy or self-government in matters relating to their internal and local affairs, and Article 9 affirms the right to "belong to an indigenous community or nation, in accordance with the traditions and customs of the community or nation concerned." Following these articles laid out by the Declaration, the Fort McKay Métis Nation has an inherent right to exist and defend their own rights.

Canada was one of four nations that rejected UNDRIP when it was adopted in 2007 due to issues around land claims and the impact of the duty to consult on resource development. Later, in 2010, Canada joined the other Anglo-settler nations (United States, Australia, and New Zealand) that had previously rejected the Declaration and approved it as an "aspirational" document. In 2016, the Canadian federal government signed UNDRIP.[29] An act creating a legislative framework to implement UNDRIP came into force on June 21, 2020, requiring the Government of Canada to act to achieve the Declaration's objectives and align federal laws with the Declaration.[30]

Larry Chartrand has examined the avenues through which the Métis must work to assert self-governance, arguing that while international law (UNDRIP) clearly and respectfully affirms the Métis right to exercise self-government, practically, the Métis have been forced to argue their rights under Canada's national legal frameworks through a colonial court system that does not view Indigenous peoples as being "civilized enough to possess legitimate international personality or competing sovereignty requiring diplomatic negotiations on the level of state-to-state relations."[31] Despite this, he argues that it is possible for the Métis to successfully claim the right to self-government within the Canadian legal framework. Chartrand details how courts often recognize the right to engage in a specific "practice, custom, or tradition" but rarely recognize the Indigenous "right to govern." To illustrate his point, Chartrand discusses the case of the Manitoba Métis Federation (MMF), where members' rights to *engage* in traditional harvesting were recognized while the MMF's right to *govern* those members' traditional harvesting was not.[32] To legally pursue the "right to govern," Chartrand points to the necessity of establishing self-governance as a traditional practice that occurred before a determined date of effective government control. This, of course, is what Fort McKay has done, building their own self-government based upon the traditional practices of the community in terms of initially managing their membership, land, and relationships with outside governments. They also worked to defend these rights as the government increasingly exerted power upon them by negotiating and defending their land, managing their membership codes, and negotiating with industry and government to protect their rights (as best as the colonial laws would allow). It is also important to note that this was often done in partnership with the Fort McKay First Nation, despite the repeated efforts of the government to deal with each group independently. And though these interventions and defences were not always successful, they do show the community has taken the steps of "just doing it," developing their self-governing processes with the federal system of government.[33]

Within Canada, the definitive national legal framework for Métis rights is Section 35 of Canada's Constitution Act, 1982, which recognizes the Aboriginal rights of First Nations, Inuit, and Métis. However, the interpretation of and the criteria for asserting Métis s.35 rights has been left to the courts and government commissions, including the 1996 Royal Commission on Aboriginal Peoples (RCAP). The RCAP provided a definition of Métis (also used by the Supreme Court in *R. v. Powley*) that emphasizes both ancestry and culture.[34] The Métis identity in s. 35 of the Constitution Act, 1982, according to the RCAP, is "not merely a question of genetics," and the term Métis does not simply refer to all individuals of mixed Indian and European ancestry. Instead, it refers to those of mixed ancestry who developed their "common culture," customs, and group identity distinct from their Indian, Inuit, and European ancestors.[35] It follows that a Métis community is a "group of Métis with a distinctive collective identity, living together in the same geographical area and sharing a common way of life."[36]

For Fort McKay, the 1996 RCAP report crucially contends that "there are many distinctive Métis communities across Canada, and more than one Métis culture as well," rather than the singular Métis Nation as advocated for by provincial Métis organizations like the MNA and supported by academic and popular writers alike. The authority to decide which nations constitute a larger Métis nation is determined by the nation and each community. The RCAP thus provides a definition of Métis that allows for multiple locally distinct Métis cultures and puts the authority to define nationhood at the community level.[37] It is important to note that this argument largely followed Justice Grammond's decision, in which he deemed it inappropriate for Canada or the MNA to represent other Métis governments, such as the Métis Settlement General Council and the Fort McKay Métis.[38] However, the parameters and thresholds for recognizing s.35 Métis rights-bearing communities have been left to the Canadian court system to define. Again, Fort McKay meets this definition of being a distinctive Métis community, evidenced by their close genealogical connections, continued defence of their self-governing community, and recent recognition by the Alberta government. Again, this line of reasoning was important to Justice Grammond, who recognized the Fort McKay Métis Nation's right to exist outside of the MNA.[39]

While the Fort McKay Métis, as well as many scholars, do not believe that the question of what is (or is not) a "Métis community" or a "Métis person" should be determined by the Canadian court system, the Supreme Court of Canada's 2003 *Powley* decision is a landmark as the first case to set out the criteria for Section 35 Métis rights, providing a test to determine whether a Métis community holds s.35 rights.[40] In *R. v. Powley*, two Ontario men charged with illegal hunting argued that their s.35 Aboriginal rights protected their hunting rights as Métis people. In 2003, the Supreme Court of Canada decided that the Powleys were lawfully exercising Métis rights and laid out ten criteria — the Powley test — determining who can hold Métis rights.[41]

Considering the right to govern, the *Powley* decision crucially established that "Aboriginal rights are communal rights: They must be grounded in the existence of a historic and present community, and they may only be exercised by virtue of an individual's ancestrally based membership in the present community."[42] For communities to claim the right to govern, they must prove that they historically existed and can be identified contemporaneously in the same geographic area (factors 2 and 3) and demonstrate a historical practice of governance (factor 5) that is integral to Métis culture (factor 6) and continues to be practiced today (factor 7). The Alberta government's credible assertion process adopts these criteria.[43]

Beyond setting the legal test for establishing Métis s.35 rights, *Powley* crucially established that Crown inaction in relation to Métis rights could not be justified by 1) difficulties in identifying Métis rights holders or 2) competing Métis representation claims. *Powley* instead recognized a positive Crown duty to negotiate with the Métis.[44] However, despite the supposed shift away from the need to prove rights before the courts to trigger Crown obligations and negotiation brought by *Powley*, the Métis face significant barriers. These include lack of jurisdictional clarity (thus, jurisdiction falls on provinces and deprives the Métis of federal services), lack of access to national treaty negotiation and dispute resolution processes, and unequal treatment across provinces.[45] In response, Bell and Seaman ask whether the shift from *proving* rights to *negotiating* credible rights claims is more theoretical than real for the Métis. In the Alberta context, Bell and Seaman argue that *Powley* has been erroneously interpreted and applied by emphasizing the "credibility (prima facie strength) of claims."[46]

As demonstrated in the above history and legal standing, it seems fair for Fort McKay to believe that Métis communities should be able to represent and govern themselves. When such a community makes the claim, the onus should fall upon the Crown to recognize the choice and work with that Métis group. The courts recognized this position, most notably in *R. v. Lizotte*, a 2009 Alberta Provincial Court case that invoked *R. v. Powley*. When dealing with the differences in the definition of Métis (as well as other inconsistencies) between *R. v. Powley* and the Métis Settlements Act, the judge decided that rather than requiring the Métis Settlements to go through an additional process, the Métis Settlements would be allowed to decide for themselves (following the process laid out in the Métis Settlements Act) who meets their membership requirements.[47] According to *R. v. Lizotte*, Métis communities that have organized themselves and that meet the conditions laid out in *Powley* should be recognized as rights-holders. Similarly, Justice Grammond asserts that "what's good for the goose is good for the gander" and that no one Métis government should be allowed to proclaim its ability to represent others "against their will."[48] This position, when applied to Fort McKay Métis Nation, seems to strengthen their argument that they should be allowed to govern themselves and not be forced to conform to a different self-governance structure because the MNA and federal government find it convenient.

This position also seems to align with several other Métis rights cases, where defendants arguing for the existence of a singular Métis Nation to be recognized as encompassing a large region such as "the entire northwest" or the "entire western plains and prairies" have repeatedly been struck down. Specifically, in cases such as *R. v. Gooden* and *R. v. Hirsekorn*, the courts found Métis communities existed in clearly defined regions.[49] Thus, despite attempts to set a precedent for recognition of one large Métis community, the courts have maintained the *Powley* definition of Métis rights as communal rights, where "a Métis community is a group of Métis with a distinctive collective identity, living together in the same geographical area and sharing a common way of life."

Of note is that among the major cases that have decided on Métis s.35 rights, there has not been a situation wherein a local community of comparable size and organization to Fort McKay have attempted to defend their Aboriginal rights in court. Rather, individual rights-bearers like Steve and Roddy Powley, have been typically supported by larger governance structures like the Manitoba Métis Federation, the Métis Nation of Ontario, the Métis Nation of Alberta, and Alberta's Métis Settlements. Thus, despite jurisprudence that supports the right of communities to self-govern, an individual Métis community has not had the opportunity to argue in the Canadian court system that the right rests with them. However, given the backing of UNDRIP, RCAP and now *Metis Settlements General Council v. Canada (Crown-Indigenous Relation), 2024 FC 487* and given Fort McKay's long history of a genealogical interconnection and self-government in a close and geographically defined community aligned with the *Powley* requirements, a continued commitment to good governance and evidence of contemporary practice of self-government, and a commitment to protecting legal rights on the land, it seems that the Fort McKay Métis Nation have a solid foundation upon which to argue for the right of self-government.

This fact was recognized when the Fort McKay Métis gained formal recognition through Alberta's credible assertion process as a historic and contemporary rights-bearing Métis community that fully meets the thresholds laid out by *R. v. Powley*.[50] As demonstrated above, the evidence makes clear that the Fort McKay Métis community was already distinct amongst the larger regional Métis community before effective European control of northeastern Alberta. Further, it demonstrates the historical and enduring connections to the Indigenous community of Fort McKay, which is made up of both Métis and First Nation members, were central to the distinctive culture of the Fort McKay Métis community. Just as in the past, Fort McKay Métis community members self-identify as local Métis community members, remain strongly connected to traditional land in the areas around Fort McKay, and see themselves as part of a distinctive community that wishes to speak for and represent itself with external governments and Indigenous organizations.

This history of self-reliance has recently, and increasingly, been challenged by the Métis Nation of Alberta, which has argued (without substantiation) that Fort McKay's leaders are not part of an independent Métis Nation, and their decision to continue defending their community's rights is driven by "oil sands money, greed and a desire to not be accountable to the Métis people."[51] It could be argued that those representatives of the Métis Nation of Alberta are worried that the provincial government's recognition of Fort McKay as a self-governing Métis Nation runs counter to their nation-building exercise. Further to this point, perhaps those MNA leaders are worried that the existence of an independent Métis Nation in Fort McKay (and potentially many other Métis Nations in Alberta's north) with a deep and long history may jeopardize the MNA's goal to develop a provincial constitution and ultimately negotiate a self-government agreement with the federal government. An agreement that would provide the MNA (whose membership has grown from 29,114 members in 2015 to over 64,000 in 2023)[52] with millions — if not billions — of dollars of funding for programs delivered provincially and overseen by a president who has been in power for over twenty-five years of an organization that saw less than 10 percent of their 50,000 members cast a vote in the 2018 MNA general election[53] and more recently less than 30 percent of the total population voting in the constitutional ratification vote despite the MNA devoting significant resources to advertising and lobbying in support of the agreement.[54] As noted by President Quintal, on behalf of Fort McKay and a number of other similarly positioned Métis communities and Nations: "We do not support their 'constitution,' we know it won't have any authority over Métis communities like ours, and we will not participate in their referendum. It is nothing more than an effort by a small group of people to amass power. But it seems to be well-funded given the amount of social media advertising we are seeing."[55]

Despite the political posturing of recent years, the story of the Fort McKay Métis Nation is illustrative. It can help show a different way of imagining the "Métis Nation" and its communities. First and foremost, it shows that to understand the contemporary Métis Nation, it is important to complete historical studies at the local community level, as many groups have unique stories worthy of deep exploration. Furthermore, Métis history and identity cannot be frozen in the eighteenth and nineteenth centuries, as for many, their identities were only fully formed due to events in the twentieth and even the twenty-first century.[56] Furthermore, Métis communities, particularly many in northern Alberta, cannot, and should not, be studied as discrete groups, separate from First Nations that were often created more through government ascription than by cultural affinity. Instead, scholars need to take time to understand these close connections and consider how government policies forced these Indigenous communities to adapt and ultimately be pushed into separate groups, even though, as demonstrated through the history of Fort McKay, those groups did not necessarily agree with this separation. And finally, particularly in places like Fort McKay, which has experienced massive disruption as a result of industrial development, scholars need to take time to consider how government policies removed Indigenous people not just from private property (as suggested through settler colonialism), but also from Crown-owned land that was managed by the government supposedly for the collective good of the province and country.

The story then of the Fort McKay Métis is one of growth and maturing, reacting to external pressures and using those pressures to form a new, stronger nation, one that is willing and able to lead a new type of Métis organization that recognizes its past and looks forward to the future. In this sense, by uncovering and emphasizing the community's local past, future generations will be able to look to Jose Grand Bouché, Isidore Lacorde, Edward Tourangeau, Earnie Lacorde, Harry MacDonald, Clara Shott, Dorothy McDonald, Emma Faichney, Henry Shott, Zachary Powder, and many others from the distant and more recent past as their role models: people from the community's history who worked with their First Nations relatives to build a Métis community that ultimately became the Fort McKay Métis Nation.

Appendix: The Fort McKay Métis Nation Position Paper on Consultation and Self-Government

By Fort McKay Métis Nation Council[1]

In February 2020, the Fort McKay Métis Nation (FMMN) was the first Métis community to "credibly assert" its Métis Aboriginal rights under the process outlined by the Government of Alberta.[2] In so doing, it joined the Alberta Métis Settlement's General Council as the only Métis organizations authorized to negotiate with the Crown in the province and for which consultation may be legally required.[3] The decision was lauded by many in the Métis community who are also seeking to be recognized and criticized by others who have a different conceptualization about who should represent Métis community rights.[4] This paper is meant to share FMMN's experience, providing their position on what they believe effective Crown consultation will look like moving forward and asserting that this recognition is a first step toward becoming a self-governing Métis Nation.

This paper is broken into three sections. First, it outlines the Fort McKay Métis Nation's history and the process that it followed to demonstrate its status. Second, it discusses the importance of consultation for Fort McKay as a key part of the Nation's move toward self-government. Finally, it outlines Fort McKay's current governance structure and its vision for the future now that the provincial government has formally recognized it as a rights-bearing Métis community through the credible assertion process.

Evolution of Fort McKay Métis Governance and Credible Assertion

Métis members in Fort McKay have organized themselves in several ways since the 1960s. They have been members of the Fort McKay Community Association, created the Red River Point Society, and constituted Métis Local 122, superseded by Métis Local 63 in 2005 within the Métis Nation of Alberta (MNA). Yet none of these societies provided the tools necessary for the Fort McKay Métis to effectively govern themselves. This is perhaps not surprising given that many of the problems experienced in Fort McKay were relatively new. The Métis Nation of Alberta bylaws were originally "formed to provide unified political advocacy on behalf of Métis communities in the face of Crown intransigence."[5] The MNA was initially imagined as an advocacy organization, not one meant to deliver the structures of self-government. Therefore, the MNA's bylaws fail to effectively explain the roles and responsibilities of the different levels of MNA government. At various times, all the levels have attempted to speak for local people in Métis communities.[6] While there have been conversations about establishing a new set of MNA bylaws or even a new constitution to clarify these (and other) deficiencies, those conversations have been ongoing since at least the 1980s, and the governing bylaws have not changed substantively since 1984.[7]

By 2010, the Fort McKay Métis had found that the MNA bylaws precluded their own effective community management. As a result, that year, they established the Fort McKay Métis Community Association (FMMCA), the precursor to today's Fort McKay Métis Nation. Throughout the process of creating the FMMCA, leadership undertook a deep engagement with community members, ensuring the new organization's bylaws met customary and conventional good-governance codes and enshrining the community's Métis identity and rights. Additionally, the leadership met with interested outside groups, most importantly the Fort McKay First Nation, to maintain the important connectedness within the larger Indigenous community of Fort McKay. This set the groundwork for the community as a whole to meet the varied and difficult challenges brought by 120 years of government interference, ensuring that "no one is left behind."

When the FMMCA was established, it was the community's hope that focusing on effective governance at the grassroots level might spark a revitalization of the MNA, encouraging the provincial organization to refocus its attention on issues of provincial importance and to support local communities in a federated governance model, where the majority of legislative power decision-making power stayed local. It was their view that Fort McKay should continue to be one of the *Otipemisiwak*, "the people who own themselves," and not beholden to rules designed by people who did not understand the unique history and culture of the Fort McKay Métis.[8]

From 2010 to 2019, the Métis of Fort McKay remained members of the MNA, though the local governance functions of the community — including the management of leased land and financial agreements — were moved over to the FMMCA. Since the mid-2000s, the Fort McKay Métis (through Métis Local 63) participated in several initiatives supporting its vision for a decentralized Métis governance structure.[9] They also participated in regional Métis groups with other like-minded Métis organizations, hoping to uplift all the members while not replacing any member's "institutional independence."[10] Unfortunately, their call for a federated governance model was largely ignored, and the MNA moved forward with its negotiations with the Alberta government based on the idea that it was the only Métis organization able to represent Métis people in the province. On 1 February 2017, in an effort to enshrine this idea, the MNA signed a Framework Agreement with the province, with a key purpose of developing a provincial Métis consultation policy.[11]

In its negotiations with the Alberta government, the MNA claimed it was the only rights-holding body in the province and no other individual group or organization could represent Métis rights without oversight from the parent organization. In preparation for the negotiations, the MNA began to amend its bylaws to reflect this centralized vision. For example, in 2016 the MNA passed a new "oath of membership" that required members to swear:

> I agree to the Métis Nation's Bylaws and policies, as amended from time to time, and, voluntarily authorize the Métis Nation to assert and advance collectively-held Métis rights, interests, and claims on behalf of myself, my community and the Métis in Alberta, including negotiating and arriving at agreements that advance, determine, recognize, and respect Métis rights. In signing this oath, I also recognize that I have the right to end this authorization, at any time, by terminating my membership within the Métis Nation.[12]

The new Oath makes the MNA the only administrative body that could represent individual Métis people or a community's rights and suggests that if individuals (or communities) disagree with it, their only means to seek redress would be to "terminate" their membership. The oath was thrust upon the membership despite opposition from several individuals and smaller dissenting Métis communities, including Fort McKay.[13] The oath also failed to recognize the authority of the Métis Settlements General Council, which had signed a consultation agreement with the province a few months earlier and was recognized as a separate Métis rights-holding body.[14]

This move to consolidate power within the MNA continued in the "Framework Agreement for Advancing Reconciliation between the Métis Nation of Alberta and Her Majesty the Queen in Right of Canada." In the document, the MNA asserted that they were the only administrative organization able to represent "collectively held Métis rights, interests and outstanding claims against the Crown" in Alberta. However, *Powley*, and nearly every court decision after that, has determined that Métis communities — much like Indigenous communities throughout Canada — are better understood as small and regional in scale and organization.[15] It is unsurprising that the federal government and MNA would propose such a solution, for, as demonstrated through the specific claims process, Crown negotiations with multiple groups representing First Nations' rights can be time-consuming and challenging.[16] The agreement has the potential to exclude from reconciliation with the Crown the Métis groups in the province that have long and verifiable histories — groups like the Fort McKay Métis Nation. It is Fort McKay Métis Nation's belief that such a move risks replacing a colonial master with a new, neo-colonial one. Their concern is that the MNA will not recognize the inherent rights-holding communities and will deny them the ability to negotiate directly with the Crown to remedy historical wrongs.

Fort McKay also believes that if Métis collectives choose to represent themselves, the Crown needs to recognize that choice and work with those groups: for, as was explicitly stated by the Supreme Court of Canada in the seminal *Powley* decision, "a Métis community is a group of Métis with a distinctive collective identity, living together in the same geographical area and sharing a common way of life." Such an approach aligns with jurisprudence that has continued to accept that Métis s.35 rights are held by local and regional communities that have a distinctive collective identity, live together in the same space, and share a common way of life.[17]

Furthermore, the *United Nations Declaration on the Rights of Indigenous Peoples* (UNDRIP) repeatedly affirms that Indigenous peoples have the right to "self-determination," "self-government," and the right to a "nationality." As per the *Declaration*, the Fort McKay Métis Nation has an inherent right to exist and to defend their own Indigenous rights; such rights cannot, and should be allowed to, "belong to an indigenous community or nation, in accordance with the traditions and customs of the community or nation concerned. No discrimination of any kind may arise from the exercise of such a right."[18]

Together, these moves seem to foreshadow the MNA's preference for a governance structure mirroring that of the Métis Nation of Ontario, where local and regional offices ultimately report to the provincial office and powers are largely centralized.[19] However, in comparison to the MNA, the Métis Nation of Ontario had a relatively shallow history (the organization was only founded in 1993) and no legacy governance structures similar to those that exist in the MNA.[20] Furthermore, the Métis of Fort McKay believe it absurd that a new centralized government model might be foisted upon them and other Métis in northeastern Alberta, particularly when the proposed centralized system failed to take into account the fact that communities like Fort McKay have been governing their own affairs throughout the community's history. In Fort McKay's view, the current governance model being proposed by the MNA, if recognized by either the federal or provincial government, would mean local communities would no longer be *Otipemisiwak* and would instead be placed under the thumb of a centralized provincial office that purports to govern previously autonomous communities.

This shift in the MNA's vision was accompanied by an increasingly interventionist stance. The MNA was beginning to participate in regulatory processes, government monitoring initiatives, and industrial negotiations that had historically never been part of its mandate.[21] Both the provincial negotiations and interventions created a great deal of uncertainty regarding how Métis consultation within Fort McKay's traditional territory should proceed. They undoubtedly caused challenges and additional uncertainty for industry and government, delaying decision-making processes for everyone involved.

Shortly after the MNA instituted its new oath of membership, the Court of Queen's Bench in Alberta issued its *Fort Chipewyan* decision.[22] Before 2016, the Government of Alberta had provided little direction to Métis groups seeking formal recognition. *Fort Chipewyan* helped to lift the veil regarding how a community might go about making a credible assertion claim, as noted by legal scholar Moira Lavoie:

> The Court in *Fort Chipewyan* set out two requirements for Métis organizations seeking to enforce the duty to consult under the Haida test, but whose governance structures are not statutorily recognized by the Crown. First, the organization must provide credible evidence that the organization's members meet the requirements of the Powley test for Métis identification. Second, the organization must provide credible evidence of its representative authority to enforce the duty to consult.[23]

Upon reviewing the decision, Fort McKay — unsure how the MNA's negotiations with the province might proceed — commissioned two reports. The first provided a thorough genealogical assessment of the Métis community, and the second reviewed the community's history. Upon receiving the reports, the community directed the FMMCA's membership registrar to undertake a comprehensive review of membership information (primarily birth records and other collected genealogical data) to compare it to the findings of the two research reports. The comparison confirmed what the community members already knew: that the FMMCA members were clearly connected through kinship to the historic community of Fort McKay and that, together with their Fort McKay First Nations relations, the group had a long history of governing themselves and representing their own Indigenous rights.

Between 2017 and 2018, and after consultation with its members, the FMMCA board took steps to formalize its governance structure to become a self-governing nation. That included developing a Fort McKay Métis Nation constitution. It also ramped up negotiations with the Alberta government to secure its land base and entered into a conversation with Alberta to determine the process by which the Nation could submit its own credible assertion claim. Through these actions, the FMMCA hoped to actualize what their research and members were telling them: that they were their own people, capable of governing themselves, and that they were unwilling to relinquish their personal and community autonomy to the MNA or anyone else.

As the Fort McKay Métis undertook these initiatives and began to assert their independence, they realized that their vision was incompatible with that of MNA, which continued in its attempt to centralize governance structures in the province. By late November 2019, the community collectively made the difficult decision to sever their relationship with the MNA.[24] Subsequently, the FMMCA's bylaws clarified that they were the only group that could represent Fort McKay Métis community members' rights. This is in contrast to the MNA bylaws, where, as the *Fort Chipwewyan* court case demonstrated, it remains unclear whether members' rights are represented at the local, regional, or provincial level. The FMMCA's bylaws helped the community to satisfy one of the more challenging aspects of Alberta's credible assertion test, demonstrating that only it was authorized to represent the contemporary Metis community in Fort McKay. This authorization, coupled with the commissioned research — which demonstrated that the vast majority (upwards of 90 percent) of members could trace their ancestry to the pre-1900 Indigenous community of Fort McKay — cemented the community's claim.[25] The evidence was reviewed by the government, which granted the Fort McKay Métis's credible assertion claim on February 13, 2020.[26]

Otipemisiwak: The People Who Govern Themselves

The major tension experienced by the Fort McKay Métis as they moved toward nationhood was the lack of clarity regarding who could represent a Métis community. The tension had existed due to the lack of federal or provincial statutes recognizing Métis governance structures.[27] While Fort McKay does not advocate for a colonial "rubber stamp" from the Canadian or Albertan government, it does believe it is necessary that the governance structures developed by any group wanting to represent a Métis collective in fact reflect the historical reality of the community over which they claim authority. Fort McKay demonstrated that they have a long history of unique Métis governance that has persisted from the mid-nineteenth century to the present. As such, Fort McKay agrees with Lavoie when she states that "we should look to the Métis communities themselves for guidance on what constitutes proper Métis representative authority, not simply the preferences of the courts or the Crown," while adding that a larger Indigenous governmental body should never be able to claim or appropriate the rights of a smaller grassroots organization. This position is not unique to Fort McKay and has been implemented by the courts, which have consistently, and without exception, found that s.35 Métis rights are held locally by communities and not by national or provincial organizations. It is also worth noting that this position is a key tenet of UNDRIP, which recognizes the authority of Indigenous communities to represent themselves. As such, when a group such as Fort McKay provides credible evidence that it exists and represents the majority of its ancestors, that authority must be recognized. It should not be subject to challenge by other groups whose claims are not as strong.[28]

Furthermore, Fort McKay also believes strongly that nationhood is practiced, not imagined in Vancouver and Toronto law offices, far from the Métis homeland. As such, the Fort McKay Métis Nation has worked hard to develop a modern governance structure that meets the needs of the membership. The community's membership code pays special attention to the unique history and culture of the community. It ensures that each member has a verifiable connection to the historic Fort McKay community or has passed a vigorous acceptance process that replicates how members would have been accepted into the community in the past. The constitution has carefully incorporated direct democracy and transparency, with members meeting quarterly to vote on key issues such as constitutional amendments, community direction, and agreements negotiated with industrial developers. Elections are carefully managed through an election code, and impartiality is maintained by an independent election officer.

In addition to enshrining the structures of good governance, the Nation takes its fiduciary responsibilities to its members extremely seriously. Annual budgets are audited by an independent third party and approved by the membership at every annual general meeting, and budgetary priorities are determined through community strategic planning on a yearly basis. Priorities in the areas of culture, health, education, land, and housing are carried out by an independent and qualified professional bureaucracy. Funding for these initiatives comes primarily from the McKay Métis Group of Companies, a social enterprise owned by community members.[29] The profits that these companies generate are reinvested in the Métis community, making it possible to provide all members with a supplemental group health plan, access to affordable housing, and bursaries for post-secondary education. The Fort McKay Métis Nation has also signed multiple agreements with the Fort McKay First Nation, and many of the services — including a daycare, nursing home, and, in the long-term, a community-managed charter school — will be jointly owned and operated by the two entities. These partnerships extend to emergency services and have allowed the community to respond in a coordinated and effective way to disasters such as the 2016 wildfire and the 2020 COVID-19 pandemic, keeping members safe regardless of whether governments deem them to be legally First Nation or Métis. In all these ways, the Fort McKay Métis leadership is fulfilling the vision of past community leaders to lift the community as a whole and ensure that no one is left behind.

As Fort McKay's history demonstrates, the community has had, at best, only weak connections to a larger regional Métis political body or a pan-Métis consciousness that seems to be much more a product of the twenty-first century than the nineteenth or twentieth.[30] Furthermore, the community's unique kinship connections and cultural history have persisted, making the formal establishment of Fort McKay Métis Nation possible. It was the local leaders who defended the community throughout the twentieth century. Thus, it is Fort McKay's position that while a larger Métis Nation may exist, it exists in the same way that a Cree or Dene Nation exists in northern Alberta: as a broad group of people connected through culture, language, and kinship, but politically represented by a number of independent First Nations in the province. The idea that the specific interests and negotiations of the Fort McKay First Nation could be taken up by a regional or provincial First Nations office would seem ludicrous to most observers, and the Fort McKay Métis Nation posits that the same level of skepticism should be levelled toward any provincial group that asserts it has the authority to represent Fort McKay Métis Nation members. In short, local communities are best positioned to represent themselves, and though regional and provincial organizations can support this work, they cannot and should not be allowed to supplant it.

When the Métis National Council was formed in 1983, it was structured as a federation, with each member maintaining its own autonomy to negotiate independently with other levels of government and each other.[31] This is the governance model that the Fort McKay Métis Nation supports and believes should be extended throughout the Métis Nation. Communities that are able to demonstrate through history, genealogy, kinship, and culture that they are *Otipemisiwak* should assume the authority to self-govern. With their status now recognized by the Alberta government, Fort McKay is poised to continue implementing its plans for self-government.[32] The Métis community has already purchased land, passed a community constitution, solidified its nation-to-nation relationship with the Fort McKay First Nation and other Indigenous groups, built a structured administration that provides services to its members, and confirmed the legitimacy of the multiple community benefit agreements it had negotiated (and continues to negotiate) with oil sands operators in the region.

The affirmation of the Fort McKay Métis Nation's status in both the eyes of the Métis national governing body and the province of Alberta has opened multiple doors for the community's future growth and prosperity. The primary purpose of this paper was to briefly provide the background regarding the Nation's journey as a model for others who may wish to undertake a similar path. Recently, Fort McKay became a founding member of the Alberta Métis Federation, which recognizes the autonomy of its member communities to represent themselves with governments, other Indigenous groups, and industrial partners.[33] Through the AMF, Fort McKay hopes to continue on its path toward Métis self-government with other like-minded communities who believe they, too, are *Otipemisiwak* and who wish to represent themselves. While it is understandable that governments and provincial groups may find it more politically expedient to deal with a single organization claiming to represent all Métis citizens and rights, this claim does not effectively take into account Fort McKay's unique history and their constitutional right to Indigenous self-government. Furthermore, this position does not face the reality that many other groups in the Métis homeland may similarly wish to become self-governing entities within the broader nation: just as many First Nations make up the Assembly of First Nations, many *Otipemisiwak* are part of the larger Métis Nation. While there can be little doubt that a larger Métis Nation of some type exists in Western Canada, it must be recognized that this nation is made up of the *Otipemisiwak*—the people who own themselves — and they will be the ones who will effectively establish new forms of Métis self-government in the twenty-first century.

Notes

NOTES TO INTRODUCTION

1. Indian Claims Commission, *Inquiry into the Treaty Land Entitlement Claim of the Fort McKay First Nation* (1995). http://iportal.usask.ca/docs/ICC/FortMckayEng.pdf.

2. Tom Flanagan provides details regarding Fort McKay First Nation's financial successes over the period in *The Community Capitalism of the Fort McKay First Nation: A Case Study* (Vancouver: Fraser Institute, 2018).

3. For more on the Alberta government's consultation policy, see Fort McKay Métis Nation, "The Fort McKay Métis Nation Position Paper on Consultation and Self Government" (Fort McKay: Fort McKay Métis Nation, 2021). This position paper by the Fort McKay Métis Nation Council is reproduced as an appendix in this book, which can be found on page 149. Also see Neil Reddekopp, "Theory and Practice in the Government of Alberta's Consultation Policy," *Constitutional Forum* 22, no. 1 (2013); Heather Devine, "The Alberta Dis-Advantage: Métis Issues and the Public Discourse in Wild Rose Country," *London Journal of Canadian Studies* 26 (2010–11): 26–62.

4. A good description of the different court decisions affecting Alberta Métis harvesters from the time is found in Devine, "The Alberta Dis-Advantage."

5. To learn more about Indigenous housing and homelessness, see Jesse Thistle, *Indigenous Definition of Homelessness in Canada* (Toronto: Canadian Observatory on Homelessness Press, 2017). Also see Peter Fortna, "How Much Longer? A Preliminary Assessment of Homelessness in Conklin, Alberta," 2018, http://www.willowspringsss.com/blog/how-much-longer-homelessness-in-conklin-alberta.

6. Many of these issues are described in Willow Springs Strategic Solutions, "2012 Fort McKay Métis Community Housing Needs Assessment," (Fort McKay: Fort McKay Métis Community, 2012).

7. Raffy Boudjikanian, "Breaking New Ground: Métis in Alberta Buy Their Land From Province For 1st Time in Canada," *CBC News*, March 28, 2018, https://www.cbc.ca/news/canada/edmonton/metis-land-purchase-mckay-alberta-1.4596299.

8. Bonita Lawrence, *"Real" Indians and Others: Mixed-Blood Urban Native Peoples and Indigenous Nationhood*, (Lincoln: University of Nebraska Press, 2004); Pamala D. Palmater, *Beyond Blood: Rethinking Indigenous Identity*, (Saskatoon: Purich Publishing Limited, 2011)

9. A selection of these reports can be found at www.willowspringsss.com.

10   It is important to note that the Alberta government did not publicly clarify *how* a Métis community might be recognized in the eyes of the government until late 2019 when it made its "Métis Credible Assertion: Process and Criteria" public. Alberta, *Métis Credible Assertion: Process and Criteria*, December 13, 2019, updated in 2023, https://open.alberta.ca/publications/metis-credible-assertion-process-and-criteria.

11   For example, see Chris Andersen, *Métis: Race, Recognition, and the Struggle for Peoplehood* (Vancouver: UBC Press 2014).

12   Lavoie, "The Right to be Heard," 1215–1219.

13   *Fort Chipewyan Métis Nation of Alberta Local #125 v. Alberta*, 2016 ABQB 713.

14   Lavoie, "The Right to Be Heard," 1213.

15   Alberta, "Credible Assertion."

16   Alberta, "Métis Organization Establishes Right to Consultation," 13 February 2020. https://web.archive.org/web/20200929224333/https://ibftoday.ca/ab-government-metis-organization-establishes-right-to-consultation//

17   Métis Nation of Alberta, "Ratified Constitution of the Otipemisiwak Government," November 22, 2022. https://albertametis.com/app/uploads/2023/09/Otipemisiwak_Metis_Government_Constitution.pdf.

18   Robert Alexander Innes, *Elder Brother and the Law of the People* (Winnipeg: University of Manitoba, 2013); Robert Alexander Innes, "Multicultural Bands on the Northern Plans and the Notion of 'Tribal' Histories," in *Finding a Way to the Heart: Feminist Writings on Aboriginal and Women's History in Canada*, eds., Robin Jarvis Brownlie and Valerie J. Korinek (Winnipeg: University of Manitoba Press, 2012). Also see Brenda L. Gunn, "Defining Métis People as a People: Moving Beyond the Indian/Metis Dichotomy," *Dalhousie Law Journal* 38 (2015) 2: 413–46; Patricia Sawchuk, "The Creation of a Non-Status Indian Population in Alberta: The Interchangeability of Status of Métis and Indians and its Effects on Future Métis Claims," in Métis Association of Alberta, *Origins of the Alberta Métis: Land Claims Research Project, 1978–79* (Edmonton: Métis Association of Alberta, March 30, 1979); Trudy Nicks, "Mary Anne's Dilemma: The Ethnohistory of an Ambivalent Identity," *Canadian Ethnic Studies* 12, no. 2 (1985): 103–14. Trudy Nicks and Kenneth Morgan, "Grande Cache: The Historic Development of an Indigenous Métis Population," in *The New Peoples: Being and Becoming Métis in North America*, eds. Jacqueline Peterson and Jennifer S.H. Brown (Winnipeg: University of Manitoba Press, 1985). This topic is dealt with more fully in the manuscript's epilogue and appendix.

19   Kenichi Matsui and Arthur J. Ray, "Delimiting Métis Economic Communities in the Environs of Ft McMurray: A Preliminary Analysis Based on Hudson's Bay Company Records," in *Fort McMurray: Historic and Contemporary Rights-Bearing Métis Community*, Tim Clark, Dermot O'Connor, and Peter Fortna (Fort McMurray: McMurray Métis, 2015); Nicole St-Onge, "Early Forefathers to the Athabasca Métis: Long-Term North West Company Employees," in *The Long Journey Home of a Forgotten People: Métis Identities & Family Histories*, ed. Ute Lischke and David T. McNab (Waterloo: Sir Wilfred Laurier Press, 2010); Stantec, *A Historical Profile of the Northeast*

Alberta Area's Mixed European–Indian or Mixed European–Inuit Ancestry Community (Ottawa: Department of Justice, 2005).

20   For example, see David Leonard and Beverly Whalen, eds., *On the North Trail: The Treaty 8 Diary of O.C. Edwards* (Edmonton: Alberta Records and Publication Board, 1998), 53. For additional context, see Patricia McCormack, *Fort Chipewyan and the Shaping of Canadian History, 1788–1920s* (Vancouver: University of British Columbia Press, 2010), 16–17. See also Patricia A. McCormack, "How the (North) West Was Won: Development and Underdevelopment in the Fort Chipewyan Region" (PhD diss., University of Alberta, 1984).

21   Gerhard Ens, "Taking Treaty 8 Scrip, 1899–1900: A Quantitative Portrait of Northern Alberta Métis Communities," in *Treaty 8 Revisited: Selected Papers of the 1999 Centennial Conference*, ed. Duff Crerar and Jaroslav Petryshyn (Grand Prairie: Grand Prairie Regional College, 1999–2000), 252. See also Neil Reddekopp and Patricia Bartko, "Distinction without a Difference? Treaty and Scrip in 1899" in *Treaty 8 Revisited*, 213–28; Reddekopp, "Research Summary"; Trudy Nicks, "Mary Anne's Dilemma."

22   J. R. Miller, "From Riel to the Metis," *Canadian Historical Review* 96, no. 1 (1988): 19. For more about the multiculturalism and Indigenous communities in the West, see Robert Alexander Innes, "Multicultural Bands on the Northern Plains and the Notion of 'Tribal' Histories" in *Finding a Way to the Heart: Feminist Writings on Aboriginal and Women's History in Canada*, eds. Robin Jarvis Brownlie and Valerie J. Korinek (Winnipeg: University of Manitoba Press, 2012).

23   Ian McKay, "The Liberal Order Framework: A Prospectus for a Reconnaissance of Canadian History," *Canadian Historical Review* 4, no. 81 (December 2000): 620.

24   McKay, "The Liberal Order Framework," 636–37. This desire to exert control over new territories is also described by Patricia McCormack as "internal colonialism" where Indigenous sovereignty is challenged and ultimately overcome by a dominating state. See "Canadian Nation-building: A Pretty Name for Internal Colonialism. Presented at Nation Building, British Association for Canadian Studies 25th Annual Conference, April 11–14, 2000, University of Edinburgh, Scotland. Also see Damien Short, "Reconciliation and the Problem of Internal Colonialism," *Journal Intercultural Studies* 26, no. 3 (August 2005): 267–82.

25   Patrick Wolfe, "Settler Colonialism and the Elimination of the Native," *Journal of Genocide Research* 8, no. 4 (2006). Also see Patrick Wolfe, *Settler Colonialism and the Transformation of Anthropology* (New York: Bloomsbury Academic, 1998); Lorenzo Veracini, *Settler Colonialism: A Theoretical Overview* (London: Palgrave MacMillan, 2010). For Canadian context see Cole Harris, *A Bounded Land: Reflections on Settler Colonialism in Canada* (Vancouver: UBC Press, 2020).

26   Allan Greer, "Settler Colonialism and Beyond," *Journal of the Canadian Historical Association* 30 (2020): 61–86. Also see the articles in *Extracting Home in the Oil Sands: Settler Colonialism and Environmental Change in Subarctic Canada*, eds. Clinton N. Westman, Tara L. Joly, and Lena Gross (London and New York: Routledge, 2020).

27   For an excellent discussion of the uses and limits of genealogical data, see Heather Devine, *The People Who Own Themselves: Aboriginal Ethnogenesis in a Canadian*

Family, 1660-1900 (Calgary: University of Calgary Press, 2004). Also see Brenda Macdougall, *One of the Family: Métis Culture in Nineteenth-Century Northwestern Saskatchewan* (Vancouver: University of British Columbia Press, 2010); Emilie Pigeon, Nicole St-Onge, and Brenda Macdougall, "A Social Network of Hunters?: Métis Mobility and New Approaches in History" (Canadian Historical Association, 2013), https://www.academia.edu/12366703/A_Social_Network_of_Hunters_Metis_Mobility_and_New_Methodological_Approaches_in_History.

28 Gerhard Ens and Joe Sawchuk, *From New People to New Nations: Aspects of Métis History and Identity from the Eighteenth to Twenty-First Centuries* (Toronto: University of Toronto Press, 2016), 131–32.

29 This process seems to mirror those described by Robert Alexander Innes in Cowessess First Nation in Saskatchewan, where a broad array of Indigenous people came together to form the Band. He effectively argues that all-encompassing "tribal histories" tend to downplay the multicultural nature of his Nation (as well as others) and fails to appreciate the fluidity that existed in the West before the treaties. See Robert Alexander Innes, *Elder Brother and the Law of the People: Contemporary Kinship and Cowessess First Nation* (Winnipeg: University of Manitoba Press, 2013); Robert Alexander Innes, "Multicultural Bands on the Northern Plains and the Notion of 'Tribal' Histories," in *Finding a Way to the Heart: Feminist Writings on Aboriginal and Women's History in Canada*, eds. Robin Jarvis Brownlie and Valerie J. Korinek (Winnipeg: University of Manitoba Press, 2012).

30 Fort McKay Tribal Administration, "From Where We Stand: Traditional Land Use and Occupancy Study of the Fort McKay First Nation" (Fort McKay: Fort McKay Tribal Administration, 1983); James N. Tanner, C. Cormack Gates, and Bertha Ganter, *Some Effects of Oil Sands Development on the Traditional Economy of Fort McKay* (Fort McKay: Fort McKay Industrial Relations Corporation, 2001). For a broader discussion on the concept, see John Lutz, *Makuk: A New History of Aboriginal-White Relations* (Vancouver: University of British Columbia Press, 2009); Liam Haggarty, "Métis Welfare: A History of Economic Exchange in Northwest Saskatchewan, 1770–1870," *Saskatchewan History* 61, no. 2 (2009): 7–17; Liam Haggarty, "Sharing and Exchange in Northwest Saskatchewan," in *Métis in Canada: History, Identity, Law, & Politics*, ed. Christopher Adams, Gregg Dahl, and Ian Peach (Edmonton: University of Alberta Press, 2013); Clark, O'Connor, and Fortna, "Fort McMurray: Historic and Contemporary Rights-Bearing Métis Community."

31 Dawn Balazs, "A Short Analysis of the Transfer of Natural Resources to Alberta in 1930 and a Preliminary Study of the Registered Trapline System," (Treaty and Aboriginal Rights Research of the Indian Association of Alberta, March 1976).

32 James C. Scott, *Seeing Like a State: How Certain Schemes to Improve the Human Condition Have Failed* (New Haven: Yale University Press, 1998) 4. For Canadian context, see Tina Loo, "High Modernism, Conflict, and the Nature of Change in Canada: A Look at Seeing Like a State," *Canadian Historical Review* 1, no. 97 (March 2016); Tina Loo, "Disturbing the Peace: Environmental Change and the Scales of Justice on a Northern River," *Environmental History*, Special Issue on Canada (October 2007); and Tina Loo, *Moved by the State: Forced Relocation and Making a Good Life in Postwar Canada* (Vancouver: UBC Press, 2019).

33   Clinton N. Westman, Tara L. Joly, and Lena Gross, "Introduction: At Home in the Oil Sands," in *Extracting Home in the Oil Sands: Settler Colonialism and Environmental Change in Subarctic Canada* eds. Clinton N. Westman, Tara L. Joly, and Lena Gross (London and New York: Routledge, 2020), 13. Also see John Sandlos and Arn Keeling, "Introduction: The Complex Legacy of Mining in Northern Canada," in *Mining and Communities in Northern Canada: History, Politics, and Memory*, eds. John Sandlos, and Arn Keeling (Calgary: University of Calgary Press, 2015).

34   Compare with Tina Loo, "Disturbing the Peace: Environmental Change and the Scales of Justice on a Northern River," *Environmental History*, Special Issue on Canada (October 2007).

35   For example, see "Fort McKay Community files," PAA, ACC GR1979.0152, box 16, item 217.

36   Patricia McCormack, *Fort Chipewyan and the Shaping of Canadian History, 1788–1920s* (Vancouver: University of British Columbia Press, 2010), 16–17. See also Patricia A. McCormack, "How the (North) West Was Won: Development and Underdevelopment in the Fort Chipewyan Region" (PhD diss., University of Alberta, 1984); James M. Parker, *Emporium of the North: Fort Chipewyan and the Fur Trade to 1835* (Saskatoon: Canadian Plains Research Centre, 1987).

37   Trudy Nicks and Kenneth Morgan, "Grande Cache: The Historic Development of an Indigenous Métis Population," in *The New Peoples: Being and Becoming Métis in North America*, ed. Jacqueline Peterson and Jennifer S. H. Brown (Winnipeg: University of Manitoba Press, 1985), 177.

38   Nicks and Morgan, "Grande Cache," 177.

39   For a broader discussion about how oral history can be used in community-based history see Clark, O'Connor, and Fortna, "Fort McMurray: Historic and Contemporary Rights-Bearing Métis Community," 10–12. For more on the role of oral history in decolonization, see Julie Cruikshank, "Oral Tradition and Oral History: Reviewing Some Issues," *Canadian Historical Review* 75, no. 3 (1994): 403–18; P. Leavy, *Oral History* (Oxford: Oxford University Press, 2011); and P. Thompson, *The Voice of the Past: Oral History* (Oxford: Oxford University Press, 2000). For epistemological, methodological, and legal debates regarding oral history and its uses, see Arthur J. Ray, *Telling It to the Judge: Taking Native History to Court* (Montreal: McGill-Queen's University Press, 2012). Also see A. Hoffman, "Reliability and Validity in Oral History," in *Oral History*, ed. D. K. Dunaway and W. K. Baum (Plymouth: Altamira Press, 1984); Thompson, *The Voice of the Past*; Signa Daum Shanks, "Mamiskotamaw: Oral History, Indigenous Method, and Canadian Law in Three Books," *Indigenous Law Journal* 3 (Fall 2004): 181–92; T. L. Charlton, L. E. Meyers, and R. Sharpless, *History of Oral History: Foundations and Methodology* (Lanham: Rowman and Littlefield, 2007); and Leavy, *Oral History*.

40   Craig Campbell, Alice Boucher, Mike Evans, Emma Faichney, Howard LaCorde, and Zachary Powder, *Mihkwâkamiwi sipîsis: Stories and Pictures from Métis Elders in Fort McKay* (Edmonton: Canadian Circumpolar Institute, 2005), https://archive.org/details/uap_9781772122091.

41	Fort McKay Tribal Administration, "From Where We Stand: Traditional Land Use and Occupancy Study of the Fort McKay First Nation" (Fort McKay: Fort McKay Tribal Administration, 1983); Fort McKay First Nations, *There Is Still Survival Out There: A Traditional Land Use and Occupancy Study of the Fort McKay First Nations* (Edmonton: Arctic Institute of North America, 1994). See also the earlier study, Edward W. Van Dyke, "Lives in Transition: The Ft. McKay Case" (Ponoka: Applied Research Associates Ltd., 1978).

42	Fort McKay Industrial Relations Corporation, "Fort McKay Specific Assessment," 2010, 1, https://fmsd.knowledgekeeper.ca/sites/default/files/fortmckay_home/documents/Fort%20McKay%20Specific%20Assessment%20-%20Final.zip.

43	Human Environment Group (HEG), "Teck Frontier Mine Project: Fort McKay Métis Integrated Cultural Assessment" (Fort McKay: Fort McKay Métis Sustainability Centre, 2016), https://open.alberta.ca/dataset/5da3a4f0-f982-4f8e-af9b-cb00c39fb165/resource/5ef5883f-c8ca-43f0-a553-183aa9d35ee8/download/fort-mckay-metis-ica-final-march-4-2016.pdf.

44	Fort McKay Industrial Relations Corporation, "The Fort McKay Cultural Heritage Assessment Baseline Pre-Development (1960s) to Current (2008), prepared as part of the Fort McKay Specific Assessment" (Fort McKay: Fort McKay Industrial Relations Corporation, 2010), https://fmsd.knowledgekeeper.ca/sites/default/files/fortmckay_home/documents/CHA%20Baseline.pdf. See also James N. Tanner, C. Cormack Gates, and Bertha Ganter, *Some Effects of Oil Sands Development on the Traditional Economy of Fort McKay* (Fort McKay: Fort McKay Industrial Relations Corporation, 2001).

45	This is one of the reasons I have chosen to publish this book with the University of Calgary Press where it is available to download for anyone with interest in the work.

46	Unless directly quoted, the author has chosen to use "Fort McKay" throughout the document instead of "Fort MacKay," which is often used in official government documentation. This is because the community prefers the former spelling, and they are working with other levels of government to standardize this in all official correspondence. A detailed explanation of the spelling of Fort McKay can be found in Neil G. Reddekopp, "Post-1915 Additions to the Membership of the Fort McKay Band," December 1994 (Indian Claims Commission, *Inquiry into the Treaty Land Entitlement Claim of the Fort McKay First Nation,* Exhibit 18, fn 2). For information on the community's modern desire to change the name to "Fort McKay" in all government correspondence, see Shari Narine, "Request Made to Change Spelling of Fort MacKay," *Alberta Sweetgrass* 19, no. 10 (2012), https://ammsa.com/publications/alberta-sweetgrass/request-made-change-spelling-fort-mackay.

NOTES TO CHAPTER 1

1	Nicole St-Onge, "Early Forefathers to the Athabasca Métis: Long-Term North West Company Employees," in *The Long Journey of a Forgotten People: Métis Identities & Family Histories*, eds. Ute Lischke and David T. McNab (Waterloo: Wilfrid Laurier Press, 2007), 109; Duckworth, "Introduction," *The English River Book*.

2   For a general history of the fur trade, see Arthur J. Ray, *Indians and the Fur Trade: Their Role as Trappers, Hunters, and Middlemen in the Lands Southwest of Hudson Bay* (Toronto: University of Toronto Press, 1974).

3   James M. Parker, *Emporium of the North: Fort Chipewyan and the Fur Trade to 1835* (Saskatoon: Canadian Plains Research Centre, 1987).

4   St-Onge, "Early Forefathers," 109.

5   McCormack, *Fort Chipewyan*.

6   Michael Forsman, "The Archaeology of Fur Trade Sites in the Athabasca District," in *Proceedings of the Fort Chipewyan and Fort Vermilion Bicentennial Conference: September 23–25, 1988*, eds. Patricia A. McCormack and R. Geoffrey Ironside (Edmonton: Boreal Institute for Northern Studies, 1990), 75–80.

7   Forsman, "The Archaeology of Fur," 75–80.

8   Forsman, "The Archaeology of Fur," 75–80.

9   Forsman, "The Archaeology of Fur," 75–80.

10 Fort Chipewyan [Wedderburn] District Report, 1819-20, HBCA, B e/4: 6-7 as cited in Matsui and Ray, 23.

11 Fort Chipewyan Report District Report [for Athabasca], 1885, HBCA B 39/e/11: 5.

12 Matsui and Ray, 31–2.

13 According to the Archives of Manitoba, "Fort McKay Started as an outpost of Fort McMurray, and was first called Little Red River. It was established at least by 1895." This record is permanently available at the following URL: http://pam.minisisinc.com/scripts/mwimain.dll/144/PAM_AUTHORITY/AUTH_DESC_DET_REP/SISN%20 1842?sessionsearch. Mention of the Little Red River post in the Fort Chipewyan Post Journal is found dating to at least 1885. See Ft Chipewyan Report District Report [for Athabasca], 1885, HBCA B 39/e/11: 5. This is also cited in Matsui and Ray, 34.

14 Ernest Voorhis, "Historic Forts and Trading Posts of the French Regime and the English Fur Trading Companies" (Ottawa: Department of the Interior, National Development Bureau, 1930): 131–32.

15 Archives of Manitoba, "Keystone Archives Descriptive Database: Fort McKay."

16 "Local," *The Edmonton Bulletin*, October 26, 1899, 5.

17 Voorhis, 131. It is important to note that the "Little Red River" that would become Fort McKay should not be confused with the better known Little Red River on the Peace River west of Wood Buffalo National Park.

18 Ft Chipewyan Report District Report [for Athabasca], 1885, HBCA B 39/e/11: 5. This is also cited in Matsui and Ray, 34.

19 It is unclear how successful the HBC post was in the face of the growing competition, but it is known that by 1896, Inspector Jarvis identified at least two competitors permanently operating at Little Red River. A. M. Jarvis, "Appendix L. Police Patrol, Athabasca District, Winter of 1896–97, North-West Mounted Police, Office of the

Commissioner, Regina, 21 December, 1896," in *Report of the Commissioner of the North-West Mounted Police, 1897* (Ottawa: Queen's Printer, 1898), 160.

20 McCormack, *Fort Chipewyan*, 147.

21 McCormack, *Fort Chipewyan*, 147. Despite Cree being the most commonly spoken language, people in Fort McKay still spoke Dené well into the twentieth century. As noted, many in Fort McKay continued to speak Cree, Dené, English, and French until at least the 1960s. For example, Ernie Lacorde remembers that his father, Isadore Lacorde, spoke "English, French, Cree, and Chipewyan" in the community and sometimes acted as an interpreter for the RCMP. Author Unknown, "The Hardships of Bush Life: Interview with Ernie Lacorde," *Fort McMurray Today*, 1978. Similarly, Emma Faichney confirms that although she had Cree and Chipewyan ancestors, they all learned to speak Cree as the primary language. Campbell et al., 45.

22 James G. E. Smith, "Western Woods Cree," in *Subarctic* 6, June Helm, editor, Handbook of North American Indians, William C. Sturtevant, general editor (Washington, DC: Smithsonian Institute, 1981): 259. Also see James G. E. Smith, "Chipewyan" in *Subarctic, vol.* 6, June Helm, editor, Handbook of North American Indians, William C. Sturtevant, general editor. Washington, DC: Smithsonian Institute, 1981: 276.

23 FMTC, *From Where We Stand*, 84; Matsui and Ray, 35–6.

24 For example, Louis Boucher explains that at the time of Treaty everyone at Fort McKay spoke "Cree, Chipewyan and English." See Louis Boucher, "Treaty and Aboriginal Rights Research Interview," February 6, 1974. http://hdl.handle.net/10294/1371. While Louis remembers only the three languages, French was also spoken by many in the community. Alice Boucher, born 1920, described her mother as "French Metis," and Isadore Lacorde, born 1882, spoke "Cree, Chipewyan, French and English." See Campbell et. al., 31; "Interview with Ernie Lacorde."

25 Matsui and Ray, 31–4.

26 29d-30 and 22d-23, HBC Archives, F.2/1. Duckworth, "Appendix B: Biographies of Voyagers and Traders," 137–38.

27 St-Onge, 132–33.

28 The HBCA biographical sheets list Jean Baptiste Boucher, another man of mixed ancestry born in Rupert's Land. He worked first for the North West Company but signed a contract with HBC in 1822, shortly after the two companies amalgamated. Perhaps he and Joseph Wakan Bouché were brothers. Hudson's Bay Company Biographical Sheet, "Jean Baptiste Boucher," 1789–1849. https://www.gov.mb.ca/chc/archives/_docs/hbca/biographical/b/boucher_jean-baptiste.pdf. It is also possible that Jean and Joseph were children of François Bouché and Jean-Marie Bouché, though the author has yet to find official documentation demonstrating this fact.

29 St-Onge, 132-3.

30 Fort McMurray Journal, HBCA B.307/a/2, 16 Jan 1882.

31 Charlot [Charles] and Chrysostome are listed in the 1881 Census of Canada, The North West Territories, 192, Athabasca T – Fort McMurray, Page 7, Household 30. Note that

the page included those living at Little Red River as it was considered an outpost of Fort McMurray.

32 The English River Book, the Account Book, 63d, HBC Archives, F.2/1, 36Ad-36B (page 75 in PDF).

33 Duckworth, "Appendix B: Biographies of Voyagers and Traders," 163.

34 Duckworth, "Appendix B: Biographies of Voyagers and Traders," 163.

35 Patricia McCormack, "Research Report: Treaty No. 8 and the Fort McKay First Nation," 2012, https://web.archive.org/web/20170726114206/https://www.ceaa-acee.gc.ca/050/documents_staticpost/59540/81946/Appendix_A_-_Treaty_No_8_and_Fort_McKay_First_Nation_Research_Report.pdf, 86–87.

36 Tourangeau, Isabelle; address: Chipewyan; born: 1867 at Chipewyan; father: Charles Piche (Métis); mother: Suzette Martin (Indian); married: 1886 at Chipewyan to Jonas Tourangeau; children living: Antoine, Louis and Isidore; scrip cert. no. 940A; claim no. 431. https://recherche-collection-search.bac-lac.gc.ca/eng/home/record?app=fonandcol&IdNumber=1515423&q=Isabelle%20Tourangeau#shr-pg0.

37 McCormack, Fort McKay First Nation Research Report," 86–87.

38 McCormack, Fort McKay First Nation Research Report, 129.

39 McCormack, Fort McKay First Nation Research Report, 87.

40 For example, as early as 1778, a basic Cree dictionary was provided to the North West Company employees. The English River Book, the Account Book, 63d, HBC Archives, F.2/1, 1A. The use of Cree continued through the nineteenth century, and it "became a regional *lingua franca*" by the end of the century." McCormack, *Fort Chipewyan*, 147.

41 See Fort McMurray Journal, HBCA B.307/a/1-4; Fort McKay Journal, HBCA 305/a/1-9. Also see Matsui and Ray, 31. While it is unclear exactly who Jose Grand Bouché was descended from, it seems highly likely that he was the descendent of one of the many Bouchés engaged in the region's fur trade as early as the late eighteenth century and in the Athabasca Region. For example, François Bouché and Jean-Marie Bouché are both referenced in the English River Book the Account Book, 29d-30 and 22d-23, HBC Archives, F.2/1. Nicole St-Onge also finds reference to Joseph and Louis Bouché in the North West Company ledgers in the late eighteenth and early nineteenth century. For more information on the early Bouché voyagers, see "Early Forefathers to the Athabasca Métis" 132–3 and Duckworth, "Appendix B: Biographies of Voyagers and Traders," 137–38.

42 "Indians at Little Red River, Athabasca River, 35 miles below Fort McMurray, 1899" as found in "Indians: Census of Indians & Halfbreeds in Peace River District" LAC, RG18, vol. 1435, file 76-1899, pt. 2. 1881 Census of Canada, Northwest Territories 192, Athabasca T – Fort McMurray, p. 7, household 30 – Piche, Chryostum; household 31 – Piche, Charlos, LAC T-6426.

43 The English River Book, the Account Book, 63d, HBC Archives, F.2/1.

44 "List of Halfbreeds at Chipewyan, 1899" as found in "Indians: Census of Indians & Halfbreeds in Peace River District" LAC, RG18, vol. 1435, file 76-1899, pt. 2. Interestingly, the NWMP census does not include a list of "halfbreeds." The police

did not create a methodology for determining who was or was not considered Métis or First Nations on their census, and furthermore, many "Indians" identified in the census chose to take scrip, and many identified as halfbreeds took treaty. Furthermore, there seems to be a strong likelihood that some families who were closely connected to the Bouchés and Pichés were missed by the census takers or lumped in with the Fort Chipewyan "Half-Breeds."

45   N.O. Cote to J.D. McLean, "RE: Claim 480970, Department of Indian and Northern Development (DIAND), file 779/30-10/174, vol. 1.

46   1881 Census of Canada, Northwest Territories 192, Athabasca T – Fort McMurray, p. 7, household 30 – Piche, Chryostum; household 31 – Piche, Charlos, LAC T-6426; Inspector Routledge, LAC, RG18, vol. 1435, no. 76, pt. 2.

47   Jonas Tourangeau, "Squatting Right's Claim," October 7, 1911. Department of Indian and Northern Development (DIAND), file 779/30-10/174, vol. 1.

48   Jonas Tourangeau Scrip cert. no. 941a, claim no. 423, August 7, 1899, https://recherche-collection-search.bac-lac.gc.ca/eng/home/record?app=fonandcol&IdNumber=1515426&q=%22Jonas%20Tourangeau%22%20Scrip.

49   Tourangeau, Isabelle; address: Chipewyan; born: 1867 at Chipewyan; father: Charles Piche (Métis); mother: Suzette Martin (Indian); married: 1886 at Chipewyan to Jonas Tourangeau; children living: Antoine, Louis and Isidore; scrip cert. no. 940A; claim no. 431, https://recherche-collection-search.bac-lac.gc.ca/eng/home/record?app=fonandcol&IdNumber=1515423&q=Isabelle%20Tourangeau#shr-pg0.

50   Appendix A: Genealogical Visual Representation of the Fort McKay Métis Nation. The deep multigenerational connections between the Boucher and Tourangeau families have meant that many members of the modern Tourangeau family, such as Edward's daughter Judy, could legally claim their First Nations status after Bill C-31. However, as per the law, those of the latest generation, such as Judy's son Jalal Bilal Eid, are not eligible for First Nations status and have joined the Fort McKay Métis Nation.

51   Heather Devine, *The People Who Own Themselves: Aboriginal Ethnogenesis in a Canadian Family, 1660–1900*, (Calgary: University of Calgary Press, 2004), 140. Also see McCormack, *Fort Chipewyan*; Patricia Sawchuk, "The Creation of a Non-Status Indian Population in Alberta: The Interchangeability of Status of Métis and Indians and Its Effect on Future Métis Claims," in *Origins of the Alberta Métis: Land Claims Research Project, 1878–79* (Edmonton: Métis Association of Alberta, 1979), 93–117; Patricia Sawchuk, "The Historic Interchangeability of Status of Metis and Indians: An Alberta Example" in *The Recognition of Aboriginal Rights*, eds. Samuel W. Corrigan and Joe Sawchuk Brandon MB: Bearpaw Publishing, 1996, 57–71.

52   Van Dyke, "Lives in Transition," 98.

53   Brenda Macdougall, "Wahkotowin: Family and Cultural Identity in Northwestern Saskatchewan Metis Communities," *Canadian Historical Review* 87, no. 3 (September 2006): 433. Also see Macdougall, *One of the Family: Métis Culture in Nineteenth-Century Northwestern Saskatchewan* (Vancouver: UBC Press, 2010). This topic is also discussed at length in Peter Fortna, "Wahkotowin, Keemooch, and Home: A History

of the Conklin Métis Community, 1886–2020," *Prairie History*, 8 (2022). For other examples see Kathleen O'Reilly-Scanlon, Christine Crow, and Angelina Weenie, "Pathways to Understanding: 'Wâhkôhtowin' as a Research Methodology," *McGill Journal of Education* 39, no. 1 (Winter 2004) ; Matthew Wildcat, "Wahkohtowin *in* Action," *Constitutional Forum Constitutionnel* 27, no. 1 (2018); Harold Cardinal and Walter Hildebrandt, *Treaty Elders of Saskatchewan: Our Dream is That Our Peoples Will One Day be Clearly Recognized as Nations* (Calgary: University of Calgary Press, 2000); Sylvia McAdam (Saysewahum), *Nationhood Interrupted: Revitalizing nêhiyaw Legal Systems* (Saskatoon: Purich Publishing, 2015).

54   Athabasca Chipewyan First Nation with Sabina Trimble and Peter Fortna, *Remembering Our Relations: Dënesųłiné Oral Histories of Wood Buffalo National Park* (Calgary: University of Calgary Press, 2023), xxi–xxii, 43. Also see Craig Candler, "Integrated Knowledge and Land Use Report and Assessment for Shell Canada's Proposed Jackmine Mine Expansion and Pierre River Mine," April 20, 2011, 2.

55   FMTA, *From Where We Stand*, 1.

56   FMTA, *From Where We Stand*, 79–82.

57   FMTA, *From Where We Stand*, 34. For a broader discussion of the Tea Dance in communities in northern Alberta, see Patrick Moore, "Tea Dance: The Circle of Community," in *Proceedings of the Fort Chipewyan and Fort Vermilion Bicentennial Conference: September 23–25, 1988*, eds. Patricia A. McCormack and R. Geoffrey Ironside (Edmonton: Boreal Institute for Northern Studies, 1990), 267–271.

58   Fort McKay Métis Nation community member as quoted in HEG, "Integrated Cultural Impact Assessment," 332.

59   Francis Orr, "Interview," in *There is Still Survival Out There*, 109.

60   Johnny Orr, "Interview," in *There is Still Survival Out There*, 86.

61   Van Dyke, "Lives in Transition," 56–57. Also see HEG, "Indicators of Cultural Change," 68.

62   Ernest Thompson Seton, *The Arctic Prairies* (New York: Charles Scribner's Sons, 1911). Originally cited in McCormack, *Fort Chipewyan*, 147. While it is true that Seton was a traveller through the area and depended upon what he was told by others, his description matches with that of the FMTA, *From Where We Stand*, 26.

63   FMTA, *From Where We Stand*, 37–42 and throughout.

64   FMTA, *From Where We Stand*, 34, 128–129.

65   Matsui and Ray, Appendix 5. Original post journals referenced by Matsui and Ray included in the document collection.

66   FMTA, *From Where We Stand*, 43–47.

67   FMFN, *There is Still Survival*, 15–29.

68   PAA, GR. 1990.377 Sheets, 84-A, 84-H, 74-E, 74-D. There is also a list of Fort McKay traplines available in FMFN, *There is Still Survival* 28–29 and HEG, "Integrated Cultural Assessment," 49.

69 Since the mid-2000s, Fort McKay (Métis and First Nation) has shared a traditional land-use map, which includes maps from *Where We Stand* and *There is Still Survival* overlayed. A version can be found at Fort McKay Sustainability Department, "Fort McKay Traditional Territory," February 2011 and is provided below. https://fmsd.knowledgekeeper.ca/sites/default/files/fortmckay_home/documents/Fort_McKay_Traditional_Territory.pdf. Also see HEG, "Integrated Cultural Assessment," 421.

70 FMTA, *From Where We Stand*, 78–79.

71 FMTA, *From Where We Stand*, 25–26.

72 FMTA, *From Where We Stand*, 79–82. Matsui and Ray, 35–36. An aspect underplayed by the Tribal Administration is the seasonal work some Fort McKay community members would likely participate in. This could include everything from provisioning the fort to participating as labourers and trackers bringing skiffs and scows back down the Athabasca River.

73 Fort McKay Sustainability Department, "Fort McKay Traditional Territory," 2011. https://fmsd.knowledgekeeper.ca/sites/default/files/fortmckay_home/documents/Fort_McKay_Traditional_Territory.pdf.

74 James Parker, 43. Also see FMTA, *From Where We Stand*, 26.

75 FMTA, *From Where We Stand*, 1. Also see Fort McKay Industrial Relations Corporation, "Cultural Heritage Assessment Baseline," 16–21.

NOTES TO CHAPTER 2

1 Canada, *Annual Report of the Department of Indians Affairs for the Year Ended June 30, 1899* (Ottawa: Queen's Press, 1900), xxxviii.

2 Donald F. Robertson to S. Bray, "Memorandum," December 23, 2015. DIAND, file 779/30-10/174, vol. 1.

3 J. A.J. McKenna to Superintendent General of Indian, Clifford Sifton, April 18, 1899. RG 10, Volume 3848, file 75,236-1.

4 Clifford Sifton to Governor General in Council, June 18, 1898. RG 10, Volume 3848, file 75,236-1.

5 Clifford Sifton to Governor General in Council, June 18, 1898. RG 10, Volume 3848, file 75,236-1.

6 As recorded in Charles Mair, *Through the Mackenzie Basin: An Account of the Signing of Treaty no. 8 and the Scrip Commission, 1899* (Edmonton: University of Alberta Press: 1999), 59–60.

7 For example, Isabelle, who was married to Jonas Tourangeau, chose to take Métis Scrip and identified her father as "Charles Piche" despite the fact that her father had signed onto Treaty 8. See Tourangeau, Isabelle; address: Chipewyan; born: 1867 at Chipewyan; father: Charles Piche (Métis); mother: Suzette Martin (Indian); married: 1886 at Chipewyan to Jonas Tourangeau; children living: Antoine, Louis and Isidore; scrip cert. no. 940A; claim no. 431. https://recherche-collection-search.bac-lac.gc.ca/eng/home/record?app=fonandcol&IdNumber=1515423&q=Isabelle%20Tourangeau#shr-pg0.

8   For example, see Devine, *People Who Own Themselves*, 141–82.

9   Order in Council 918, "Half breed commission appointing James Walker and Joseph Arthur Cole as Commrs [Commissioners] to investigate half breed claims Athabaska. May 6, 1899. LAC, R.G. 2, Series 1, Vol 796.

10 Dennis K. Madill, "Treaty Research Report: Treaty Eight (1899)" (Ottawa: Treaties and Historical Research Centre, Indian and Northern Affairs Canada, 1986), 23–26.

11 Metis Association of Alberta, Joe Sawchuk, Patricia Sawchuk, Theresa Ferguson, *Metis Land Rights in Alberta* (Edmonton: Metis Association of Alberta, 1981), 127–30.

12 Unfortunately for the scrip recipients, the scrip speculators rarely (if ever) provided fair value, and scrip fraud remained a major issue into the 1920s before the government instituted a statute of limitations banning future fraud claims. See Metis Association of Alberta et. al., *Metis Land Rights in Alberta,* 130–140.

13 The scrip process is described at length in Metis Association of Alberta et. al., *Metis Land Rights in Alberta*, 87–158, while the Treaty process is described by Madill.

14 For example, Charles Mair's Treaty 8 memoir only makes passing reference to the commission passing by Little Red River and Fort McMurray, and the official report only lists the signatories. See Mair, 120–21; Canada, *Treaty No. 8, Made June 21, 1899 and Adhesions, Reports, Etc.* (Ottawa: Queen's Printer and Controller of Stationary, 1966 [1899]), 18.

15 Canada, *Treaty No. 8,* 18.

16 Canada, *Treaty No. 8,* 18.

17 Jonas Tourangeau Scrip cert. no. 941a.

18 Reddekopp, "The First Survey of Reserves for the Cree-Chipewyan Band of Fort McMurray," January 1995. Indian Claims Commission, Inquiry into the Treaty Land Entitlement Claim of the Fort McKay First Nation, Exhibit 17, 12–14. Expansion of the community's land-use areas to include Moose Lake to the west, Lake Claire to the north, Willow Lake to the south, and the east side of the Athabasca River, a territory the people have maintained into the twentieth century. FMFN, *There Is Still Survival Out There;* FMTA, *From Where We Stand*; Fort McKay Industrial Relations Corporation, "The Fort McKay Cultural Heritage Assessment Baseline."

19 Reddekopp, "First Survey," 12–14.

20 Ft Chipewyan Report District Report [for Athabasca], 1885, HBCA B 39/e/11: 5. Jarvis, "Appendix L. Police Patrol, Athabasca District, Winter of 1896–97," 160.

21 John McDonald was hired on with the Hudson's Bay Company in 1874 and worked at various posts in the Athabasca District, from Fort McMurray to Fort Vermilion. He was born in 1854 at St. Andrew's Parish at the Red River, Manitoba, as the "English halfbreed" son of Duncan McDonald and Elizabeth Tait. He signed a "Labourer/Horsekeeper" contract at the Fort McMurray Hudson's Bay Company post by the late 1870s and was described in the HBC 1889 inspection report for Fort McMurray as an "[i]nterpreter, [who] talks English & Cree. 14 years service; wife and 7 children; in charge of outpost in winter." It seems likely that John was in a position of significance at the Fort McKay post by the late 1880s as he was later described by government

surveyor Donald Robertson in 1915 as "one of the first, if not the first man in charge of the trading post at Ft. McKay for the Hudson's Bay company." While John was clearly working in the community, there is little evidence that he and his family members permanently integrated into the community, and he and his family would later settle in Fort McMurray. John McDonald, ("C" or "K") Hudson's Bay Company Biographical Sheet, https://www.gov.mb.ca/chc/archives/_docs/hbca/biographical/mc/mcdonald_john-c1874-1889.pdf; Donald F. Robertson to S. Bray, "Memorandum," December 23, 2015. DIAND, file 779/30-10/174, vol. 1; Fred McDonald, "Interview Transcript: Métis 1935 'Mark of the Métis' Heritage Study Pilot Project' Interviewed by Sara Loutitt and Sherri Labour, March 30, 2007.

22 For more about Louison Fosseneuve see Gregory A. Johnson, *Lac La Biche Chronicles: Early Years* (Lac La Biche: Portage College, 1999), 176–83.

23 For example, see Fort McKay Post Journal, October 29, 1911. HBCA, B/305/a/9; Ray and Matsui, "Delimiting Métis Economic Communities," 38. John Cowie's mother was likely Susan Cree, a daughter of Seapotainum Cree, who signed the Treaty 8 adhesion at Fort McMurray on behalf of the Cree of the area. John Cowie entered treaty with his grandfather and disappeared from the paylists about the time of his grandfather's death in 1911. Reddekopp, "First Survey," 44.

24 Reddekopp, "First Survey," 27.

25 FMFN, *There Is Still Survival Out There*, 67, 92.

26 FMFN, *There Is Still Survival Out There*, 80.

27 Personal Correspondence with Billie Fortier, July 2024.

28 Fort McKay Genealogy, Appendix A.

29 "A Stand for Fort McKay," *Alberta Report*, January 31, 1983, 37.

30 Appendix A: Genealogical Visual Representation of the Fort McKay Métis Nation.

31 Department of the Interior, Dominion Lands Branch, North-West Territories Metis scrip applications, Alberta or Bernard Lapoudre, Claim 771, Volume 1354, LAC C-14981.

32 Alphonse was born in 1890, while Modest was born in 1900. See 1906 Census of the Northwest Provinces, Alberta, Edmonton 20, Sub-district 8 – Lac La Biche, page 7, household 62. Lapoudre, Abel. LAC T-19362.

33 Devine, *The People Who Own Themselves*, 194, 186–94. For more on the Lac La Biche exodus into northern Alberta see Patricia McCormack, "How the (North) West was One: Development and Underdevelopment in the Fort Chipewyan Region" (Edmonton: University of Alberta PhD Thesis, 1984), 108–11; Fortna, "Wahkotowin, Keemooch, and Home," 2022.

34 For example, this practice was well documented to the east in La Loche by Macdougall in *One of the Family*, 2011.

35 FMFN, *There Is Still Survival Out There*, 65–66, 71–72, 81, 84, 86–87, 105.

36 PAA, GR. 1990.377 Sheets 84-A, 84-H, 74-E, 74-D.

37 Zachary Powder to Stan Daniels, April 12, 1973, Glenbow Museum and Archives, M4755, file 470.

38 Liam Harrap, "Fractured Forest: Alberta's Seismic Lines Dilemma" in *Alberta Views*, May 1, 2020, https://albertaviews.ca/fractured-forest/. For a description of the economic discrepancies between the Fort McKay First Nation and Métis Nation from the 1990s forward, see Fort McKay, "Position Paper," 2021.

39 Fort McKay Métis Nation, Membership List, 2023.

40 Appendix A: Genealogical Visual Representation of the Fort McKay Métis Nation.

41 Macdougall, *One of the Family*, 229–31.

42 Margie Wood "Interview Transcript: Métis 1935 'Mark of the Métis' Heritage Study Pilot Project'" Interviewed by Sara Loutitt and Sherri Labour, March 30, 2007, 72–74. https://www.acee-ceaa.gc.ca/050/documents/45006/45006F.pdf; Ray and Matsui, "Delimiting Métis Economic Communities," 474. Brenda Macdougall noted that Pascal Janvier's brother, Louison would also trade in Fort McMurray, obtaining trading goods in Lac La Biche to take into the region around the same time. Macdougall, *One of the Family*, 229–30.

43 Isadore and Catharine's grandfathers were brothers Pascal and Louison Janvier. See Macdougall, *One of the Family*, 230.

44 "The Hardships of Bush Life: Interview with Ernie Lacorde."

45 "Fort McKay Community files," PAA, ACC GR1979.0152, box 16, item 217.

46 Appendix A: Genealogical Visual Representation of the Fort McKay Métis Nation.

47 FMFN, *There Is Still Survival Out There*, 90–91.

48 Fort McKay Métis Nation Membership List.

49 Fort McKay Métis Nation Membership List.

50 FMFN, *There Is Still Survival Out There*, 80. Many members of the Fort McKay Indigenous community can trace their roots back to the Wabasca/Chipewyan Lakes area. For example, the Ahyasou and Orr families originated from Chipewyan Lakes and were accepted into the band by Adam Boucher in the early 1900s. FMFN, *There Is Still Survival Out There*, 78; Reddekopp, "Post 1915 Additions," 26–27

51 1911 Census of Canada, Alberta, Victoria 7, Sub-district Chipewyan Lake, page 74, household 192 - Beaver, Julian. LAC T-20333. Also see Highwood Environmental Group, "Family History of RFMA 2137," 3.

52 Jeannette Reva Sinclair, "On the Role of Nehiyaw'skwewak in Decision Making among Northern Cree" (master's thesis, University of Alberta, 1999), 145.

53 Reddekopp, "Post-1915 Additions," 19–21.

54 It is also possible that Felix was not allowed to join the local First Nation because Felix's family chose to take Métis scrip at Wabasca in 1899–1900. While possible, this does not seem likely as neither of their names were included in Matthew LaCompte et al.'s review of the Wabasca-Desmarais scrip records (though many other Beaver and Cardinals were included) or a search of Library and Archives Canada. See Matthew LaCompte,

Carol Hodgson, William Cornish, Jonathan Hart, and Joan Holmes "Historical Profile of the Wabasca-Desmarais Area's Mixed European-Indian Ancestry Community," (Ottawa: Research and Statistics Division & Aboriginal Law and Strategic Policy Group, 2005), 76–82.

55 Highwood Environmental Group, "Traditional Ecological Knowledge and Family History for RFMA 2137," (Fort McKay: Fort McKay Industrial Relations Corporation, 2001), 3.

56 Francois Boucher, 1916 Census of Alberta, Saskatchewan and Manitoba, Alberta, Edmonton East E-20 – Fort McKay, page 17, household 179 – Boucher, Francois. LAC T-21950.

57 Francois was also Joseph Robillard's brother-in-law, having married the latter's sister, Rosalie. Reddekopp, "The First Survey of Reserves," 26–27.

58 Highwood Environmental Group, 3.

59 Highwood Environmental Group, 3.

60 Highwood Environmental Group, 3.

61 For example, see Brandi Morin, "Fort McKay First Nation, holding onto nature in the middle of the tar sands," *APTN National News*, June 26, 2015. https://www.aptnnews.ca/national-news/fort-mckay-first-nation-holding-onto-nature-middle-tar-sands/; Janelle Marie Baker and the Fort McKay Berry Group, "Cranberries are Medicine: Monitoring, Sharing, and Consuming Cranberries in Fort McKay," in *Wisdom Engaged: Traditional Knowledge for Northern Community Well-Being*, ed. Leslie Main Johnson (Edmonton: University of Alberta Press, 2019).

62 Baker and the Fort McKay Group, "Cranberries." Also see Campbell et al., preface; FMFN, *There Is Still Survival Out There*, 30.

63 Fort McKay Métis Nation Membership List; FMFN, "Strong Governance," 2022. http://fortmckaymetis.com/strong-governance/.

64 Van Dyke, *Lives in Transition*, 52.

NOTES TO CHAPTER 3

1 Arthur Ray, *Indians in the Fur Trade: Their Roles as Trappers, Hunters, and Middlemen in the Lands Southwest of Hudson Bay, 1660–1870* (Toronto: University of Toronto Press, 2015; first published 1974); Arthur Ray, *The Canadian Fur Trade in the Industrial Age* (Toronto: University of Toronto Press, 1990).

2 McCormack, *Fort Chipewyan and the Shaping of Canadian History*, 159–69, 223. Descriptions of these early white trappers coming into the region can be found in the Edmonton Bulletin, with the first description coming as early as 1896. See Author Unknown, "Local" *Edmonton Bulletin*, September 17, 1896, 1.

3 Fort McKay Tribal Administration, "From Where We Stand," 31. Also see, Author Unknown, "Fur Plentiful but Hard to Trap Owing to Late Snowfall," *Edmonton Bulletin*, December 6, 1917, 7; Bustane Martin and William Whitehead to D. C. Scott,

Superintendent General, July 5, 1927, LAC, RG10, vol. 6732, file 420-2B, reel C8094, pp. 6–9.

4   Indigenous people and government officials colloquially use the term "trapline" to describe registered fur management areas, or "RFMAs."

5   Gerald Card, Indian Agent, to D. C. Scott, Superintendent General, May 22, 1924, LAC, RG10, vol. 6732, file 420-2B. Also see Sabina Trimble, and Peter Fortna, "A History of Wood Buffalo National Park's Relations with the Denésuliné" (Fort Chipewyan: Willow Springs Strategic Solutions, 2021).

6   Alberta Aboriginal Affairs and Northern Development, *The Alberta Natural Resources Act, Assented to April 3, 1930, Chapter 21, Alberta, An Act Respecting the Transfer of the Natural Resources of Alberta.*

7   H. W. Theisen, *Trapping the Buffalo Head Hills & Utikuma Uplands* (Edmonton: Bear Trap Trappers' Committee, 2006), 73. Also see McCormack, "How the (North) West Was Won."

8   "Legislative Debate over the Creation of Trap-lines," PAA, acc. 70.427/409, box 23. For more on the trapline system implemented in British Columbia see Glenn Iceton, "Many Families of Unseen Indians": Trapline Registration and Understandings of Aboriginal Title in the BC-Yukon Borderlands," *BC Studies* no. 201 (Spring 2019).

9   For a good description of the implementation of the Registered Fur Management System in Alberta see Theisen, *Trapping the Buffalo Head Hills*, 122–27. Also see Balazs, "A Short Analysis."

10 P. W. Head to Department of Mines and Resources – Indian Affairs Branch, February 2, 1940, pp. 22–24 in LAC, RG10, vol. 6733, file 420-2-2 1, reel C8095.

11 Maclean, Robinson, "Crees and Chipewyans Explain their Trouble," *Ottawa Citizen*, July 19, 1939. https://www.newspapers.com/clip/114884970/1939-07-19-crees-and-chipewyans/.

12 N. E. Tanner to M. Christianson, March 15, 1938. LAC, RG10, vol. 6733, file 420-2-2 1, reel C8095.

13 P. W. Head to C. Schmidt, February 2, 1940. LAC, RG10, vol. 6733, file 420-2-2 1, reel C8095.

14 P. W. Head to Department of Mines and Resources – Indian Affairs Branch, February 2, 1940, pp. 22–24 in LAC, RG10, vol. 6733, file 420-2-2 1, reel C8095.

15 C. Schmidt to Department of Mines and Resources – Indian Affairs Branch, February 13, 1940, LAC, RG10, vol. 6733, file 420-2-2 1, pp. 22–24, reel C8095.

16 J. L. Grew to D. J. Allen, "Memorandum," December 19, 1944, LAC, RG10, vol. 6734, 420-2-2 3, pp. 73–86, reel C8095.

17 LAC, RG10, vol. 6733, file 420-2-2 1, p. 29, reel C8095. It should also be noted that within the context of the memorandum, Mr. Grew was attempting to identify areas they could "lease from the Province" to solve the "Indian trapping situation." As such, he was constrained as much by potential cost as by the desire to map the Fort McKay traditional territory effectively, and therefore, these areas are much smaller than those

identified in sources such as "From Where We Stand" and *There Is Still Survival Out There*.

18   J. L. McGrew, "Report on Registered Trap Lines and General Trapping Conditions," August 14, 1945, LAC, RG10, vol. 6734, file 420-2-2 3, p. 42, reel C8095. This process was detailed with regards to the Boucher/Beaver/Faichney family in Highwood Environmental Group, "Traditional Ecological Knowledge and Family History for RFMA 2137" (Fort McKay: Fort McKay Industrial Relations Corporation, 2001).

19   Originally, Fort McKay First Nation was part of the "Cree-Chipewyan Band of Fort McMurray" even though they were largely independent groups. It was officially divided between 1949 and 1951. See Reddekopp, "Post 1915 Additions," 1–2.

20   Fort McKay Tribal Administration, *From Where We Stand*, 32. See also Balazs, "A Short Analysis." Monique Passelac-Ross suggests that by 2005, an informal policy for transferring open lines to First Nations had developed in government, but that they were unwilling to formalize a process to ensure Indigenous traplines stay with the community. However, an informal system had developed where "the transfer of a licence from an Aboriginal trapper to a non-Aboriginal trapper usually involes the approval of the band." See Monique Passelac-Ross, "The Trapping Rights of Aboriginal Peoples in Northern Alberta" (Calgary: Canadian Institute of Resource Law, 2005), 49. https://cirl.ca/sites/default/files/teams/1/Occasional%20Papers/Occasional%20Paper%20%2315.pdf.

21   W. B. Skead, "Annual Report – Alberta Fur Supervisor," 1948, LAC, RG10, vol. 6734, file 420-2-1-3, p. 26, reel C8096.

22   PAA, acc. GR 1990.377 – Trapping Maps and Index Cards.

23   Fort McKay Tribal Administration, "From Where We Stand," 99.

24   This list is slightly different than the list provided in the Fort McKay Integrated Cultural Assessment. For the purpose of this report, the author has taken a conservative approach, though it seems likely additional connections will be identified through further research. See HEG, "Teck Frontier Mine Project," 46–50.

25   Fort McKay Tribal Administration, "From Where We Stand," 96–97.

26   Fort McKay Tribal Administration, "From Where We Stand," 99.

27   Fort McKay, *There Is Still Survival Out There*, 27–30. In addition to these founding families, other Métis families owned traplines in the Fort McKay traditional territory, particularly in the south. They included Cooper, Flobert, Golosky, and Auger, all identified as belonging to the Fort McKay Indigenous community. While this is not particularly surprising given the close relationship between Indigenous communities in Fort McMurray and Fort McKay, it is likely the result of later marriages between members of each group. The histories of the Cooper, Flobert, Golosky, and Auger families are covered at length in Clark et al., "Fort McMurray: Historic and Contemporary Rights-Bearing Métis Community."

28   The Fort McKay Tribal Administration stated that while a "Native Trapping Policy" was developed by the Alberta government, it did not meet the needs of the community [any idea why not?], Fort McKay Tribal Administration, "From Where We Stand," 109–14.

It is unclear what happened to this policy, but Passelac-Ross explains that by 2005, Fish and Wildlife officers were using an informal system "to the extent it is possible" to offer traplines as they become available to the Band that "claims" them. She makes no reference to how officers might deal with potential conflicts between Indigenous communities or whether officers would recognize Métis claims to such areas. Passelac-Ross, "The Trapping Rights of Aboriginal Peoples," 49.

29 Agricultural Committee Debate Regarding Traplines, 1933. PAA, Acc. 70.427/409, box 23, pages 10-11.

30 J. I. Donnanco to G. W. Pollock, November 23, 1967, PAA, acc. 91-270, file T.4, V9, box 65.

31 Balazs, "A Short Analysis."

32 Fort McKay Tribal Administration, "From Where We Stand," 112. See also Fort McKay, *There Is Still Survival Out There*, 31; M. Fox and W.A. Ross, *The Influence of Oil Sands Development on Trapping in the Fort McMurray Region* (Edmonton: Alberta Oil Sands Environmental Research Program, 1979).

33 HEG, "Integrated Cultural Impact Assessment," 64, 46–92.

34 G. A. Kemp to David Neave, "Re: Liabilities of Industry or Government to Renewable Resource Permit and License Holders," November 9, 1972, PAA, acc. 91-270, file T.4, V7, box 64.

35 Kemp, and Neave, "Re: Liabilities," 1972.

36 Syncrude Public Affairs Department, "Compensation for Native Trappers on Lease #17: A Report to the Executive Committee," October 22, 1974, as found in Terry Garvin Personal Papers.

37 Syncrude, "Compensation."

38 Syncrude, "Compensation."

39 J. J. Barr to R. R. Goforth, "Syncrude Canada Lt. Inter Office Correspondence" October 23, 1974. Terry Garvin Personal Papers.

40 Syncrude Public Affairs, "Compensation," Terry Garvin Personal Papers. This decision also seemed to spur the government to explore the issue of trapper compensation more formally, commissioning a series of discussion papers and beginning to work with the Alberta Trappers Association. For example, see Native Secretariat, "Providing Compensation to Trappers: A Discussion Paper," August 16, 1979, in PAA, acc. 1990.0071, file 70 box 13, page 15, where they specifically consider applying the "formula developed by Syncrude" to compensate trappers affected by industrial development.

41 E. A. Reilly to Mr. J. C. Bjornson, "Subject Vincent Boucher Trap Line," Syncrude Canada Ltd. Inter Office Correspondence, January 10, 1975. Terry Garvin Personal Papers.

42 E. A. Reilly to T. Garvin, "Theodore Boucher Settlement," Syncrude Canada Ltd. Inter Office Correspondence, February 21, 1975. Terry Garvin Personal Papers. It is worth noting that this episode is also recorded in Fox and Ross, *The Influence of Oil Sands*

Development on Trapping, where they state, based on personal conversations with T. Garvin, that the two trappers were compensated $6,500 and $10,000. However, there is no corroborating evidence provided. Fox and Ross, *The Influence of Oil Sands Development on Trapping*," 67.

43 "Dorothy Keeps on Swinging," *Fort McMurray Express*, January 19, 1983; Brian Laghi and Doug Tattrie, "Dump Allegations Exaggerated," *Fort McMurray Today*, February 24. 1983.

44 For more on this topic, see Hereward Longley, "Conflicting Interests: Development Politics and the Environmental Regulation of the Alberta Oil Sands Industry, 1970–1980, *Environment and History*, https://doi.org/10.3197/096734019X15463432086919; Larry Pratt, *The Tar Sands: Syncrude and the Politics of Oil* (Edmonton: Hurtig, 1976). This attitude began to change in the late 1970s as trappers in and around the proposed Cold Lake leases controlled by Esso began to agitate in the region. For example, see David J. Unger to Gordon R. Kerr, "Meeting with Esso Resources on Trapping Compensation," October 9, 1979. PAA, acc. 1990.0071, file 70 box 13.

45 Fox and Ross, *The Influence of Oil Sands Development on Trapping*, 67.

46 Fox and Ross, *The Influence of Oil Sands Development on Trapping*, 98–99. Also see Tanner et al., *Some Effects of Oil Sands Development on the Traditional Economy of Fort McKay*.

47 Fox and Ross, *The Influence of Oil Sands Development on Trapping*, 100.

48 Fox and Ross, *The Influence of Oil Sands Development on Trapping*, 100–101.

49 This point is the thesis of Tanner, et al., *Some Effects of Oil Sands Development on the Traditional Economy of Fort McKay*.

50 Brock Volman, "Local Trappers Say Their Industry is in Trouble." *Fort McMurray Today*, December 16, 1986, 3. Also see Willy Barth, "Traplines Have Trouble," *Fort McMurray Today*, Feb. 22, 1980.

51 HEG, "Teck Frontier Mine Project," 46–92.

52 HEG, "Teck Frontier Mine Project," 47, 54–64.

53 Fort McKay, *There Is Still Survival Out There*, 2. Also see Tanner, et al., *Some Effects of Oil Sands Development on the Traditional Economy of Fort McKay*. For a broader conversation about the importance of trapping to Indigenous peoples see Hugh Brody, *Maps and Dreams: Indians and the British Columbia Frontier* (Vancouver: Douglas & McIntyre, 1981).

NOTES TO CHAPTER 4

1 Fort McKay Tribal Administration, "From Where We Stand," 1. Also see Fort McKay Industrial Relations Corporation, "Cultural Heritage Assessment Baseline: Pre-development (1960s) to Current (2008), 16–21. https://fmsd.knowledgekeeper.ca/sites/default/files/fortmckay_home/documents/CHA%20Baseline.pdf.

2 Dennis F. K. Madill, "Treaty Research Report: Treaty Eight (1899)" (Ottawa: Treaties and Historical Research Centre, 1986), 49.

3   James Ross, as quoted in Charles Mair, *Through the Mackenzie Basin: A Narrative of the Athabasca and Peace River Treaty Expedition* (Toronto: William Briggs, 1908), 61.

4   Dennis F. K. Madill, "Treaty Research Report: Treaty Eight (1899)" (Ottawa: Treaties and Historical Research Centre, 1986), 71. See also: Richard Daniel, "The Spirit and Terms of Treaty Eight," in *The Spirit of the Alberta Indian Treaties*, ed. Richard Price (Edmonton: Pica Pica Press, 1987), 47–101.

5   Rupert's Land Centure for Métis Research and the Métis Archival Project, *Métis Scrip in Alberta* (Edmonton: Rupertsland Centre for Métis Research, 2018), https://www.ualberta.ca/native-studies/media-library/rcmr/publications/rcmr-scrip-booklet-2018-final-150dpi.pdf. Also see Frank Tough and Erin McGregor, "'The rights to the land may be transferred:' Archival Records as Colonial Text – A Narrative of Metis Scrip," *The Canadian Review of Comparative Literature* 31, no. 1 (2007).

6   Fort McKay Tribal Administration, "From Where We Stand," 26.

7   The *Edmonton Bulletin* is full of stories detailing the economic potential of the land near Fort McMurray and Fort McKay: "The North Country," *Edmonton Bulletin*, October 5, 1906; "Railway to Fort McMurray and the Country It Will Open Up;" *Edmonton Bulletin*, May 11, 1907. "Alberta's Rich Hinterland" *Edmonton Bulletin* July 31, 1908; "McMurray Region Second Cobalt: Prospectors Returned from Clear Water River Say Silver and Copper Float Abundant," *Edmonton Journal* July 28, 1910.

8   "Surveyor's Tragic Death Affects McMurray Claims," *Edmonton Journal,* Sept 1, 1910.

9   "Surveyor's Tragic Death," *Edmonton Journal,* 1910. Also see "Staked Claims in Fort McMurray," *Edmonton Journal,* August 17, 1910; Judy Larmour, *Laying Down the Lines: A History of Land Surveying in Alberta* (Calgary: Brindle & Glass, 2005), 117–19.

10 David J. Hall, "Oliver, Frank (Francis Robert Bowsfield, Bossfield, or Bousfield)," in *Dictionary of Canadian Biography*, vol. 16, (Toronto/Quebec City: University of Toronto/Université Laval, 2003). http://www.biographi.ca/en/bio/oliver_frank_16E.html.

11 Frank Oliver, originally cited in Larmour, *Laying Down the Lines*, 118.

12 "Surveyor's Tragic Death Affects McMurray Claims," *Edmonton Journal,* Sept 1, 1910; "May not Require Second Survey of McMurray Mines," *Edmonton Journal,* Oct 13, 1910.

13 "Fort McMurray: Every Lot a Gold Mine," *Edmonton Journal* June 22, 1912.

14 Larmour, *Laying Down the Lines,* 119–21.

15 Reddekopp, "First Survey," 21.

16 J. H. Lewis, *Survey Records Search of the Surveys Branch of Indians Affairs: Its Creation, Operations and Demise with Respect to the Prairie Provinces* (Ottawa: Department of Indian and Northern Affairs, 1993), 251.

17 Donald F. Robertson, "Survey Report," January 7, 1916. LAC, RG10, vol. 4065, file 412,786-4. A copy of the report was also included in the Annual Report of the Department of Indian Affairs, Part II, p. 27.

18 Donald F. Robertson to S. Bray, "Memorandum," December 23, 2015. DIAND, file 779/30-10/174, vol. 1. This letter is also cited in Fort McKay Tribal Administration, "From Where We Stand," 26–27. For additional context see Reddekopp, "First Survey," 21–32.

19 Reddekopp, "First Survey," 22–23.

20 Author unknown, "Memorandum to the Deputy Minister, Re: Fort McKay Settlement, Athabaska, Alberta," June 19, 1958. DIAND, file 779/30-10/174, vol. 1. Donald Robertson DLS to Secretary, Department of Indian Affairs, January 7, 1916. DIAND, file 779/30-10/174, vol. 1.

21 For example, see Campbell et al., *mihkwâkamiwi sîpîsis*, 43. As described in the excerpt, wage labour was the exception and not the rule in Fort McKay until the 1960s.

22 N.O. Coté to J.D. McLean, "Re: Part Lot 10, McKay Settlement, Alberta, Area 32.7 acres, 29 November 1922. DIAND, file 779/30-10/174, vol. 1. Also see N.O. Coté to J.D. McLean, Re: Part of Lot 7, McKay Settlement, Alberta, lying between the roadway crossing this lot and the left bank of the Athabasca River. Containing an area of 5.55 acres. DIAND, file 779/30-10/174, vol. 1; J.D. McLean to N.O. Coté, "Your file No. 2618128," 24 October 1923. DIAND, file 779/30-10/174, vol. 1.

23 For example, Victoria McDonald describes her experience going to residential school in Fort Chipewyan. Fort McKay, *There Is Still Survival Out There*, 64–65.

24 Rod Hyde, Personal Correspondence, August 5, 2020.

25 Chartran et al., *Métis History and Experience and Residential Schools in Canada*, 126–28.

26 The majority of the Elders interviewed for *There Is Still Survival Out There* provide stories about moving to Fort McKay for schooling. Similarly the Elders interviewed for *mihkwâkamiwi sîpîsis* describe their moves to Fort McKay, most often to attend school. See Fort McKay, *There Is Still Survival Out There*, 27, 57–58, 73, 81, 84, 97, 98, 107, 111, 117, 119; Campbell et al., *mihkwâkamiwi sîpîsis*, 7, 24, 38. Fred Macdonald "Interview Transcript," 38, 49. http://www.acee-ceaa.gc.ca/050/documents/45006/45006F.pdf.

27 Francis Orr as quoted in Heather Deighton and Carl R. Surrendi, *From Traplines to Pipelines: A Socio-Economic Impact Assessment of the Proposed Shell Lease 13 Project on the Community of Fort McKay* (Fort McKay: Fort McKay Environmental Services Ltd. 1998), 67.

28 H. Soley, "RE: Lot 10, Fort McKay Settlement, August 7, 1958, DIAND, file 779/30-10/174, vol. 1

29 Alberta's threats are documented in R. F. Battle to H.G. Jensen, December 27, 1957. DIAND, file 779/30-10/174, vol. 1.

30 R. F. Battle to H.G. Jensen, December 27, 1957. DIAND, file 779/30-10/174, vol. 1.

31 H.M. Jones to N. G. Jensen, August 22, 1958, DIAND, file 779/30-10/174, vol. 1.

32 R.F. Battle to H.G. Jensen, April 24, 1958. DIAND, file 779/30-10/174, vol. 1.

33 W.C. Bethune, "Fort McKay Settlement," April 11, 1958. DIAND, file 779/30-10/174, vol. 1.

34 Reddekopp, "First Survey," 59.

35 As of 1978, only two individual miscellaneous leases from the provincial government were recognized in the community; one to Métis member Narcisse Shott and the other to J. "Torchy" Peden, who operated the local café and store in the community. Van Dyke, *Lives in Transition*, 13.

36 Fort McKay Tribal Administration, "From Where We Stand," 88. For a full description of this process see 79–117. Grande Cache had a very similar experience to Fort McKay, which is described at length in Nicks and Morgan, "Grande Cache" as well as Joe Sawchuk, Patricia Sawchuk, Theresa Ferguson, and the Metis Association of Alberta, *Metis Land Rights: A Political History* (Edmonton: The Metis Association of Alberta, 1981).

37 Ben Tierney, "Oil Sands Spawn Boom Town in the Bush: Hopes Galore, Headaches, Too As Fort McMurray Awakens,"

38 Eaton Howitt, "McMurray Hardly Recognizable: Oil Sands Boom Changing Face of the Town," *Edmonton Journal*, November 18, 1965; Ovi Baril, "McMurray Caught in Great Boom," *Edmonton Journal*, March 18, 1965. For additional examples, see PAA ACC GR76.502 box 40 file 15 for various news stories from the mid-1960s as well as Terry Garvin's Newspaper Scrapbook (2 volumes). For a broader context, see Clark et al. *Mark of the Métis*, 85–95 and Hereward Longley and Tara Joly, "The Moccasin Flats Evictions: Métis Home, Forced Relation, and Resilience in Fort McMurray, Alberta" (Fort McMurray: McMurray Métis, 2018), 44–84.

39 Harassed New Resident, "Letter to the Editor Re: McMurray Indians," *Edmonton Journal*, September 14, 1964 as found in the Terry Garvin Newspaper Scrapbook, volume 2, p. 40 and also found in PAA, GR76.502, box 40 file 15 – Clippings. While the letter is anonymous, given it was saved by Mr. Garvin, there is a strong likelihood that he penned it as he was seconded in July 1964 from the RCMP to work in Fort McMurray as a community development officer, and shortly thereafter, worked to establish the Nistowoyou Housing Co-Op to help individuals who were being displaced in the city.

40 "Tenders Called on North Span" *Edmonton Journal*, Sept. 7, 1966, suggests that the bridge was scheduled to be completed in March 1967. Community members remember it being completed in 1966, see Campbell et. al., *mihkwâkamiwi sîpîsis*, 11.

41 Fort McKay Tribal Administration, "From Where We Stand," 35.

42 For a fuller description of the impacts of "high-modernity" on Indigenous communities the work of Tina Loo is illustrative, see for example: Tina Loo, "High Modernism, Conflict, and the Nature of Change in Canada: A Look at Seeing Like a State," *Canadian Historical Review* 1, no. 97 (March 2016); Tina Loo, "Disturbing the Peace: Environmental Change and the Scales of Justice on a Northern River" *Environmental History*, Special Issue on Canada (October 2007); Tina Loo, *Moved by the State: Forced Relocation and Making a Good Life in Postwar Canada* (Vancouver: UBC Press, 2019). For a broader conversation, also see James C. Scott, *Seeing Like a State: How Certain Schemes to Improve the Human Condition Have Failed* (New Haven: Yale University Press, 1998) and for the contextualization of the impact of neo-liberalism on the creation of the modern Canadian state see Ian McKay, "The Liberal Order Framework:

A Prospectus for a Reconnaissance of Canadian History," *Canadian Historical Review* 4, no. 81 (December 2000). Nicks and Morgan argue that the Indigenous community of Grande Cache felt a similar impact in the 1960s that contributed to forming the community's identity. See Nicks and Morgan, "Grande Cache," 172–78.

43   Fox and Ross, *The Influence of Oil Sands Development on Trapping*, 98–101; Longley, "Conflicting Interests."

44   Fort McKay Tribal Administration, "From Where We Stand," 88.

45   Theresa Grandjambe on behalf of the Fort McKay Association, February 16, 1967. PAA, GR1979.0152 box 16, item 217. It seems likely that the issue of secure water was brought to the Department of Indian Affairs in December 1966 and was responded to internally, describing the land-tenure situation with a commitment that even if the lands in Fort McKay settlement were not "reserve land" they were still "federal Crown lands" and the federal government "should be in a position to negotiate the extension of services and where necessary issue permits." H.T. Vergette to R.D. Ragan, "Water Supply System, McKay Settlement," 13 January 1967, DIAND, file 779/30-10/174, vol. 1.

46   C. L. Pearson to Allan Kerr, "Re: Fort McKay Settlement," May 31, 1973. GR1979.0152 box 16, item 217. L. Gareau to G. R. Sterling, "Re: Fort McKay Water Problem," July 6, 1967. PAA, GR1979.0152 box 16, item 217.

47   Max Foran, "1967: Embracing the Future . . . at Arm's Length," in *Alberta Formed: Alberta Transformed,* ed. Michael Payne, Donald Wetherell, Catherine Cavanaugh (Edmonton: University of Alberta Press, 2006), 632.

48   L. Gareau to G. R. Sterling, "Re: Fort McKay Water Problem," July 6, 1967. PAA, GR1979.0152 box 16, item 217.

49   L. Gareau to G. R. Sterling, "Re: Fort McKay," 1967.

50   James R. Whitford to Ernie Lacorde, March 16, 1967. PAA, GR1979.0152 box 16, item 217.

51   S. J. Sinclair to J. R. Whitford, "Re: Fort McKay," June 7, 1967. PAA, GR1979.0152 box 16, item 217.

52   Van Dyke, *Lives in Transition: The Fort McKay Case,* 11–14.

53   With the lease to Narcisse Shott being the lone exception. Van Dyke, *Lives in Transition*, 13.

54   Fort McKay First Nation successfully negotiated a treaty land entitlement agreement with the federal government that included reserve land within the hamlet of Fort McKay. This process began in 1987 and was only concluded by a 1995 agreement, with the community only selecting an additional 20,000 acres of land in 2006. Tom Flanagan, *The Community Capitalism of the Fort McKay First Nation: A Case Study* (Vancouver: Fraser Institute, 2018), 6. https://www.fraserinstitute.org/sites/default/files/community-capitalism-of-the-fort-mckay-first-nation.pdf. The Fort McKay Métis decided in 2018 to buy the land in the community from the Government of Alberta in 2018 for 1.6 million dollars, thus avoiding a lengthy legal case. For more, see Raffy Boudjikanian, "Breaking New Ground: Métis in Alberta Buy Their Land from Province

for 1st Time in Canada," March 28, 2018, *CBC News*, https://www.cbc.ca/news/canada/edmonton/metis-land-purchase-mckay-alberta-1.4596299.

55 "Summary Minutes of Meeting between Delegates from Fort McKay and Government Representatives," October 23, 1968. PAA, GR1979.0152 box 16, item 217.

56 "Summary Minutes of Meeting," 1968.

57 Again, this is not a situation unique to Fort McKay and is well covered by Patricia Sawchuk in her article "The Creation of a Non-Status Indian Population in Alberta," 1979. There are also many parallels to the experience of the Indigenous community in Grande Cache, which is described in detail by Trudy Nicks and Kenneth Morgan in "Grande Cache" and by Joe Sawchuk et. al. *Metis Land Rights*.

58 G. W. Fyfe to F. W. Picard, "Re: Fort McKay," October 17, 1968. PAA, GR1979.0152 box 16, item 216.

59 D. J. Armstrong to J. E. Oberholtzer, "Re: Temporary Committee – Fort McKay." PAA, GR1979.0152 box 16, item 217. The committee members included Chairman Francis Orr, Sub-Chairmen Andrew Boucher, Zachery Powder, James Grandjambe, and Secretary Teresa Grandjambe.

60 R. H. Botham to file, "Re: Fort McKay," November 13, 1968. GR1979.0152, box 16, item 216.

61 B. R. Orysiuk to N. F. W. Picard, "Re: Fort McKay," November 15, 1968. GR1979.0152, box 16, item 216. Of course, remember that the federal government had committed to providing supplies to the First Nations members separately.

62 Roy L. Piepenburg to T. G. Armstrong, "Bus Transportation for Workers, Fort McKay, Alberta. 9 January 1969." PAA, GR1979.0152 box 16, item 217. In the meeting, Wilfred Granjamb represented the First Nations, while Henry Shott and Percy Lacorde represented Métis interests. See "Fort McKay," Glenbow Museum and Archives, M4755, file 470.

63 Noel Dant to George Armstrong, November 26, 1968. PAA, GR76.502, box 15, Community Development – Fort MacKay.

64 J. E. Oberholtzer to G. J. Armstrong, "Re: Fort MacKay," March 10, 1969. PAA, GR1979.0152 box 16, item 217; the same letter is also found in PAA, GR76.502, box 15, Community Development – Fort MacKay.

65 C. J. McAndrews to J. E. Oberholtzer, "Re: Fort McKay," May 13, 1970. PAA, GR1979.0152, box 16, item 217.

66 Unfortunately, there is very little biographical information available regarding Jim Ducharme, although a man by the same name, shortly after this episode, became the president of the Métis Association of Alberta (1971–1972), and it seems highly likely that this was the same person. Lawrence J. Barkwell, *Métis Dictionary of Biography, Volume D* (Winnipeg: Louis Riel Institute, 2015), 118.

67 J. Ducharme to G. J. Armstrong, "Re: Fort McKay," July 6, 1970. PAA, GR1979.0152 box 16, item 217.

68 J. Ducharme to G. J. Armstrong, "Re: Fort McKay," July 6, 1970.

69 Premier Harry Strom to Stan Daniels, "Suggested Draft Reply," July 8, 1970. PAA, GR1979.0152 box 16, item 217.

70 G. J. Armstrong and J. A. Ducharme to Honorable R.A. Speaker, "Re: Fort McKay Recommendations," October 9, 1970. PAA, GR1979.0152 box 16, item 217.

71 AHURC is an acronym for Alberta Housing and Urban Renewal Corporation. Provincial Archives of Alberta, *An Administrative History of the Government of Alberta* (Edmonton: Provincial Archives of Alberta, 2006), 329.

72 G. J. Armstrong and J. A. Ducharme to Honorable R. A. Speaker, "Re: Fort McKay Recommendations," October 9, 1970. PAA, GR1979.0152, box 16, item 217.

73 G. J. Armstrong and J. A. Ducharme to Honorable R. A. Speaker, "Re: Fort McKay," 1970.

74 A. C. Towill to G. J. Armstrong, "Re: Fort McKay – Assistant H.R.O. – George Sanderson," November 9, 1970. PAA, GR1979.0152 box 16, item 217.

75 G. J. Armstrong to Phillip McDonald, January 13, 1971. PAA, GR1979.0152 box 16, item 217; G.J. Armstrong to Ed Tourangeau, January 13, 1971. PAA, GR1979.0152 box 16, item 217. At the time, the government was in discussions with a number of isolated northern Indigenous communities about creating land or housing co-ops. In total, the government created twelve such co-ops, with the one at Peerless Lake being the first. For more on this topic see: Public Lands Division, "Isolated Native Communities in Northern Alberta – Implications of Land Tenure Alternatives," April 1973. PAA ACC PR1987.0303 - File 59.

76 G. J. Armstrong to J. E. Oberholtmer, "Re: Fort McKay," December 1, 1971. PAA, GR1979.0152 box 16, item 217.

77 T. F. Roach to G.J. Armstrong "Memorandum," November 22, 1971. PAA, GR1979.0152 box 16, item 217.

78 T. F. Roach to G.J. Armstrong "Memorandum," November 22, 1971.

79 T. F. Roach to G.J. Armstrong "Memorandum," November 22, 1971.

80 Government of Alberta Land Use Secretariat, Understanding Land Use in Alberta (Edmonton: Government of Alberta, 2007), 9.

81 Edward W. Van Dyke and Carmon Loberg, *Community Studies: Fort McMurray, Anzac, Fort MacKay*, (Edmonton: Alberta Oil Sands Environmental Research Program, 1978), 126–29. Also see, Peter Fortna, "'A moral if not legal responsibility:' Métis Land Tenure in Northern Alberta, 1965–2000," Canadian Historical Association Annual Conference, 2021.

82 G. J. Armstrong to J. E. Oberholtmer, "Re: Fort McKay," November 24, 1971. PAA, GR1979.0152 box 16, item 217.

83 J. E. Oberholtzer to Armstrong, "Re: Fort McKay," November 30, 1971. PAA, GR1979.0152 box 16, item 217.

84 G. J. Armstrong to J. E. Oberholtmer, "Re: Fort McKay," December 1, 1971. PAA, GR1979.0152, box 16, item 217.

85   Métis Association of Alberta, "The Métis People and the Land Question in Alberta," 1971, PAA GR1979.0152, Métis-Societies, "Métis Association of Alberta file," box 8. While this shift accelerated after the election of the PC government, it began in the late 1960s when the Métis Association of Alberta (MAA) was able to secure significant funding (nearly $250,000 in 1969 and $450,000 in 1970 and 1971) from the Alberta government. With the funding, the MAA positioned itself as representing the collective voice of all Métis in the province, though in actuality, particularly in the early years, it was a somewhat fragmented and new organization. For more on the early history of the MAA see Joe Sawchuk, *The Dynamics of Native Politics: The Alberta Experience* (Saskatoon: Purich Publishing, 1998), 49–69.

86   T. F. Roach, "Memo for file, Re: Metis Residents – Fort McKay," May 24, 1972. PAA, GR1979.0152, box 16, item 217.

87   T. F. Roach, "Memo for file."

88   Zachary Powder to Stan Daniels, April 12, 1973, Glenbow Museum and Archives, M4755, file 470; Stan Daniels to Zachary Powder, April 18, 1973. Glenbow Museum and Archives, M4755, file 470.

89   Edward Tourangeau to Stan Daniels, July 27, 1973, Glenbow Museum and Archives, M4755, file 470.

90   Edward Tourangeau to Stan Daniels, August 23, 1973, Glenbow Museum and Archives, M4755, file 470.

91   Metis Association of Alberta, "Definition of Native Housing Conditions" N.D. PAA, GR1979.0152, box 14 item 169.

92   Alberta Housing Corporation Metis Housing Program. N.D. PAA, GR1979.0152, box 14 item 169.

93   Alberta Northern Alberta Development Council, *Annual Report, 1973–1974* (Edmonton: ANADC, 1974), 20.

94   Honourable Robert Bogle, "Request for Cabinet Decision: Land Tenure Secretariat" May 8, 1975. GR1979.0152, box 13 item 158.

95   The Metis Association of Alberta, "A Submission for a Housing Program for Metis and Non-Status Indians in the Province of Alberta," April 1, 1974. PAA ACC GR1979.0152, Box 1, Item 1.

96   H. Jane Fournier to S. J. Sinclaire, March 27, 1974. Glenbow Museum and Archives, M4755, file 968; Red River Point Society to Alberta Housing Corporation, April 8, 1974. Glenbow Museum and Archives, M4755, file 968.

97   Van Dyke, *Lives in Transition*, 17, 41.

98   Van Dyke, *Lives in Transition*, 74.

99   Van Dyke, *Lives in Transition*, 75.

100 Peter Fortna, "Wahkotowin, Keemooch, and Home: A History of the Conklin Métis Community, 1886–2020" in *Prairie History* 8 (Summer 2022): 55–71. To understand the impacts of this policy, see Peter Fortna, "How Much Longer?" A Preliminary

Assessment of Homelessness in Conklin, Alberta," (Conklin: Conklin Resource Development Advisory Committee, 2018).

101 Van Dyke, *Lives in Transition*, 18.

102 John Goddard, *Last Stand of the Lubicon Cree* (Vancouver/Toronto: Douglas & McIntyre, 1992), 49.

103 *John Goddard, *Last Stand*, 1992, 49–52. Also see Tom Flanagan, "Lubicon Lake: The Success and Failure of Radical Activism," in *Blockades or Breakthroughs?: Aboriginal Peoples Confront the Canadian State*, eds. Yale D. Belanger and P. Whitney Lackenbauer (Montreal & Kingston: McGill-Queen's University Press, 2014); Christine Mary Smillie, "The People Left Out of Treaty 8" (master's thesis, University of Saskatchewan, 2005), 65–71.

104 Geoff White, "Accord on Land Claim Reached With Two Northern Native Groups" *Calgary Herald* October 13, 1978.

105 Ian Williams, "Small Alberta Community Faces Pressure-filled Future" *Edmonton Journal,* June 6, 1979.

106 Marvin E. Moore to Dorothy McDonald, April 10, 1980. PAA ACC PR. 1993.362 File 1081.

107 Fortna, "Fort McKay Métis Community."

108 Dorothy McDonald to Marvin Moore, Minister of Municipal Affairs, July 10, 1981. PAA, Acc PR1993.0362, file 1079.

109 Fortna, "Wahkotowin, Keemooch, and Home."; "Fortna, "How Much Longer.;" RMWB, "Briefing Note."

110 The Red River Point Society was formally dissolved in 1988, replaced by the Métis Local 122. The *Alberta Gazette*, PART 1 vol. 91, Edmonton, Tuesday, January 31, 1995. http://www.qp.alberta.ca/documents/gazette/1995/text/0131_i.cfm.

111 Alberta Municipal Affairs, Local Government Services Division, Fort McKay Métis Local #122 Lease, Agreement No. AMA 2001-001, Hamlet of Fort McKay, 2001, Fort McKay Métis Nation Archive. While the original 1987 lease agreement has been lost, it was explained that the 2001 agreement was a continuation of the five-year leases that began in 1987 with nearly identical terms and conditions.

112 Van Dyke, *Life in Transition*, 75.

113 Tom Flanagan, *The Community Capitalism of the Fort McKay First Nation* (Vancouver: Fraser Institute, 2018).

114 Personal Correspondence, Ron Quintal, July 25, 2019. It is also worth mentioning that this situation was not fully addressed until the management of the lease was transferred from Métis Local 122 to Métis Local 63.

115 *The Alberta Gazette*, Part 1, June 14, 2003 http://www.qp.alberta.ca/documents/gazette/2003/text/0614_i.cfm.

116 In 1991, the Métis Association of Alberta changed its name to the Métis Nation of Alberta . Métis Nation of Alberta, "Timeline," https://albertametis.com/metis-in-alberta/timeline/.

117 Pearl Calahasen to Calvin Kennedy, March 15, 2006. Fort McKay Métis Nation Archive.

118 Brian Quickfall to Ron Qutinal, April 25, 2006. Fort McKay Métis Nation Archive.

119 Brian Quickfall to Ron Qutinal, April 25.

120 Norma Chitrena to Cort Callup, "FW: Fort McKay Sustainable Remote Housing," January 8, 2007. Fort McKay Métis Nation Archive.

121 Alberta Municipal Affairs and Housing, Local Services Division, September 21, 2007, Memorandum of Lease Agreement between Her Majesty the Queen in Right of Alberta as Represented by the Minister of Municipal Affairs and Housing and Fort McKay Métis Local 63. Fort McKay Métis Nation Archive.

122 Wayne Jackson to Ron Quintal, "Fort McKay Lease," June 9, 2009. Fort McKay Métis Nation Archive.

123 Wayne Jackson to Ron Quintal, "Re: Moving Forward," January 9, 2010. Fort McKay Métis Nation Archive.

124 Thomas Droege to Donavon Young, "Re: Fort McKay Visit," March 8, 2012. Fort McKay Métis Nation Archive. It seems that a copy of this email that was exchanged between Thomas Droege and Donovan Young, was given to Ron Quintal by Nicole Budgell who was initially copied on the correspondence.

125 This topic is explored more fully in Fort McKay Métis Nation, "The Fort McKay Métis Nation Position Paper on Consultation and Self-Government," which is included as an appendix in this volume.

126 Fort McKay Métis Nation, "'History Has Been Made': Fort McKay Métis First in Canadian History to Adopt a Constitution and Declare Self-Governance," May 24, 2019. https://www.newswire.ca/news-releases/-history-has-been-made-fort-mckay-metis-first-in-canadian-history-to-adopt-a-constitution-and-declare-self-governance-895627043.html.

127 Raffy Boudjikanian, "Breaking New Ground: Métis in Alberta Buy Their Land From Province for 1st Time in Canada." *CBC News,* March 28, 2018. https://www.cbc.ca/news/canada/edmonton/metis-land-purchase-mckay-alberta-1.4596299.

NOTES TO CHAPTER 5

1 Larry Pratt, *The Tar Sands: Syncrude and the Politics of Oil* (Edmonton: Hurtig Publishers, 1976); Liza Piper and Heather Green, "A Province Powered by Coal: The Renaissance of Coal Mining in Late Twentieth-century Alberta," *The Canadian Historical Review* 98, no. 3 (2017).

2 Tina Loo, "High Modernism, Conflict, and the Nature of Change in Canada: A Look at Seeing Like a State," *Canadian Historical Review* 1 (March 2016), 97; Tina Loo, "Disturbing the Peace: Environmental Change and the Scales of Justice on a Northern River." *Environmental History,* Special Issue on Canada (October 2007); James L.

Kenny and Andrew Secord, "Engineering Modernity: Hydro-Electric Development in New Brunswick, 1945–70," *Acadiensis* 39, no. 1 (2010); Liza Piper and Heather Green, "A Province Powered by Coal: The Renaissance of Coal Mining in Late Twentieth-century Alberta," *The Canadian Historical Review* 98, no. 3 (2017); Philip Van Huizen, "Building a Green Dam: Environmental Modernism and the Canadian-American Libby Dam Project," *Pacific Historical Review* 79, no. 2 (2010). Daniel Sims "Ware's Waldo: Hydroelectric Development and the Creation of the Other in British Columbia," in *Sustain the West: Cultural Responses to Canadian Environments*, ed. Liza Piper and Lisa Szabo-Jones (Waterloo: Wilfred Laurier Press, 2015).

3   For example, Tina Loo, *Moved by the State: Forced Relocation and Making a Good Life in Postwar Canada* (Vancouver: UBC Press, 2019); John Sandlos and Arn Keeling, "The Giant Mine's Long Shadow: Arsenic Pollution and Native People in Yellowknife, Northwest Territories," in *Mining North America: An Environmental History since 1522*, ed. J. R. McNeill and George Vrtis (Oakland: University of California Press, 2017).

4   Fort McKay Community Committee, "Intervention Filed with the Energy Resources Conservation Board by the Fort McKay Community Committee in Relation to the Proposed GCOS Expansion Application 780318." *Energy Resources Conservation Board*, Application No. 780318, January 19, 1979, 2. Also see Hereward Longley, "Indigenous Battles for Environmental Protection and Economic Benefits during the Commercialization of the Alberta Oil Sands, 1967–1986," in *Mining and Communities in Northern Canada: History, Politics and Memory*, ed. Arn Keeling and John Sandlos (Calgary: University of Calgary Press, 2015), 213–15.

5   This is not to say that the community of Fort McKay did not have to deal with the provincial and federal governments before building the modern oil sands developments. However, those interactions did not require society to be "turned upside down" and could be managed using traditional structures. The coming of the major oil sands projects forced many of these structures to be remade through the 1960s, 1970s, and 1980s.

6   Van Dyke, *Life in Transition*, 88.

7   Van Dyke and Loberg, *Community Studies*. For the broader context see for example, David DesBrisay, "The Impact of Major Resource Development Projects on Aboriginal Communities: A Review of the Literature," *Royal Commission on Aboriginal People* (Feb. 1994); Angela C. Angell and John R. Parkins, "Resource Development and Aboriginal Culture in the Canadian North," *Polar Record*, 47, no. 1 (Jan. 2011); Ginger Gibson and Jason Klinck, "Canada's Resilient North: The Impact of Mining on Aboriginal Communities" *Pimatisiwin* 3 (2005); Claudia Notzke, *Aboriginal People and Natural Resources in Canada* (North York: Captus Press Inc., 1996).

8   Van Dyke, *Lives in Transition*, 131–37. Also see Edward W. Van Dyke and Jane Lee Van Dyke, *Ft. McKay Needs Assessment and Planning Study* (Calgary: Bear-Spike Holdings Ltd., 1990).

9   Energy Resources Conservation Board, "Oil Sands, Tar Island Area, Application No. 78318, Notice of Hearing." Energy Resources Conservation Board, Application No. 780318, December 11, 1978.

10 Fort McKay Community Committee, "Intervention Filed with the Energy Resources Conservation Board by the Fort McKay Community Committee in Relation to the Proposed GCOS Expansion Application 780318." *Energy Resources Conservation Board*, Application No. 780318, January 19, 1979.

11 Ian Williams, "Small Alberta Community Fights for Rights," *Edmonton Journal*, June 6, 1979.

12 A point also emphasized by Van Dyke in his community analysis. See Van Dyke, *Lives in Transition*.

13 Longley, "Indigenous Battles," 213.

14 Fort McKay Community Committee, "Intervention 780318," 4.

15 Bobbi Lambright, "GCOS and ERCB Responsibility Raises Concerns at Hearings," *Fort McMurray Today*, February 1, 1979, 3.

16 Lambright, "GCOS and ERCB Responsibility."

17 Lambright, "GCOS and ERCB Responsibility."

18 Longley, "Indigenous Battles," 214. Also, remarks in later submissions and testimony to environmental impact assessments for later oil sands projects point to ongoing problems in all these areas.

19 As quoted in Longley, "Indigenous Battles," 217.

20 Graeme Bethell, *Preliminary Inventory of the Environmental Issues and Concerns Affecting the People of Fort MacKay, Alberta* (Brentwood Bay, BC, Bethell Management Ltd., 1985), 38.

21 Bethell, "Preliminary Inventory," 39.

22 Bethell, "Preliminary Inventory," 39.

23 Bethell, "Preliminary Inventory," 39. This story is also discussed at length in Longley, "Indigenous Battles."

24 "Suncor Admits Dumping Oil, Grease into River," *The Red Deer Advocate*, February 26, 1982.

25 "Firm Too Busy to Report Pollution: Province, Indians Take Action," *Edmonton Journal*, March 1, 1982.

26 "Suncor Spends Millions on Waste Water System," *Fort McMurray Today*, June 18, 1982.

27 Longley, "Indigenous Battles," 216.

28 Mark Dent, "Will Prosecutor Be Ready at Suncor Trial?" *Fort McMurray Today*, January 21, 1983. Rod Hyde notes that this was perhaps an exaggeration, as McDonald more accurately "stomped" out of the courtroom.

29 Editorial, "Explanations, Please," *Edmonton Journal*, October 30, 1982.

30 Ken Nelson, "The Case Against Suncor," *Fort McMurray Today*, October 26, 1982.

31 Longley, "Indigenous Battles," 216.

32 Dent, "Will Prosecutor Be Ready."

33   Jackie MacDonald, "McKay Band to 'Intervene in Suncor Plan,'" August 24, 1982.

34   Van Dyke, *Ft. McKay Needs Assessment*.

35   Shortly after this, Mr. Boucher was elected as a councillor, though it seems he continued to support community interventions through the 1980s.

36   For more concerning the history of Bill C-31 see Gerard Hartley, *The Search for Consensus: A Legislative History of Bill C-31, 1969–1985* (London, ON: Aboriginal Policy Research Consortium International, 2007). Additionally see Bonita Lawrence, *"Real" Indians and Others: Mixed-Blood Urban Native Peoples and Indigenous Nationhood* (Vancouver: UBC Press, 2004); Pamela D. Palmater, *Beyond Blood: Rethinking Indigenous Identity* (Saskatoon: Purich Publishing Ltd. 2011).

37   "Natives Abandon Sexist Provision," *Toronto Globe and Mail*, April 9, 1982.

38   "Natives Abandon Sexist Provision."

39   Gabrielle Donnelly, *Indigenous Women in Community Leadership Case Studies: Fort McKay First Nation, Alberta* (Antigonish, NS, Coady International Institute, 2012), 5

40   "Natives Abandon Sexist Provision."

41   Palmater, *Beyond Blood*," 30.

42   Van Dyke *Ft. McKay Needs Assessment*.

43   Van Dyke *Ft. McKay Needs Assessment*, 15.

44   Doug Tattrie, "MacKay Indians Setup Blockade," *Fort McMurray Today*, January 14, 1983.

45   Doug Tattrie, "Natives Protest Logging Plan," *Fort McMurray Today*, December 23, 1982. Unfortunately, I have not yet been able to locate a copy of the original press release, though it is cited extensively verbatim in the Tattrie news article.

46   Tattrie, "MacKay Indians Setup Blockade."

47   Barry Nelson, "Road Ban Halts Clash of Cultures," *Globe and Mail*, January 22, 1983, 8; "A Stand at Fort MacKay: Northern Indians Claim a Blockade Victory," *Alberta Report*, January 31, 1983; Larry Tucker, "Female Chief Attacks Red Tape," *Edmonton Sun*, March 3, 1984; Gordon Legge and Peter O'Neil, "The Band That Pushed Back," *Maclean's*, January 31, 1983. Rod Hyde also explained that most, if not all, of the TV and radio programs also picked up the story.

48   Brian Laghi, "Shields Condemns Protest," *Fort McMurray Today*, January 18, 1983.

49   Ed Struzik and Duncan Thorne, "Natives Callous, Pahl says," *Edmonton Journal*, January 18, 1983.

50   Legge and O'Neil, "The band That Pushed Back."

51   Ed Struzik, "Survival More Than Safety Roadblock Issue, Chief Says," *Edmonton Journal*, January 14, 1983.

52   Doug Tattrie, "Tentative Pact OK'd: Protestors to Vote on Offer," *Fort McMurray Today*, January 20, 1983.

53   Tattrie, "Tentative Pact OK'd."

54 Jackie MacDonald, "Indian Chief Dorothy McDonald: Fierce Fighter of Rights," *Calgary Sun*, August 7, 1983.

55 "Dorothy Keeps on Swinging," *Fort McMurray Express*, January 19, 1983.

56 Brian Laghi and Doug Tattrie, "Dump Allegations Exaggerated," *Fort McMurray Today*, February 24, 1983.

57 "McKay Band Wins Appeal to Delay Hearing on New Syncrude Dump," *Edmonton Journal*, January 24, 1983.

58 Brian Laghi, "Syncrude Waste Dump 'No Health Risk' – Gov't," *Fort McMurray Today*, February 28, 1983.

59 Michael Moralis, "Chief Could Delay Expansion," *Fort McMurray Today*, June 6, 1984.

60 Michael Moralis, "Environment Data Poor," *Fort McMurray Today*, June 15, 1984.

61 Michael Moralis, "ERCB Holds the Cards in Syncrude's Hearing," June 16, 1984.

62 Michael Board, "ERCB Move Will Stall Expansion," *Fort McMurray Today*, August 22, 1984.

63 Michael Board, "ERCB Approves Syncrude Expansion," *Fort McMurray Today*, October 5, 1984. Interestingly, this remains an ongoing challenge as companies complain that many legitimate community concerns remain outside the regulator's purview. For a discussion of this issue, see Pat McCormack, "Studying the Social and Cultural Impacts of 'Extreme Extraction' in Northern Alberta" in *Extracting Home in the Oil Sands: Settler Colonialism and Environmental Change in Subarctic Canada*, eds. Clinton N. Westman, Tara L. Joly, and Lena Gross (London and New York: Routledge, 2020).

64 The Ft. McKay Community, *A Review of the Biophysical Impact Assessment and Reclamation Plan for New Mining Areas in Support of Approved New Facilities at the Syncrude Canada Ltd. Mildred Lake Plant*, (Fort McKay, January 1986), i.

65 Dorothy McDonald to Vern Millard, "Re: A Review of the Biophysical Impact Assessment and Reclamation Plan for New Mining Areas in Support of Approved New Facilities at the Syncrude Canada Ltd. Mildred Lake Plant," January 31, 1986, as found in The Ft. McKay Community, *A Review of the Biophysical Impact Assessment and Reclamation Plan for New Mining Areas in Support of Approved New Facilities at the Syncrude Canada Ltd. Mildred Lake Plant* (Fort McKay, January 1986).

66 For example, see Graeme Bethell, *Preliminary Inventory*, ii–iii.

67 Dayle Hyde, personal correspondence, August 6, 2020.

68 Ken Younger, "New Chief Promises Conciliatory Approach: A Number of Projects Scheduled for Fort MacKay Band," *Fort McMurray Today*, August 6, 1986.

69 Tom Flanagan, *The Community Capitalism of the Fort McKay First Nation* (Vancouver: Fraser Institute, 2018).

70 Mike Mercredi, Director of the Athabasca Native Development Corporation, in LAC, Royal Commission on Aboriginal People Testimony, Fort McMurray, ALTA 92-06-16, p. 140. http://www.bac-lac.gc.ca/eng/discover/aboriginal-heritage/royal-commission-aboriginal-peoples/Pages/item.aspx?IdNumber=38.

71 Wood Buffalo Environmental Association, "History and Evolution." https://web.archive.org/web/20220817080309/https://wbea.org/about/history-and-evolution/; Regional Aquatics Monitoring Program, "About," http://www.ramp-alberta.org/ramp.aspx; Cumulative Environmental Management Association, "About CEMA," https://web.archive.org/web/20180929181544/http://cemaonline.ca/index.php/about-us/cema-history. Also see Peter Fortna, "Incorporating the Findings from the CEMA Indigenous Traditional Knowledge Framework into the Alberta Environmental Monitoring, Evaluation, and Reporting Agency: Key Findings and Recommendations." A Report Submitted to AEMERA, June 25, 2016, p. 6–12. http://www.willowspringsss.com/blog/report-incorporating-the-findings-from-the-cema-indigenous-traditional-knowledge-framework-into-the-alberta-environmental-monitoring-evaluation-reporting-agency-key-findings-and-recommendations.

72 Syncrude Expansion Review Group, "A report of the Syncrude Expansion Review Group Regarding the Mildred Lake Plant Expansion, Application No. 870593 to the Energy Resources Conservation Board" (March 1988), 37. Also see Longley, "Indigenous Battles," 223.

73 Tom Flanagan estimates that the Fort McKay First Nation's Group of Companies grew in revenue from $120,000 in the first year to $6 million in 1996 to $150 million in 2004. Flanagan, *Community Capitalism*, 4–5.

74 Ian Urquhart, "Between the Sands and Hard Place? Aboriginal Peoples and the Oil Sands," Working Paper No. 10-005. Evanston, IL.: Buffet Centre for International and Comparative Studies Working Paper: Energy Series, 2010, 19. https://doi.org/10.21985/N2BB4K.

75 Urquhart, "Between the Sands." While the three-year agreement was signed in 1999, the Fort McKay IRC was incorporated approximately a year prior. See Kelly Vivier, "Environmental Students Stop in Fort McKay," *Fort McKay Today,* May 16, 1998. https://www.newspapers.com/article/fort-mcmurray-today/124985242/.

76 Fort McKay Métis Nation, "Position Paper."

77 Fort McKay Industry Relations Corporation Agreement – Fort McKay and Mobil Oil Canada Properties, Shell Canada Limited, Suncor Energy Inc., & Syncrude Canada Ltd., August 5, 1999, 12.

78 Fort McKay Industry Relations, 2.

79 Heather Devine, "The Alberta Dis-Advantage: Métis Issues and the Public Discourse in Wild Rose Country." *London Journal of Canadian Studies* 26 (2010/11): 37–53. FMMN, "Position Paper."

80 Urquhart, "Between the Sands," 2010, 22.

81 Carol Christian, "Métis Group Disputes Syncrude's Claim of Aboriginal Investment," *Fort McMurray Today*, November 7, 2008.

82 Fort McKay Métis Position Paper; Ron Quintal Interview, October 26, 2022.

83 Tom Flanagan estimates that the Fort McKay First Nation's Group of Companies grew in revenue from $120,000 in the first year to $6 million in 1996 to $150 million in 2004. Flanagan, *Community Capitalism*, 4–5. It is also worth noting that while the

First Nation's Group of Companies was experiencing exponential growth, the Métis Group of Companies was dealing with the fallout from the Solv-Ex bankruptcy, which hindered its ability to capitalize on the opportunities available in the region. Urquhart estimates the amount to only be "$100 million" in 2004, but regardless, the First Nation's companies were exceptionally successful in the new millennium. Urquhart, 23

84 Fort McKay First Nation, *Annual Report 2018*, (Fort McKay: Fort McKay First Nation, 2019 https://www.fortmckay.com/app/uploads/2020/01/FMFN_2018AnnualReport.pdf.

85 Patrick Nichol, "Native Firms Hired on by Solv-Ex," *Fort McMurray Today*, July 19, 1996.

86 Nichol, "Native Firms," 1996.

87 Manuel P. Asensio with Jack Barth, *Sold Short: Uncovering Deception in the Markets* (Danvers, MA: John Wiley & Sons, Inc., 2001), 75.

88 Patrick Nichol, "Solv-Ex Faces Class-action Lawsuit Again,"

89 Irene Thomas, "Solv-Ex Creditors Not Optimistic," *Fort McMurray Today*, August 26, 1997.

90 Ron Quintal "Interview," 2.

91 When the original twenty-five-year lease between the Red River Point Society and the provincial government expired in 1987, it was transferred to the Fort McKay Métis Local 122 on a new five-year lease with similar terms. Alberta Municipal Affairs Agreement No. AMA 2001-001, Hamlet of Fort McKay, 2001.

92 Ron Quintal "Interview," 11.

93 Ron Quintal "Interview," 11.

94 Flanagan, *Community Capitalism*, 4–5.

95 Flanagan, *Community Capitalism*, 4–5.

96 The Fort McKay Métis Nation does not have records to determine how many members joined the First Nation since Bill C-31 was first introduced. However, community estimates are that between 20% and 40% of community members have chosen to join. Interestingly, as the law is currently drafted, many of the children of First Nations members who rejoined the FMFN through Bill C-31 (and Bill C-3) will not qualify for First Nation status as the laws are currently drafted. It is expected that the majority of these people will rejoin the Fort McKay Métis Nation should they chose to complete an application. For more on this topic see HEG, "Integrated Cultural Assessment," 262–68.

97 Ron Quintal, "Interview," 45–46; Alberta Municipal Affairs and Housing, Local Services Division, September 21, 2007, Memorandum of Lease Agreement between Her Majesty the Queen in Right of Alberta as Represented by the Minister of Municipal Affairs and Housing and Fort McKay Métis Local 63.

98 Human Environment Group, "Indicators of Cultural Change (1960 to 2009): A Framework for Selecting Indicators Based on Cultural Values in Fort McKay" (Fort McKay: Fort McKay Industrial Relations Corporation, 2009), 8–9.

99 Human Environment Group, "Indicators," 55–57.

100 McKay Métis Nation-Local 63, "5-Year Strategic Plan," 1–2.

101 McKay Métis Nation-Local 63, "5-Year Strategic Plan," 1–2.

102 Métis Nation of Alberta, "Bylaws of the Métis Nation of Alberta Association," updated October 28, 2010.

103 For example, see Métis Nation of Alberta, "Policy Guidelines Regarding the Duty to Consult and Accommodate Métis Aboriginal Rights and Interests in Alberta," July 2009, 2. This shift is described in the Fort McKay Métis Nation's "Position Paper."

104 Ron Quintal, "Interview," 20. Also see FMMN, "Position Paper."

105 Ron Quintal, "Interview," 20

106 Fort McKay Métis Nation, "Fort McKay Métis Community: Bylaw Summary PowerPoint Presentation," 2011.

107 Fort McKay Métis Nation, "Position Paper," 11.

108 Fort McKay Métis Nation, "Position Paper," 11.

109 Fort McKay Métis Nation, "Position Paper," 11–12.

110 Fort McKay Métis Nation, "Position Paper."

111 At a community meeting on November 28, 2018, the Fort McKay Métis Local 63 members in attendance unanimously voted to dissolve the organization. See Ron Quintal to Alberta Corporate Registries, "Re: Dissolution of The Metis Nation of Alberta, Association Local Council #63 of Fort McKay, Corporate Access #509974226," December 5, 2018. In the following months, former members of Métis Local 63 formally terminated their membership in the MNA. See Métis Nation of Alberta, Métis Local 63 "Termination Letters." For news coverage see Shari Narine, "Metis Local in Limbo as Government Policy Forces Members to Choose Who Represents Them," *Windspeaker*, 1 April 2019. https://windspeaker.com/news/windspeaker-news/metis-local-limbo-government-policy-forces-members-choose-who-represents-them.

112 Ron Quintal letter "Re: Fort McKay Metis Community Association Special Meeting – May 23, 2019" to Fort McKay Metis Community Association Members, April 25, 2019. Also see Fort McKay Métis Nation, "Position Paper," 15–16.

113 Boudjikanian, "Breaking New Ground," March 28, 2018.

114 Fort McKay Métis Nation, "'History Has Been Made:' Fort McKay Métis First in Canadian History to Adopt a Constitution and Declare Self-governance," May 24, 2019. https://www.newswire.ca/news-releases/-history-has-been-made-fort-mckay-metis-first-in-canadian-history-to-adopt-a-constitution-and-declare-self-governance-895627043.html. For the meeting details see Fort McKay Métis Community Association, "Member Package: Declaration of Self-Government: Fort McKay Métis Nation (Amendments to the bylaws of the Fort McKay Metis Community Association), May 23, 2019; Fort McKay Métis Community Association, "Special Meeting Minutes," May 23, 2019.

115 Alberta, "Métis Organization Establishes Right to Consultation," 13 February 2020, https://www.alberta.ca/release.cfm?xID=6861188357C08-C734-DA8D-FD73A149425FFE3D.

116   Chris Nelson, "Fort McKay Métis Nation Builds Booming Business in Oilsands Sector," *Calgary Herald* April 14, 2021. https://calgaryherald.com/news/local-news/fort-mckay-metis-nation-builds-booming-business-in-oilsands-sector.

NOTES TO EPILOGUE

1. Métis Nation of Alberta, "Public Notice: Re: Ron Quintal No Longer Ft. McKay Métis Local President," Paid Advertisement, *Fort McMurray Today,* March 2019, 24–28, https://shopping.fortmcmurraytoday.com/places/view/483/m_tis_nation_of_alberta.html.

2. Vincent McDermott, "Quintal Rejects MNA's Claims of 'Abandoning His Post' as McKay Métis President," *Fort McMurray Today*, March 28, 2019, https://www.fortmcmurraytoday.com/news/local-news/quintal-rejects-mnas-claims-of-abandoning-his-post-as-mckay-metis-president.

3. McDermott, "Quintal Rejects MNA's Claims," 2019. Also see Fort McKay Metis Community Association, "Press Statement: Reports that Fort McKay Metis President Ron Quintal Has Resigned False," *Windspeaker,* March 27, 2019, https://windspeaker.com/news/opinion/press-statement-reports-fort-mckay-metis-president-ron-quintal-has-resigned-false. Fort McKay Métis, "Correction Notice: Re: False Reports that Fort McKay Metis President Ron Quintal Resigns" Paid Advertisement, *Fort McMurray Today*, March 26, 2019.

4. Bianca Mazziotti, "Both Sides in Metis Governance Case See Judge's Response as Good News for Future Plans," *Lakeland Today* Jan. 29, 2020. https://www.lakelandtoday.ca/lac-la-biche-news/both-sides-in-metis-governmance-case-see-judges-response-as-good-news-for-future-plans-2037113.

5. Alberta, "Métis Organization Establishes Right to Consultation." February 13, 2020. https://web.archive.org/web/20200929224333/https://ibftoday.ca/ab-government-metis-organization-establishes-right-to-consultation//. The provincial government's Aboriginal Consultation Office confirmed the decision on March 26, 2020. See Alberta, "Fort McKay Metis Community Credible Assertion," March 26, 2020. https://www.alberta.ca/indigenous- consultation-notices-and-information-updates.aspx.

6. James. A. Cardinal and Jason Ekeberg, "Statement by the Métis Nation of Alberta Region One President & Vice President," February 13, 2020, https://web.archive.org/web/20210301123914/http://albertametis.com/2020/02/. Emphasis in the original.

7. Métis Nation of Alberta "Appalled by Alberta Decision on Métis Consultation 'It's a Breach of the Honour of the Crown,'" February 13, 2020, https://web.archive.org/web/20210301123914/http://albertametis.com/2020/02/. Also see Audrey Poitras, "Province is Siding With Wrong Métis Representatives," *Edmonton Journal,* February 21, 2020.

8. Métis Nation of Alberta "Appalled by Alberta Decision on Métis Consultation," February 13, 2020. Madden's position is more fully articulated in Jason Madden, "The Re-Emergence of Previously Slayed Metis Rights-Denial Dragons: The Dangers and Duplicity in Fort Chipewyan Métis Nation of Alberta Local# 125 v Alberta." *Osgoode Hall Law Journal* 57, no. 1 (2020): 195–229.

9   Métis Nation of Alberta, "Self-Governance," www.albertametis.com/governance. For an alternative interpretation of Otipemisiwak see Fort McKay, "The Fort McKay Métis Nation Position Paper on Consultation and Self-Government," which is included as an appendix in this volume.

10 For example, see Jean Teillet, *The North-West is our Mother: The Story of Louis Riel's People* (Toronto: Harper Collins Canada, 2019); Chris Andersen, *Métis: Race, Recognition and the Struggle for Indigenous Peoplehood* (Vancouver: UBC Press, 2014); Kelly Saunders and Janique Dubois, *Métis Politics and Governance in Canada* (Vancouver: UBC Press, 2019); the articles in *A People and a Nation: New Directions in Contemporary Métis Studies*, eds. Jennifer Adese and Chris Andersen (Vancouver: UBC Press, 2021).

11 For example, see Adam Gaudry, "Communing with the Dead: The "New Métis," Métis Identity Appropriation, and the Displacement of Living Métis Culture," *The American Indian Quarterly* 42, no. 2 (Spring 2018).

12 For example, see Jennifer Adese and Chris Andersen, "Introduction: A New Era of Métis Studies Scholarship," in *A People and a Nation: New Directions in Contemporary Métis Studies*, eds. Jennifer Adese and Chris Andersen (Vancouver: UBC Press, 2021).

13 Robert Alexander Innes, "Challenging a Racist Fiction: A Closer Look at Métis-First Nations Relations," *A People and a Nation: New Directions in Contemporary Métis Studies*, eds. Jennifer Adese and Chris Andersen (Vancouver: UBC Press, 2021), 94. Also see Innes, *Elder Brother and the Law of the People*, 2013, 83–89.

14 Innes, "Challenging a Racist Fiction."

15 Ens and Sawchuk, *From New Peoples to New Nations*, 493.

16 In many respects, this argument is not a new one and was well articulated as "Red River Myopia" by J. R. Miller in "From Riel to the Metis," *Canadian Historical Review,* 96, 1 (1988).

17 Justin Trudeau to Carolyn Bennett, "Minister of Indigenous and Northern Affairs Mandate Letter," Nov. 12, 2015, https://pm.gc.ca/en/mandate-letters/2015/11/12/archived-minister-indigenous-and-northern-affairs-mandate-letter. Emphasis added. Also see Kelly Saunders and Janique Dubois, *Métis Politics and Governance in Canada* (Vancouver: UBC Press, 2019), xii–xiii.

18 In comparison, the Federal government currently recognizes 634 First Nations in Canada and has multiple agreements (treaties, self-government, special claims, etc.) with many, if not all, of them. By limiting their negotiations to only the five members of the Métis National Council (based in British Columbia, Alberta, Saskatchewan, Manitoba, and Ontario), the federal government would minimize the potential risk associated with having potentially hundreds of negotiating tables with many communities all with deferent interests and negotiating mandates.

19 Canada, "Historic Self-government Agreements Signed with the Métis Nation of Alberta, the Métis Nation of Ontario and the Métis Nation-Saskatchewan," June 27, 2019, https://www.canada.ca/en/crown-indigenous-relations-northern-affairs/news/2019/06/historic-self-government-agreements-signed-with-the-metis-nation-of-

alberta-the-metis-nation-of-ontario-and-the-metis-nation-saskatchewan.html. The federal government has yet to sign a similar agreement with the Métis Nation of British Columbia. However, in 2018, they signed an MOU that would place "it on a path to self-determination." See Canada, "Canada and Métis Nation of British Columbia Solidify Their Relationship," July 25, 2018, https://www.canada.ca/en/crown-indigenous-relations-northern-affairs/news/2018/07/canada-and-metis-nation-british-columbia-solidify-their-relationship.html.

20 Canada, Manitoba Métis Self-Government Recognition and Implementation Agreement, July 6, 2021. https://www.rcaanc-cirnac.gc.ca/eng/1641476532215/1641476589226. Also see *CBC News*, "Manitoba Metis Federation signs self-government agreement with feds," July 6, 2021, https://www.cbc.ca/news/canada/manitoba/manitoba-metis-federation-self-government-agreement-1.6092332.

21 Métis Nation of Alberta, "Otipemsiwak Métis Government Constitution: The Government of the Métis Nation within Alberta," November 2022. https://albertametis.com/app/uploads/2023/09/Otipemisiwak_Metis_Government_Constitution.pdf.

22 Métis Nation of Alberta, "Governance," https://albertametis.com/governance/.

23 Métis Nation of Alberta, "Métis Government Recognition and Self-Government Agreement Frequently Asked Questions," https://albertametis.com/app/uploads/2019/08/MNA-MGRSA-FAQ-DOCUMENT-FINAL.pdf. It is worth noting that the Métis Nation of Alberta's Constitutional Committee previously stated on their Frequently Asked Questions webpage that the MNA was "only representative of Métis in Alberta that has signed a self-government agreement with Canada." The page, previously found at http://www.albertametisgov.com/faq/, has since been removed from the internet and scrubbed from www.archive.org.

24 While Fort McKay is one group questioning the MNA's authority to make such claims, they are not the only one. Some of these groups have joined together to create the Alberta Métis Federation. See Vincent McDermott, "Six Métis Communities Form Alberta Métis Federation, Breaking From Métis Nation of Alberta," *Fort McMurray Today*, Feb. 27, 2020, https://www.fortmcmurraytoday.com/news/local-news/six-metis-communities-form-alberta-metis-federation-breaking-from-metis-nation-of-alberta. Also see Alberta Métis Federation, https://albertametisfederation.ca/. The MNA also elides over the fact that the Alberta Métis Settlements General Council has been self-governing since at least the 1930s and has multiple agreements with both federal and provincial governments. To this point, the MNA states that "nothing prevents members of the Métis Settlements from registering as MNA citizens" and that they believe that their agreement with Canada provides them with the mandate "to represent all citizens of the Métis Nation within Alberta in asserting our inherent right to self-government." The Métis Nation of Alberta, https://albertametis.com/metis-settlements/#:~:text=The%20MGRSA%20is%20clear%20that,inherent%20right%20to%20self%2Dgovernment.

25 The Métis Nation of Alberta, "Other Métis Governments and 'Métis' Organizations," https://albertametis.com/other-metis-governments-and-metis-organizations/. Also see Métis Nation of Alberta, "Métis Government Recognition and Self-Government Agreement Frequently Asked Questions," https://albertametis.com/app/uploads/2019/08/MNA-MGRSA-FAQ-DOCUMENT-FINAL.pdf.

26 See the Court's Judgement, section 2 in *Metis Settlements General Council v. Canada (Crown-Indigenous Relation), 2024 FC 487I*, https://decisions.fct-cf.gc.ca/fc-cf/decisions/en/item/525306/index.do#_Toc162431652.

27 Court's Judgement, section 2 in *Metis Settlements*," especially paragraphs 57–65.

28 UN General Assembly, *United Nations Declaration on the Rights of Indigenous Peoples: Resolution / Adopted by the General Assembly*, (UNDRIP) 2 October 2007, A/RES/61/295, https://www.un.org/development/desa/indigenouspeoples/wp-content/uploads/sites/19/2018/11/UNDRIP_E_web.pdf.

29 Canada, "Canada Becomes a Full Supporter of the United Nations Declaration on the Rights of Indigenous Peoples," May 10, 2016, https://www.canada.ca/en/indigenous-northern-affairs/news/2016/05/canada-becomes-a-full-supporter-of-the-united-nations-declaration-on-the-rights-of-indigenous-peoples.html.

30 Department of Justice Canada, "Legislation to Implement the United Nations Declaration on the Rights of Indigenous Peoples Becomes Law," June 22, 2020, https://www.canada.ca/en/department-justice/news/2021/06/legislation-to-implement-the-united-nations-declaration-on-the-rights-of-indigenous-peoples-becomes-law.html.

31 Larry Chartrand, "'We Rise Again:' Métis Traditional Governance and the Claim to Métis Self-Government," in *Aboriginal Self-government in Canada: Current Trends and Issues*, eds. Ned Belanger and Yale Deron (Saskatoon: Purich Publishing, 2008), 147.

32 Chartrand, "'We Rise Again," 2008, 149.

33 Janique Dubois and Kelly Saunders, "'Just Do It!': Carving Out Space for Métis in Canadian Federalism," *Canadian Journal of Political Science/ Revue canadienne de science politique* 46, no. 1 (2013). https://www.jstor.org/stable/43298128.

34 Canada. Royal Commission on Aboriginal Peoples (RCAP), "Métis Perspectives." Vol. 4, *Perspectives and Realities*. In *Report of the Royal Commission on Aboriginal Peoples*. Ottawa: Ottawa: Canada Communications Group, 1996, 201, 202. https://data2.archives.ca/e/e448/e011188230-04.pdf.

35 RCAP, "Métis Perspectives," 187.

36 *Powley*, 2–3.

37 RCAP, "Métis Perspectives," 190, 193.

38 *Metis Settlements General Council v. Canada (Crown-Indigenous Relation), 2024 FC 487*

39 *Metis Settlements*, par. 26–27, 38–41, 87, 93, 114, 119.

40 For example, see Chris Andersen, *Métis: Race, Recognition, and the Struggle for Peoplehood* (Vancouver: UBC Press 2014).

41 A good summary of the Powley Test can be found at Métis Nation of Ontario, "Establishing a Métis Right," https://www.metisnation.org/registry/the-powley-case/establishing-a-metis-right-the-powley-test/.

42 *Powley*, para. 24.

43 Alberta, "Métis Credible Assertion: Process and Criteria," 2020. https://open.alberta.ca/dataset/e74ec17c-9cf6-4f2c-8dde-1cae21ae6b0c/resource/19a86947-5798-46e3-a150-a436ccfb2f6a/download/ir-metis-credible-asssertion.pdf.

44 Jason Madden, "The Re-Emergence of Previously Slayed Metis Rights-Denial Dragons: The Dangers and Duplicity in Fort Chipewyan Métis Nation of Alberta Local# 125 v Alberta." *Osgoode Hall Law Journal* 57, no. 1 (2020): 195–229.

45 Catherine Bell and Paul Seaman. "A New Era for Métis Constitutional Rights? Consultation, Negotiation and Reconciliation." *Manitoba Law Journal* 38, no. 1 (2014): 38.

46 Bell and Seaman. "A New Era," 42, 48.

47 *Lizotte 2009* paras. 26, 27, 29.

48 *Metis Settlements General Council v. Canada (Crown-Indigenous Relation), 2024 FC 487.* Especially paras. 57, 137, 160–68.

49 For a more in-depth discussion on this topic see Patricia McCormack, "The Willow Lake Métis," Report submitted as part of the Alberta Credible Assertion Process, 2020, 15–49.

50 R. v. Powley, 2003, SCC 43 (CanLII).

51 James. A. Cardinal and Jason Ekeberg, "The Real Issues Emerging in Northeastern Alberta: Oil Sands Money, Greed and Unaccountable, "Métis Community Associations," February 13, 2020, https://web.archive.org/web/20210301123914/http://albertametis.com/2020/02/. Emphasis in the original.

52 See the population numbers as presented by the MNA in Métis Nation of Alberta, "Governance," 16 Feb 2018, (https://web.archive.org/web/20180216105354/https://albertametis.com/governance/) when compared to the numbers given in 2023 (https://albertametis.com/governance/).

53 For example, in the 2018 election, 3,821 members cast ballots for the position of president, though the organization claims to have "almost 50,000" registered members of the Métis Nation of Alberta. Official Results as issued by the Chief Electoral Officer, Election 2018, https://albertametis.com/app/uploads/2018/09/Official-Results-All-Candidates-2018.pdf. This was a significant jump from the previous two elections, which only saw 1,533 votes in 2014 and 2,024 votes in 2010. See Métis Nation of Alberta, "Audrey Poitras Re-elected as Provincial President of the Métis Nation of Alberta," September 5, 2014, https://www.newswire.ca/news-releases/audrey-poitras-re-elected-as-provincial-president-of-the-metis-nation-of-alberta-515450541.html; Clint Buehler, "Alberta Métis Re-Elect Audrey Poitras, *First Nations Drum*, September 10, 2011, http://www.firstnationsdrum.com/2011/09/alberta-metis-re-elect-audrey-poitras/. Recently, the MNA claimed to have slightly under 64,000 members, though it is difficult to verify this number as the membership list is not publicly available. Metis Nation of Alberta, "Governance," https://albertametis.com/governance/. It should be noted that in 2023, Poitras did step down, though the candidate she endorsed, Andrea Sandmaier, handily won the election with 5,693 of a possible 64,000 votes. Chris Steward, "Outgoing

president of the Métis Nation of Alberta says she faced a 'man's world' when first elected," *APTN News*, September 18, 2023. https://www.aptnnews.ca/national-news/outgoing-president-of-the-metis-nation-of-alberta-says-she-faced-a-mans-world-when-first-elected/; Métis Nation of Alberta,"Métis Nation within Alberta Citizens elect new President and Citizens' Council, formally becoming the Otipemisiwak Métis Government," *Press Release,* September 21, 2023. https://www.newswire.ca/news-releases/metis-nation-within-alberta-citizens-elect-new-president-and-citizens-council-formally-becoming-the-otipemisiwak-metis-government-818765383.html.

54   Westey Simpson-Denig, "Constitutional Crisis at the Métis Nation of Alberta," *Yellowhead Institute* February 9, 2023. https://yellowheadinstitute.org/2023/02/09/mna-constitutional-crisis/. While it is difficult to determine exactly how much the MNA spent on advertising for the constitutional vote, it is known that they purchased advertising newspapers, radio, and television. Additionally, they paid for billboards in major cities and advertisements on social media. To view the *Meta* advertisements see https://www.facebook.com/ads/library/?active_status=all&ad_type=all&country=CA&view_all_page_id=339682308115&sort_data[direction]=desc&sort_data[mode]=relevancy_monthly_grouped&search_type=page&media_type=all.

55   Ron Quintal, "The Métis Nation of Alberta Do Not Need the Proposed Constitution," *Calgary Herald*, November 17, 2022, https://calgaryherald.com/opinion/columnists/opinion-the-metis-of-alberta-do-not-need-the-proposed-constitution. The opinion piece was written on behalf of the Fort McKay Métis Nation as well as the Lac Ste. Anne Métis Community Association, Cadotte Lake Métis Nation Association, Willow Lake Métis Association, The Athabasca Landing Métis Nation, The Chard Métis Nation, Lakeland Métis Community, Owl River Métis Community, Edmonton Métis Community.

56   This point is made by Michel Houge, who argues that "the very existence of Métis communities across much of the twentieth century have largely remained invisible to many historians, archivists, and others in the scholarly community merits closer attention." Michel Hogue, "Still Hiding in Plain Sight?: Historiography and Métis archival memory," *History Compass*, 18, no. 2 (2020). Also see Ens and Sawchuk, *From New Peoples to New Nations*, esp. 490–507.

NOTES TO APPENDIX

1   This paper represents the position of the Fort McKay Métis Nation Council and they share it with the hope that it might spark a broader conversation about Métis governance. The Council would like to offer special thanks to Eddison Lee-Johnson and Peter Fortna, who helped to organize and present these positions in this paper, and Emily Boak, who produced the attached map. In addition, it would like to thank the multiple reviewers for providing additional perspectives, including Clayton Leonard, Patricia McCormack, Aron Taylor, and Anjalika Rogers. While the paper represents the opinions of the Nation, it is not meant as a legal document and should be used without prejudice.

The Fort McKay Métis Nation (FMMN) has been registered as a trade name for the community and is in the process of being officially recognized by Alberta and Canada.

FMMN replaces the Fort McKay Métis Community Association (FMMCA), which was the primary vehicle for representing the community from 2010 to 2020.

The position paper was originally published on the Fort McKay Métis Nation website February 2021. Where possible, weblinks were updated in May 2024.

2   Government of Alberta, "Métis Credible Assertion," https://open.alberta.ca/publications/metis-credible-assertion-process-and-criteria.

3   Alberta, "Métis Organization Establishes Right to Consultation," 13 February 2020, https://web.archive.org/web/20200929224333/https://ibftoday.ca/ab-government-metis-organization-establishes-right-to-consultation//.

4   Numerous Métis people and groups sent their congratulations, both publicly and privately through social media platforms, phone calls, and emails. In particular, a number of the future members of the Alberta Métis Federation sent their well wishes, and those conversations have led a number of those groups to explore the possibility of charting a similar path through the credible assertion process. Beyond Métis groups, the Fort McKay First Nation also offered their congratulations: "Fort McKay First Nation Congratulates Fort McKay Métis," Media Release, 14 February 2020, https://fortmckay.com/news/fort-mckay-first-nation-congratulates-fort-mckay-metis/. Much of the criticism levelled against the Fort McKay Métis Nation has come from the Métis Nation of Alberta, and can be found at https://web.archive.org/web/20210301123914/http://albertametis.com/2020/02/. In particular see releases from 26 February 2020; 13 February 2020; and 2 December 2019. A good summary of the current situation is provided by Shari Narine, "Metis Nation of Alberta Now Fighting on Three Fronts," *Windspeaker*, 14 February 2020, https://windspeaker.com/news/windspeaker-news/metis-nation-alberta-now-fighting-three-fronts.

5   Lavoie, "The Right to Be Heard," 1215.

6   This point was made explicit in *Fort Chipewyan*, para. 423.

7   For example see: Metis Association of Alberta, "Principles & Parameters of Metis Self-Government in Alberta, (1986); Metis Nation of Alberta Association, "Final Report Metis Nation of Alberta Association: Royal Commission on Aboriginal People, (1995); Alberta Metis Otipemisiwak Commission, "Final Report," (1995); Alberta Metis Association, "'A New Direction:' A Metis Governance Plan for Alberta (2008) and Jobin, Lindquist, and Letendre, "Métis Nation of Alberta Governance Framework Review Community Report," (2017). A good summary of the situation is provided in Shari Narine, "MNA Member Not Confident Review of Structure Will Bring Necessary Changes," *Alberta Sweetgrass* 24, no. 4 (2016). More recently, the MNA has begun the push toward an Alberta Métis Constitution, the details of which can be reviewed at www.albertametisgov.com. It is as yet unclear whether this latest process will have more success than others launched over the last thirty-plus years.

8   Jen Gerson, "Métis Have Long Fared Better than Status Indians, So Why Do They Want to be Treated the Same?," *National Post*, 26 January 2013. https://nationalpost.com/news/canada/metis-have-long-fared-better-than-status-indians-so-why-do-they-want-to-be-treated-the-same.

9   Committees to which the Fort McKay Métis participated included: The Métis Nation of Alberta Region 1, Consultation Protocol Committee (2012–2014), the MNA Consultation Technical Committee (2016–2017).

10 Fort McKay helped to reinitiate the Wood Buffalo Métis Corporation as a group to advocate for the rights of Métis people in the Regional Municipality of Wood Buffalo. The group's founding memorandum of understanding can be found here: https://web.archive.org/web/20240227123402/https://fdocuments.in/download/memorandum-of-understanding-wood-buffalo-metis.

11 Métis Nation of Alberta – Government of Alberta, Framework Agreement, 1 February 2017, https://open.alberta.ca/dataset/eac3e6c9-e54f-4d4c-81f7-a47b8e39d7e9/resource/de6ebd40-9bbb-41ea-8ec2-fa4f06ebf607/download/mna-framework-agreement-jan-31-2017.pdf. The framework agreement was followed by a series of meetings where the development of the Alberta Métis consultation policy was discussed. A summary of these meetings can be found at Métis Nation of Alberta, "Developing a Métis Consultation Policy: Key highlights from meeting with Métis Nation of Alberta and Minister of Indigenous Relations," 6 October 2017, https://web.archive.org/web/20180609095008/http://albertametis.com/2017/10/developing-metis-consultation-policy-key-highlights-meeting-metis-nation-alberta-minister-indigenous-relations/. Authors Kelly Saunders and Janique Dubois discuss how the question of how power should be centralized or decentralized within Métis governments has remained a "point of contention in Métis political circles." *Métis Politics and Governance in Canada* (Vancouver: UBC Press, 2019), 58–59.

12 Métis Nation of Alberta, *Advancing Métis Rights and Claims in Alberta: Understanding the New Objective and Oath of Membership in the Métis Nation of Alberta's Bylaws* (Edmonton: Métis Nation of Alberta, 2017), https://web.archive.org/web/20210121044703/http://albertametis.com/wp-content/uploads/2013/08/Advancing-M%C3%A9tis-Rights-and-Claims-in-Alberta.pdf.

13 For example, see Donald McCargar, "Donald McCargar speaks out on case that proved Metis Nation of Alberta (MNAA) neither a nation nor a governing body—launches further appeal to further define the limited role of the MNAA," 30 August 2018, https://www.newswire.ca/news-releases/donald-mccargar-speaks-out-on-case-that-proved-metis-nation-of-alberta-mnaa-neither-a-nation-nor-a-governing-body---launches-further-appeal-to-further-define-the-limited-role-of-the-mnaa-692081591.html . A number of communities, including Fort McKay, expressed concern with the oath at the 2016 Métis Nation of Alberta general assembly, where ultimately a majority of the .5% of the membership that were present passed the changes to the bylaws.

14 For more on the early history of Métis Settlement governance in the province see: Thomas C. Pocklington, *The Government and Politics of the Alberta Métis Settlements* (Regina: Canadian Plains Research Center, Regina); Catherine Bell, *Alberta's Metis Settlements Legislation: An Overview of Ownership and Management of Settlement Lands* (Regina: Canadian Plains Research Centre, 1994); and Nicole O'Byrne, "'No other weapon except organization': The Métis Association of Alberta and the 1938 *Métis Population Betterment Act*," *Journal of the Canadian Historical Association* 24, no. 2 (2013): 311–52.

15   Patricia McCormack provides a good summary of the Court decisions in "The Willow Lake Métis: A Distinctive Métis Community." (Edmonton: Native Bridges Consulting Inc., 2020).

16   See: Jane E. Dickson, *By Law or In Justice: The Indian Specific Claims Commission and the Struggle for Indigenous Justice* (Vancouver: Purich Books, 2018).

17   In the cases of *Gooden and Hirsekorn,* the Courts found Métis communities existed in clearly defined regions, even as the defendants' pushed for the acceptance of "the entire northwest" or the "entire western plains and prairies" in their claims. Furthermore, as demonstrated in *Lizotte 2009 ABPC 287* asserted that Métis communities that have organized themselves and that meet the conditions laid out in Powley should be recognized as being a rights holder. For a more in-depth discussion on this topic see McCormack, "The Willow Lake Métis," 15–49.

18   While these statements are found throughout the document, in particular see articles 1-9. UN General Assembly, *United Nations Declaration on the Rights of Indigenous Peoples: Resolution / Adopted by the General Assembly*, 2 October 2007, A/RES/61/295, https://www.refworld.org/docid/471355a82.html.

19   Lavoie, "The Right to Be Heard," 1222.

20   Joe Sawchuk, *The Dynamics of Native Politics: The Alberta Metis Experience* (Saskatoon: Purich Publishing, 1998); Joe Sawchuk, Patricia Sawchuk, and Theresa Ferguson, *Métis Land Rights in Alberta: A Political History* (Métis Association of Alberta: Edmonton, 1981).

21   For example see: Mix 103.7, "Fort McKay Metis React to Alberta Court Lawsuit Dismissal against MNA," 3 December 2019, https://www.play1037.ca/2019/12/03/80552/.

22   *Fort Chipewyan Métis Nation of Alberta Local #125 v Alberta*, 2016 ABQB 713. https://www.canlii.org/en/ab/abqb/doc/2016/2016abqb713/2016abqb713.html.

23   Lavoie, "The Right to Be Heard," 1213.

24   At a community meeting on 28 November 2019, 7 of the 10 members in attendance at the last meeting of the Fort McKay Métis Local 63 unanimously voted to dissolve the organization. Shari Narine, "Metis Local in Limbo as Government Policy Forces Members to Choose Who Represents Them," *Windspeaker*, 1 April 2019. https://windspeaker.com/news/windspeaker-news/metis-local-limbo-government-policy-forces-members-choose-who-represents-them.

25   Fortna, "Genealogical Narrative," 17.

26   Alberta, "Métis Organization Establishes Right to Consultation," 13 February 2020, https://www.alberta.ca/release.cfm?xID=6861188357C08-C734-DA8D-FD73A149425FFE3D

27   Lavoie, "The Right to Be Heard," 1216.

28   Lavoie, "The Right to Be Heard," 1219.

29   To learn more about the McKay Métis Group please visit https://www.mckaymetisgroup.com/. A good definition of "social enterprise" is provided by Adam Barone, "Social Enterprise" *Investopedia,* 3 February 2020, https://www.investopedia.

com/terms/s/social-enterprise.asp#:~:text=A%20social%20enterprise%20or%20social,used%20to%20fund%20social%20programs.

30 Ens and Sawchuk, *From New People to New Nations*, 2016; Sawchuk, "Negotiating an Identity: Metis Political Organizations, the Canadian Government, and Competing Concepts of Aboriginality." *American Indian Quarterly* 25, no. 1 (Winter 2001): 73–92.

31 Mary Agnes Welch with updates by David Gallant, "Métis National Council," The Canadian Encyclopedia, 2019, https://www.thecanadianencyclopedia.ca/en/article/metis-national-council.

32 Justin Giovannetti, "Alberta Métis Community Declares Self-Government," *The Globe and Mail*, 24 May 2019. https://www.theglobeandmail.com/canada/alberta/article-alberta-metis-community-declares-self-government/. FMMN President Ron Quintal spoke on this topic at the Metis National Council organized "Building Wealth for the Métis Nation" conference held March 3–5, 2020 and the Fort McKay Métis Nation were active participants at the most recent MNC National Convention, held in Saskatoon, Saskatchewan, March 9–10, 2020.

33 Vincent McDermott, "Six Métis Communities Form Alberta Métis Federation, Breaking from the Métis Nation of Alberta," 27 February 2020, https://www.fortmcmurraytoday.com/news/local-news/six-metis-communities-form-alberta-metis-federation-breaking-from-metis-nation-of-alberta.

Bibliography

Primary Sources

CENSUS OF CANADA

1870 Census of Manitoba, St. Andrew. LAC C-2170. http://www.collectionscanada.gc.ca/lac-bac/anc.

1881 Census of Canada, Northwest Territories, Athabasca T – Fort McMurray. T-6426.

1901 Census of Canada, The Territories, Unorganized Territories 206, Athabaska A-6, Fort McMurray. LAC T-6555.

DEPARTMENT OF INDIAN AFFAIRS AND NORTHERN DEVELOPMENT

File 779/30-10/174, vol. 1.

FORT MCKAY HISTORY PROJECT INTERVIEWS, 2017.

GLENBOW MUSEUM AND ARCHIVES, CALGARY, ALBERTA

M4755, file 470, "Métis Association of Alberta Papers, 1892–1979," accession no. M5006.

M4755, file 968.

GOVERNMENT OF CANADA VOTERS LISTS.

Fort McKay 1958, 1962, 1963, 1965. http://ancestry.ca.

LIBRARY AND ARCHIVES CANADA (LAC)

RG10, vol. 6732, file 420-2B, reel C8094.

RG10, vol. 6733, file 420-2-2 1, reel C8095.

RG10, vol. 6734, 420-2-2-3, reel C8095.

RG10, vol. 6734, file 420-2-1-3, reel C8096.

RG15, vol. 1369.

RG18, vol. 1435, file 76-1899, pt. 2.

"MacKay Settlement Alberta, and surrounding area," n.d., MIKAN no. 4141022.

Royal Commission on Aboriginal People Testimony, Fort McMurray, ALTA 92-06-16. http://www.bac-lac.gc.ca/eng/discover/aboriginal-heritage/royal-commission-aboriginal-peoples/Pages/item.aspx?IdNumber=38.

PROVINCIAL ARCHIVES OF ALBERTA (PAA)

GR1979.0152, box 13, item 158.

GR1979.0152, box 14.

GR1979.0152, box 8.

GR1979.0152, box 16, item 216.

GR1979.0152, box 16, item 217.

GR 1990.377, Trapping Maps and Index Cards.

GR76.502, box 40, file 15.

GR76.502, box 15, Community Development – Fort MacKay.

70.427/409, box 23.

91-270, file T.4, V7, box 64.

91-270, file T.4, V9, box 65.

96-32, file 65E, vis 2-11-6.

NEWSPAPERS / PERIODICALS (INCLUDES CLIPPINGS FOUND IN THE *ROD HYDE NEWSPAPER COLLECTION*, FORT MCKAY, ALBERTA)

Alberta Gazette

Alberta Report

AMMSA

Calgary Sun

CBC News

Edmonton Bulletin

Edmonton Journal

Edmonton Sun

Fort McMurray Express

Fort McMurray Today

Globe and Mail

Maclean's

Red Deer Advocate

SASKATCHEWAN CATHOLIC CHURCH RECORDS
Mission de la Visitation, La Loche, 1905.

TREATY AND ABORIGINAL RIGHTS RESEARCH PROGRAM
Louis Boucher, tape number IH.259, transcript disc 29, 1974,http://hdl.handle.net/10294/1371.

Phillip Macdonald, tape number IH-297, transcript disk 40, 1973, http://ourspace.uregina.ca/handle/10294/1564.

TERRY GARVIN PERSONAL PAPERS UNIVERSITY OF CALGARY ARCHIVES
Correspondence (ca. 1975).

Photo Collection.

Terry Garvin Newspaper Scrapbook (2 volumes).

OTHER INTERVIEWS [WHERE ARE THEY]
Fred Macdonald, "Interview Transcript: Métis 1935 'Mark of the Métis' Heritage Study Pilot Project,'" Interviewed by Sara Loutitt and Sherri Labour, March 30, 2007. http://www.acee-ceaa.gc.ca/050/documents/45006/45006F.pdf.

Margie Wood, "Interview Transcript: Métis 1935 'Mark of the Métis' Heritage Study Pilot Project,'" Interviewed by Sara Loutitt and Sherri Labour, March 30, 2007. http://www.acee-ceaa.gc.ca/050/documents/45006/45006F.pdf.

FORT MCKAY MÉTIS NATION ARCHIVE. FORT MCKAY, ALBERTA.

COURT DECISIONS
R. v. Powley, 2003, SCC 43 (CanLII).

Fort Chipewyan Métis Nation of Alberta Local #125 v. Alberta, 2016 ABQB 713.

Secondary Sources

Adese, Jennifer, and Chris Andersen, eds. *A People and a Nation: New Directions in Contemporary Métis Studies.* Vancouver: UBC Press, 2021.

Alberta. "Métis Credible Assertion: Process and Criteria." December 13, 2019. https://open.alberta.ca/publications/metis-credible-assertion-process-and-criteria.

Alberta Aboriginal Affairs and Northern Development. *The Alberta Natural Resources Act, Assented to April 3, 1930, Chapter 21, Alberta, An Act Respecting the Transfer of the Natural Resources of Alberta.*

Alberta Finance. *Government of Alberta's Strategic Business Plan, 2008–2011.* April 2008.

Alberta Municipal Affairs, Local Government Services Division. Fort McKay Métis Local #122 Lease, Agreement No. AMA 2001-001, Hamlet of Fort McKay, 2001.

Alberta Northern Alberta Development Council, *Annual Report, 1973-1974.* Edmonton: ANADC, 1974.

Andersen, Chris. *Métis: Race, Recognition, and the Struggle for Peoplehood.* Vancouver: UBC Press, 2014.

Andersen, Chris. "Settling for Community? Judicial Visions of Historical Métis Collectivity In and After R. v. *Powley.*" In *Contours of a People: Métis Family, Mobility, and History,* edited by Nicole St. Onge, Carolyn Podruchny, and Brenda Macdougall. Norman: University of Oklahoma Press, 2012.

Angell, Angela C., and John R. Parkins. "Resource development and aboriginal culture in the Canadian north." *Polar Record,* 47, no. 1 (Jan. 2011).

Asensio, Manuel P., with Jack Barth. *Sold Short: Uncovering Deception in the Markets.* Danvers, MA: John Wiley & Sons, Inc., 2001.

Balazs, Dawn. "A Short Analysis of the Transfer of Natural Resources to Alberta in 1930 and a Preliminary Study of the Registered Trapline System." Treaty and Aboriginal Rights Research of the Indian Association of Alberta, March 1976.

Barkwell, Lawrence J. *Métis Dictionary of Biography, Volume D.* Winnipeg: Louis Riel Institute, 2015.H.W. Theisen, *Trapping the Buffalo Head Hills & Utikuma Uplands.* Edmonton: Bear Trap Trappers' Committee, 2006.

Bell, Catherine and Paul Seaman. "A New Era for Métis Constitutional Rights? Consultation, Negotiation and Reconciliation." *Manitoba Law Journal* 38, no. 1 (2014).

Bethell, Graeme. *Preliminary Inventory of the Environmental Issues and Concerns Affecting the People of Fort MacKay, Alberta.* Brentwood Bay, BC, Bethell Management Ltd., 1985.

Brody, Hugh. *Maps and Dreams: Indians and the British Columbia Frontier.* Vancouver: Douglas & McIntyre, 1981.

Canada. Royal Commission on Aboriginal Peoples (RCAP), "Métis Perspectives." Vol. 4, *Perspectives and Realities.* In *Report of the Royal Commission on Aboriginal Peoples.* Ottawa: Ottawa: Canada Communications Group, 1996.

Canada, Department of Justice. "Legislation to Implement the United Nations Declaration on the Rights of Indigenous Peoples Becomes Law," June 22, 2020.

Campbell, Craig, Alice Boucher, Mike Evans, Emma Faichney, Howard LaCorde, and Zachary Powder. *Mihkwâkamiwi sîpîsis: Stories and Pictures from Métis Elders in Fort McKay.* Edmonton: Canadian Circumpolar Institute, 2005. https://archive.org/details/uap_9781772122091.

Charlton, T. L., L. E. Meyers, and R. Sharpless. *History of Oral History: Foundations and Methodology.* Lanham, MD: Rowman and Littlefield, 2007.

Chartrand, Larry N., Tricia E. Logan, and Judy D. Daniels. *Métis History and Experience and Residential Schools in Canada.* Ottawa: Aboriginal Healing Foundation, 2006.

Chartrand, Larry. "'We Rise Again': Métis Traditional Governance and the Claim to Métis Self-Government." In Aboriginal Self-government in Canada: Current Trends and Issues, edited by Ned Belanger and Yale Deron. Saskatoon: Purich Publishing, 2008.

Clark, Tim, Dermot O'Connor, and Peter Fortna. *Fort McMurray: Historic and Contemporary Rights-Bearing Métis Community*. Fort McMurray: McMurray Métis, 2015.

Cruikshank, Julie. "Oral Tradition and Oral History: Reviewing Some Issues." *Canadian Historical Review* 75, no. 3 (1994): 403–18.

Daniel, Richard. "The Spirit and Terms of Treaty Eight." In *The Spirit of the Alberta Indian Treaties*, edited by Richard Price. Edmonton: Pica Pica Press, 1987.

Deighton, Heather, and Carl R. Surrendi. *From Traplines to Pipelines: A Socio-Economic Impact Assessment of the Proposed Shell Lease 13 Project on the Community of Fort McKay*. Fort McKay: Fort McKay Environmental Services Ltd. 1998.

DesBrisay, David. "The Impact of Major Resource Development Projects on Aboriginal Communities: A Review of the Literature." *Royal Commission on Aboriginal People* (Feb. 1994). https://data2.archives.ca/rcap/pdf/rcap-51.pdf.

Devine, Heather. "The Alberta Dis-Advantage: Métis Issues and the Public Discourse in Wild Rose Country." *London Journal of Canadian Studies* 26 (2010/11): 37–53.

———. *The People Who Own Themselves: Aboriginal Ethnogenesis in a Canadian Family, 1660–1900*. Calgary: University of Calgary Press, 2004.

Donnelly, Gabrielle. *Indigenous Women in Community Leadership Case Studies: Fort McKay First Nation, Alberta*. Antigonish, N.S., Coady International Institute, 2012.

Duckworth, Harry, ed. *The English River Book: A North West Company Journal and Account Book of 1786*. Montreal and Kingston: McGill-Queen's University Press, 1990.

Dubois, Janique, and Kelly Saunders. "'Just Do It!': Carving Out Space for Métis in Canadian Federalism." *Canadian Journal of Political Science/ Revue canadienne de science politique* 46, no. 1 (2013).

Energy Resources Conservation Board, "Oil Sands, Tar Island Area, Application No. 78318, Notice of Hearing." Energy Resources Conservation Board, Application No. 780318, December 11, 1978.

Ens, Gerhard. "Taking Treaty 8 Scrip, 1899–1900: A Quantitative Portrait of Northern Alberta Métis Communities." In *Treaty 8 Revisited: Selected Papers of the 1999 Centennial Conference*, edited by Duff Crerar and Jaroslav Petryshyn. Grand Prairie, AB: Grand Prairie Regional College, 1999–2000.

Ens, Gerhard, and Joe Sawchuk. *From New People to New Nations: Aspects of Métis History and Identity from the Eighteenth to Twenty-First Centuries*. Toronto: University of Toronto, 2016.

Flanagan, Tom. *The Community Capitalism of the Fort McKay First Nation: A Case Study*. Vancouver: Fraser Institute, 2018. https://www.fraserinstitute.org/sites/default/files/community-capitalism-of-the-fort-mckay-first-nation.pdf.

———. "Lubicon Lake: The Success and Failure of Radical Activism," in *Blockades or Breakthroughs?: Aboriginal Peoples Confront the Canadian State*, edited by Yale D. Belanger and P. Whitney Lackenbauer. Montreal and Kingston: McGill-Queen's University Press, 2014.

Ft. McKay Community. *A Review of the Biophysical Impact Assessment and Reclamation Plan for New Mining Areas in Support of Approved New Facilities at the Syncrude Canada Ltd. Mildred Lake Plant.* Fort McKay, January 1986.

Fort McKay Community Committee, "Intervention Filed with the Energy Resources Conservation Board by the Fort McKay Community Committee in Relation to the Proposed GCOS Expansion Application 780318." *Energy Resources Conservation Board*, Application No. 780318, January 19, 1979.

Fort McKay First Nations. *There Is Still Survival Out There: A Traditional Land Use and Occupancy Study of the Fort McKay First Nations.* Edmonton: Arctic Institute of North America, 1994.

Fort McKay First Nation, "Moose Lake: Our Commitment to Protection." https://web.archive.org/web/20190123030300/http://fortmckay.com/moose-lake/.

Fort McKay Métis Nation, "The Fort McKay Métis Nation Position Paper on Consultation and Self Government." Fort McKay: Fort McKay Métis Nation, 2021.

Fort McKay Industrial Relations Corporation. "The Fort McKay Cultural Heritage Assessment Baseline Pre-Development (1960s) to Current (2008), prepared as part of the Fort McKay Specific Assessment." Fort McKay: Fort McKay Industrial Relations Corporation, 2010.

Fort McKay Industrial Relations Corporation. *Fort McKay Specific Assessment.* Fort McKay, 2010.

———. "Memorandum of Understanding between Fort McKay Industry Relations Corporation and Fort McKay Métis Local 63." October 2008.

Fort McKay Sustainability Department. "Place Names Map." https://fmsd.knowledgekeeper.ca/placenames-map

Fort McKay Tribal Administration. "From Where We Stand: Traditional Land Use and Occupancy Study of the Fort McKay First Nation." Fort McKay: Fort McKay Tribal Administration, 1983.

———. *Incorporating the Findings from the CEMA Indigenous Traditional Knowledge Framework into the Alberta Environmental Monitoring, Evaluation & Reporting Agency: Key Findings and Recommendations.* A Report Submitted to AEMERA June 25, 2016.

———. "'How Much Longer?': A Preliminary Assessment of Homelessness in Conklin, Alberta." Conklin: Conklin Resource Development Advisory Committee, 2018.

Fox, M., and W. A. Ross. *The Influence of Oil Sands Development on Trapping in the Fort McMurray Region.* Edmonton: Alberta Oil Sands Environmental Research Program, 1979.

Foran, Max. "1967: Embracing the Future… at Arm's Length," in *Alberta Formed: Alberta Transformed,* edited by Michael Payne, Donald Wetherell, and Catherine Cavanaugh. Edmonton: University of Alberta Press, 2006.

Garvin, T., S. Nelson, E. Ellehoj, and B. Redmond. *A Guide to Conducting a Traditional Knowledge and Land Use Study.* Edmonton: Canadian Forest Service, 2001.

Gaudry, Adam. "Communing with the Dead: The 'New Métis,' Métis Identity Appropriation, and the Displacement of Living Métis Culture." *The American Indian Quarterly* 42, no. 2 (Spring 2018).

Goddard, John. *Stand of the Lubicon Cree*. Vancouver/Toronto: Douglas & McIntyre, 1992.

Gibson Ginger and Jason Klinck. "Canada's Resilient North: The Impact of Mining on Aboriginal Communities." *Pimatiswin* 3 (2005).

Government of Alberta. "Métis Harvesting in Alberta July 2007 – Updated June 2010." https://open.alberta.ca/dataset/57bdd5ba-d024-4c06-b3aa-b9cbf8c513ca/resource/b0da0882-4ddc-4886-abc1-b6d3ab6f485e/download/metisharvestinginalberta-jun2010.pdf.

Government of Alberta. "Métis Harvesting in Alberta Policy, 2018." https://open.alberta.ca/publications/metis-harvesting-in-alberta-policy-2018#:~:text=Description,fish%20and%20trap%20for%20food.

Government of Alberta Land Use Secretariat. "Understanding Land Use in Alberta." Edmonton: Government of Alberta, 2007.

Greer, Allan. "Settler Colonialism and Beyond." *Journal of the Canadian Historical Association* 30 (2020).

Gunn, Brenda L. "Defining Métis People as a People: Moving Beyond the Indian/Metis Dichotomy." *Dalhousie Law Journal* 38, no. 2 (2015).

Haggarty, Liam. "Métis Welfare: A History of Economic Exchange in Northwest Saskatchewan, 1770–1870." *Saskatchewan History* 61, no. 2 (2009): 7–17.

———. "Sharing and Exchange in Northwest Saskatchewan." In *Métis in Canada: History, Identity, Law, & Politics*, edited by Christopher Adams, Gregg Dahl, and Ian Peach. Edmonton: University of Alberta Press, 2013.

Hall, David J. "Oliver, Frank" (Francis Robert Bowsfield, Bossfield, or Bousfield)." In *Dictionary of Canadian Biography*, vol. 16. Toronto/Quebec City: University of Toronto/Université Laval, 2003. http://www.biographi.ca/en/bio/oliver_frank_16E.html.

Hanowski, Laura. "Fort McKay Métis Community Genealogies." Fort McKay: Fort McKay Métis Community Association, 2017.

———. "Personal Correspondence." 27 April 2017.

Hartley, Gerard. *The Search for Consensus: A Legislative History of Bill C-31, 1969-1985*. London, ON: Aboriginal Policy Research Consortium International, 2007.

Harris, Cole. *A Bounded Land: Reflections on Settler Colonialism in Canada*. Vancouver: UBC Press, 2020.

Highwood Environmental Group. "Traditional Ecological Knowledge and Family History for RFMA 2137." Fort McKay: Fort McKay Industrial Relations Corporation, 2001.

Hoffman, A. "Reliability and Validity in Oral History." In *Oral History*, edited by D. K. Dunaway and W. K. Baum. Plymouth, MA: Altamira Press, 1984.

Hogue, Michel. "Still Hiding in Plain Sight?: Historiography and Métis Archival Memory," *History Compass* 18, no. 7 (2020).

Human Environment Group (HEG). "Indicators of Cultural Change (1960 to 2009): A Framework for Selecting Indicators Based on Cultural Values in Fort McKay." Fort McKay: Fort McKay Industrial Relations Corporation, 2009.

———. "Teck Frontier Mine Project: Fort McKay Métis Integrated Cultural Assessment." Fort McKay: Fort McKay Métis Sustainability Centre, 2016.

Indian Claims Commission. *Inquiry into the Treaty Land Entitlement Claim of the Fort McKay First Nation*. 1995. http://iportal.usask.ca/docs/ICC/FortMckayEng.pdf.

Innes, Robert Alxander. *Elder Brother and the Law of the People*. Winnipeg: University of Manitoba, 2013.

Innes, Robert Alexander. "Multicultural Bands on the Northern Plans and the Notion of 'Tribal' Histories." In *Finding a Way to the Heart: Feminist Writings on Aboriginal and Women's History in Canada*, edited by Robin Jarvis Brownlie and Valerie J. Korinek. Winnipeg: University of Manitoba Press, 2012.

Innes, Robert Alexander. "Challenging a Racist Fiction: A Closer Look at Métis-First Nations Relations." In *A People and a Nation: New Directions in Contemporary Métis Studies* Jennifer Adese and Chris Andersen eds. Vancouver: UBC Press, 2021.

Jarvis, A. M. "Report of Inspector Jarvis re: Northern Patrol." In "Report of the Commissioner of the North-West Mounted Police, 1897." Ottawa: Queen's Printer, 1898.

Johnson, Gregory A. *Lac La Biche Chronicles: Early Years*. Lac La Biche: Portage College, 1999.

Keeling, Arn, and John Sandlos, eds. *Mining and Communities in Northern Canada: History, Politics, and Memory*. Calgary: University of Calgary Press, 2015.

Kenny, James L., and Andrew Secord. "Engineering Modernity: Hydro-Electric Development in New Brunswick, 1945–70," *Acadiensis* 39, no. 1 (2010).

Labour, Sherri, and Barb Hermansen. *The Last Woman to Raise Children on the Athabasca River*. Fort Chipewyan: Fort Chipewyan Métis Local 125, 2011.

Laird, David, J. H. Ross, J. A. J. McKenna. "Report of Commissioners for Treaty No. 8." In *Treaty No. 8 Made June 21, 1899 and Adhesions, Reports, Etc*. Ottawa: Queen's Printer and Controller of Stationery, 1899 [reprint 1966]. https://www.rcaanc-cirnac.gc.ca/eng/1100100028813/1581293624572#chp6.

Larmour, Judy. *Laying Down the Lines: A History of Land Surveying in Alberta*. Calgary: Brindle & Glass, 2005.

Lavoie, Moira. "The Right to be Heard: Representative Authority as a Requirement in Enforcing Métis Consultation." *Alberta Law Review* 56, no. 4 (2019): 1209–27. http://www.albertalawreview.com/index.php/ALR/article/view/2549.

Lawrence, Bonita. *"Real" Indians and Others: Mixed-Blood Urban Native Peoples and Indigenous Nationhood*. Vancouver: UBC Press, 2004.

Leonard, David, and Beverly Whalen, eds. *On the North Trail: The Treaty 8 Diary of O.C. Edwards*. Edmonton: Alberta Records and Publication Board, 1998.

Leavy, P. *Oral History*. Oxford: Oxford University Press, 2011.

Lewis, J. H. *Survey Records Search of the Surveys Branch of Indians Affairs: Its Creation, Operations and Demise with Respect to the Prairie Provinces*. Ottawa: Department of Indian and Northern Affairs, 1993.

Longley, Hereward. "Conflicting Interests: Development Politics and the Environmental Regulation of the Alberta Oil Sands Industry, 1970–1980." *Environment and History* (April 2, 2019). https://doi.org/10.3197/096734019X15463432086919.

———. "Indigenous Battles for Environmental Protection and Economic Benefits During the Commercialization of the Alberta Oil Sands, 1967–1986." In *Mining and Communities in Northern Canada: History, Politics and Memory*, edited by Arn Keeling and John Sandlos. Calgary: University of Calgary Press, 2015.

Longley, Hereward, and Tara Joly. "The Moccasin Flats Evictions: Métis Home, Forced Relation, and Resilience in Fort McMurray, Alberta." Fort McMurray: McMurray Métis, 2018.

Loo, Tina. "High Modernism, Conflict, and the Nature of Change in Canada: A Look at Seeing Like a State." *Canadian Historical Review* 1 (March 2016): 97.

———. "People in the Way: Modernity, Environment, and Society on the Arrow Lakes." *BC Studies* 142/43 (Summer/Autumn 2004).

———. "Disturbing the Peace: Environmental Change and the Scales of Justice on a Northern River." *Environmental History*, Special Issue on Canada (October 2007).

———. *Moved by the State: Forced Relocation and Making a Good Life in Postwar Canada*. Vancouver: UBC Press, 2019.

Lutz, John. *Makuk: A New History of Aboriginal–White Relations*. Vancouver: University of British Columbia Press, 2009.

Macdougall, Brenda. *One of the Family: Métis Culture in Nineteenth-Century Northwestern Saskatchewan*. Vancouver: University of British Columbia Press, 2010.

Madden, Jason. "The Re-Emergence of Previously Slayed Metis Rights-Denial Dragons: The Dangers and Duplicity in Fort Chipewyan Métis Nation of Alberta Local# 125 v Alberta." *Osgoode Hall Law Journal* 57, no. 1 (2020).

Madill, Dennis F.K. "Treaty Research Report: Treaty Eight (1899)." Ottawa: Treaties and Historical Research Centre, 1986.

Matsui, Kenichi, and Arthur J. Ray. "Delimiting Métis Economic Communities in the Environs of Ft McMurray: A Preliminary Analysis Based on Hudson's Bay Company Records." In *Fort McMurray: Historic and Contemporary Rights-Bearing Métis Community*, edited by Tim Clark, Dermot O'Connor, and Peter Fortna. Fort McMurray: McMurray Métis, 2015.

McCormack, Patricia. *Fort Chipewyan and the Shaping of Canadian History, 1788–1920s*. Vancouver: University of British Columbia Press, 2010.

———. "How the (North) West Was Won: Development and Underdevelopment in the Fort Chipewyan Region." PhD diss., University of Alberta, 1984.

———. *Research Report: Treaty No. 8 and the Fort McKay First Nation*. 2012. https://web.archive.org/web/20170726114206/http://ceaa-acee.gc.ca/050/documents_staticpost/59540/81946/Appendix_A_-_Treaty_No_8_and_Fort_McKay_First_Nation_Research_Report.pdf

———. "Defining Effective Control for Métis Communities." 2021.

———. "Studying the Social and Cultural Impacts of 'Extreme Extraction' in Northern Alberta." In *Extracting Home in the Oil Sands: Settler Colonialism and Environmental Change in Subarctic Canada*, edited by Clinton N. Westman, Tara L. Joly, and Lena Gross. London and New York: Routledge, 2020.

McDonald, Dorothy to Vern Millard. "Re: A Review of the Biophysical Impact Assessment and Reclamation Plan for New Mining Areas in Support of Approved New Facilities at the Syncrude Canada Ltd. Mildred Lake Plant." In *The Ft. McKay Community, A Review of the Biophysical Impact Assessment and Reclamation Plan for New Mining Areas in Support of Approved New Facilities at the Syncrude Canada Ltd. Mildred Lake Plant*. Fort McKay, January 1986.

McKay, Ian. "The Liberal Order Framework: A Prospectus for a Reconnaissance of Canadian History." *Canadian Historical Review* 81 (2000).

Moberly, Henry John, in collaboration with William Blaisdell Cameron. *When Fur Was King*. London and Toronto, 1929.

Miller, J.R. "From Riel to the Metis." *Canadian Historical Review* 96, no. 1 (1988).

Nicks, Trudy. "Mary Anne's Dilemma: The Ethnohistory of an Ambivalent Identity." *Canadian Ethnic Studies* 12, no. 2 (1985): 103–14.

Nicks, Trudy, and Kenneth Morgan. "Grande Cache: The Historic Development of an Indigenous Métis Population." In *The New Peoples: Being and Becoming Métis in North America*, edited by Jacqueline Peterson and Jennifer S.H. Brown. Winnipeg: University of Manitoba Press, 1985.

Notzke, Claudia. *Aboriginal People and Natural Resources in Canada*. North York: Captus Press Inc., 1996.

Palmater, Pamela D. *Beyond Blood: Rethinking Indigenous Identity*. Saskatoon: Purich Publishing Ltd. 2011.

Parker, James M. *Emporium of the North: Fort Chipewyan and the Fur Trade to 1835*. Saskatoon: Canadian Plains Research Centre, 1987.

———. *History of the Athabasca Oil Sands Region, 1890–1960s, Volume II: Oral History*. Edmonton: Athabasca Oil Sands Environmental Program, 1980.

Passelac-Ross, Monique. "The Trapping Rights of Aboriginal Peoples in Northern Alberta." Calgary: Canadian Institute of Resource Law, 2005. https://prism.ucalgary.ca/items/1bb9b414-8c51-4db6-b54c-dd603ddb9d7b.

Peyton, Jonathan. *Unbuilt Environments: Tracing Postwar Development in Northwest British Columbia*. Vancouver: UBC Press, 2017.

Pigeon, Emilie, Nicole St-Onge, and Brenda Macdougall. "A Social Network of Hunters?: Métis Mobility and New Approaches in History." Canadian Historical Association, 2013. https://www.academia.edu/12366703/A_Social_Network_of_Hunters_Métis_Mobility_and_New_Methodological_Approaches_in_History.

Piper, Liza. *The Industrial Transformation of Subarctic Canada*. Vancouver: UBC Press, 2010.

Piper, Liza, and Heather Green. "A Province Powered by Coal: The Renaissance of Coal Mining in Late Twentieth-century Alberta." *The Canadian Historical Review* 98, no. 3 (2017).

Pratt, Larry. *The Tar Sands: Syncrude and the Politics of Oil*. Edmonton: Hurtig, 1976.

Provincial Archives of Alberta, *An Administrative History of the Government of Alberta*. Edmonton: The Provincial Archives of Alberta, 2006.

Quintal, Ron. "Personal Correspondence." July 25, 2019.

Ray, Arthur. *The Canadian Fur Trade in the Industrial Age*. Toronto: University of Toronto Press, 1990.

———. *Indians in the Fur Trade: Their Roles as Trappers, Hunters, and Middlemen in the Lands Southwest of Hudson Bay, 1660–1870*. First published 1974. Reprint, Toronto: University of Toronto Press, 2015.

———. *Telling It to the Judge: Taking Native History to Court*. Montreal and Kingston: McGill-Queen's University Press, 2012.

Reddekopp, G. Neil. "Personal Correspondence." April 25, 2017.

———. "Conklin as an Aboriginal Community: Legal Analysis." Conklin: Conklin Resource Development Advisory Committee, 2009.

———. "The First Survey of Reserves for the Cree-Chipewyan Band of Fort McMurray," January 1995. Indian Claims Commission, *Inquiry into the Treaty Land Entitlement Claim of the Fort McKay First Nation*, Exhibit 17.

———. "Post-1915 Additions to the Membership of the Fort McKay Band." December 1994. Indian Claims Commission, *Inquiry into the Treaty Land Entitlement Claim of the Fort McKay First Nation*, Exhibit 18.

———. "Theory and Practice in the Government of Alberta's Consultation Policy." *Constitutional Forum* 22, no. 1 (2013): 47–62.

———. "Research Summary Dated December 6, 2006, Summarizing the Status of Research Being Conducted on Métis Historical Issues, Prepared by Neil Reddekopp." *Sessional Papers 2007*, Legislature Assembly of Alberta 1044/2007.

Reddekopp, G. Neil, and Patricia Bartko. "Distinction without a Difference? Treaty and Scrip in 1899." In *Treaty 8 Revisited: Selected Papers of the 1999 Centennial Conference*, edited by Duff Crerar and Jaroslav Petryshyn. Grand Prairie: Grand Prairie Regional College, 1999–2000.

Sandwell, Ruth, ed., *Powering Up Canada: The History of Power, Fuel, and Energy from 1600*. Montreal and Kingston: McGill-Queen's University Press, 2016.

Sandlos, John, and Arn Keeling, eds. *Mining and Communities in Northern Canada: History, Politics, and Memory.* Calgary: University of Calgary Press, 2015.

Sandlos, John, and Arn Keeling. "The Giant Mine's Long Shadow: Arsenic Pollution and Native People in Yellowknife, Northwest Territories." In *Mining North America: An Environmental History since 1522,* edited by J. R. McNeill and George Vrtis. Oakland: University of California Press, 2017.

Saunders, Kelly, and Janique Dubois. *Métis Politics and Governance in Canada.* Vancouver: UBC Press, 2019.

Sawchuk, Joe, Patricia Sawchuk, Theresa Ferguson, and the Metis Association of Alberta. *Metis Land Rights: A Political History.* Edmonton: the Metis Association of Alberta, 1981.

Sawchuk, Joe. *The Dynamics of Native Politics: The Alberta Experience.* Saskatoon: Purich Publishing, 1998.

Sawchuk, Patricia. "The Creation of a Non-Status Indian Population in Alberta: The Interchangeability of Status of Métis and Indians and Its Effects on Future Métis Claims." in Métis Association of Alberta, *Origins of the Alberta Métis: Land Claims Research Project, 1978–79.* Edmonton: Métis Association of Alberta, March 30, 1979.

Scott, James C. *Seeing Like a State: How Certain Schemes to Improve the Human Condition Have Failed.* New Haven: Yale University Press, 1998.

Seton, Ernest Thompson. *The Arctic Prairies.* New York: Charles Scribner's Sons, 1911.

Shanks, Signa Daum. "Mamiskotamaw: Oral History, Indigenous Method, and Canadian Law in Three Books." *Indigenous Law Journal* 3 (Fall 2004): 181–92.

Shipley, Ken, "Creating Circles of Understanding: All Parties Core Agreement – Feedback and Recommendations Report." Fort McMurray: Shipley Management Consulting, 2004.

Short, Damien. "Reconciliation and the Problem of Internal Colonialism." *Journal Intercultural Studies* 26, no. 3 (August 2005).

Simard, Deanna. "Memorandum on Fort McKay Métis Community Association Membership." April 11, 2017.

Sims, Daniel. "Ware's Waldo: Hydroelectric Development and the Creation of the Other in British Columbia." In *Sustain the West: Cultural Responses to Canadian Environments,* edited by Liza Piper and Lisa Szabo-Jones. Waterloo: Wilfred Laurier Press, 2015.

Sinclair, Jeannette Reva. "On the Role of Nehiymv'skwewak in Decision Making among Northern Cree." MA thesis, University of Alberta, 1999.

Smillie, Christine Mary. "The People Left Out of Treaty 8." MA thesis, Saskatoon: University of Saskatchewan, 2005.

Smith, James G. E. "Western Woods Cree," in *Subarctic,* vol. 6, June Helm, editor, *Handbook of North American Indians,* William C. Sturtevant, general editor. Washington, DC: Smithsonian Institute, 1981.

Stantec. *A Historical Profile of the Northeast Alberta Area's Mixed European–Indian or Mixed European–Inuit Ancestry Community*. Ottawa: Department of Justice, 2005.

St-Onge, Nicole. "Early Forefathers to the Athabasca Métis: Long-Term North West Company Employees." In *The Long Journey Home of a Forgotten People: Métis Identities and Family Histories*, edited by Ute Lischke and David T. McNab. Waterloo: Sir Wilfred Laurier Press, 2010.

Syncrude Expansion Review Group. "A Report of the Syncrude Expansion Review Group regarding the Mildred Lake Plant Expansion, Application No. 870593 to the Energy Resources Conservation Board." March 1988.

Tanner, James N., C. Cormack Gates, and Bertha Ganter. *Some Effects of Oil Sands Development on the Traditional Economy of Fort McKay*. Fort McKay: Fort McKay Industrial Relations Corporation, 2001.

Teillet, Jean. *Métis Law in Canada*. Vancouver: Pape Salter Teillet Law, 2013.

———. *The North-West is our Mother: The Story of Louis Riel's People*. Toronto: Harper Collins Canada, 2019.

Thistle, Jesse. *Indigenous Definition of Homelessness in Canada*. Toronto: Canadian Observatory on Homelessness Press, 2017.

Thompson, P. *The Voice of the Past: Oral History*. Oxford: Oxford University Press, 2000.

Tobias, Terry N. *Living Proof: The Essential Data-Collection Guide for Indigenous Use-and-Occupancy Map Surveys*. Vancouver: Ecotrust Canada / Union of British Columbia Indian Chiefs, 2009.

Tough Frank, and Erin McGregor. "'The Rights to the Land May be Transferred:' Archival Records as Colonial Text – A Narrative of Metis Scrip." *The Canadian Review of Comparative Literature* 31, no. 1 (2007).

UN General Assembly, *United Nations Declaration on the Rights of Indigenous Peoples: Resolution / Adopted by the General Assembly*, (UNDRIP). 2 October 2007, A/RES/61/295.

Urquhart, Ian. "Between the Sands and Hard Place?: Aboriginal Peoples and the Oil Sands." *Working Paper No. 10-005*. Evanston, IL.: Buffet Centre for International and Comparative Studies Working Paper: Energy Series, 2010.https://doi.org/10.21985/N2BB4K

Van Dyke, Edward W. "Lives in Transition: The Ft. McKay Case." Ponoka, IL: Applied Research Associates Ltd., 1978.

Van Dyke, Edward W., and Carmon Loberg, *Community Studies: Fort McMurray, Anzac, Fort MacKay*. Edmonton: Alberta Oil Sands Environmental Research Program, 1978.

Van Dyke, Edward W., and Jane Lee Van Dyke. *Ft. McKay Needs Assessment and Planning Study*. Calgary: Bear-Spike Holdings Ltd., 1990.

Van Huizen, Philip. "Building a Green Dam: Environmental Modernism and the Canadian-American Libby Dam Project." *Pacific Historical Review* 79, no. 2 (2010).

Veracini, Lorenzo. *Settler Colonialism: A Theoretical Overview*. London: Palgrave MacMillan, 2010.

Voorhis, Ernest. *Historic Forts and Trading Posts of the French Regime and the English Fur Trading Companies*. Ottawa: Department of the Interior, National Development Bureau, 1930.

Westman, Clinton N. Tara L. Joly, and Lena Gross eds. *Extracting Home in the Oil Sands: Settler Colonialism and Environmental Change in Subarctic Canada*. London and New York: Routledge, 2020.

Williams, Brian, and Mark Riley. "The Challenge of Oral History to Environmental History." *Environment and History*, 26, no. 2 (2020).

Wolfe, Patrick. "Settler Colonialism and the Elimination of the Native." *Journal of Genocide Research* 8, (2006): 4.

Wolfe, Patrick. *Settler Colonialism and the Transformation of Anthropology*. New York: Bloomsbury Academic, 1998.

Index

Note: Page numbers in **bold** refer to photos and maps. Pages numbers followed by "*n*" refer to a numbered note in the endnotes.

A

Aboriginal consultation policy. *See* consultation policy
Ahyasou, Marcel, 110
Ahyasou family, 44
Alberta court cases, 7–9, 114–115, 144, 153–154
Alberta government
    disqualifies Fort McKay from community improvement, 77–78
    environmental monitoring and reporting criticisms, 115, 120
    housing programs, 81–85, 93–94
    land use policies, 86, **87**, 88–90, 94–99, 101–105
    and logging truck blockade, 118–119
    meetings with Fort McKay community, 76, 77, 78–81, 112
    Métis consultation and credible assertion, 7–8, 133, 135–136, 151, 154–155
    natural resources legislation, 50–51
    northern industrial development potential, 14, 107–108
    sells reserve lands to federal government, 72
    in trapline compensation negotiations, 60–63
    trapping areas and trapline system, 13–14, 51–52, 54–56, **57**, 58–60
Alberta Métis Study Task Force, 86, 89–90
Alberta Rural Development Administration, 77–78
Alsands project hearing, 112–113
Armstrong, G. J., 82, 84, 85–86, 88
Asensio, Manuel P., 129
Athabasca Chipewyan First Nation, 28
Athabasca Native Development Corporation, 125

Athabasca region. *See also* Indigenous northern communities
    communities, 16, 21–22, 24, 30–31, 49
    fur trade sites, **23**
Athabasca Regional Issues Working Group. *See* Oil Sands Developer Group (OSDG)
Athabasca River
    pollution, 76
    settlement and posts along, 21–22, 24, 27, 67
    travel on, 39, 43, 44, 69, **70**, 74
    water pollution, 113–114
    water treatment, 84
Audibert, J., 79

B

Balazs, Dawn, 59
Barr, J.J., 60–61
Barr, John, 122–123
Barth, Jack, 129
Battle, R. F., 71–72
Beaver, Felix, 43–44, **45**
Beaver, Marianne, 44, **45**, **46**
Beaver, Mary, **45**
Beaver family, **33**, 34, 43–45, **45**, **46**
Bechtel company, 76
Begin, Father, 69, 70
Bell, Catherine, 144
Beren's House, 22
Bethune, W. C., 72
Bill C-31, 4, 100–101, 130, 168*n*50, 193*n*96. *See also* Indian Act
blockades, 118–121, **120**
Bonko, Bill, 101
Botham, R. J., 81
Boucher, Adam, 26, 36, 38, 68
Boucher, Alex, **44**, 81
Boucher, Clara. *See* Shott, Clara (formerly Boucher)
Boucher, Jim, 96, 110, 111–112, 116, 118, 124
Boucher, Theodore, 60–61

219

Boucher, Vincent, 60–61
Boucher (Bouché) family, 21, 24–26, 27, 34, 36, 38, 39–40, 43, 44, 81
bush economy
   decline and destruction, 74–76
   descriptions of, 24, 29, 30–31, 63–64
   and fur trade, 13, 21
business ventures
   Fort McKay First Nation, 1–2, 124, 125, 128
   Fort McKay Métis Nation, 133, 156–157
   Solv-Ex scam, 128–129

C

Calahasen, Pearl, 101
Canadian government. *See also* Bill C-31; Department of Indian Affairs; Indian Act; Supreme Court of Canada
   First Nations consultation requirements, 126, 128
   Lot 10 purchase, 71–72
   maps and surveys commissioned, 31, 67–68
   Métis nationhood mandate, 138–139
   natural resources transfer to provinces, 50, 72
   as project of rule, 11–12
   Royal Commission on Aboriginal Peoples, 142–143
   treaty and scrip commissions, 10, 35–38
   and UNDRIP, 141
capacity-building agreements, 126–128
Cardinal, James (Jimmy), 135
Cary, Bill, 114
census and population reports, 26, 27, 52, 54, 77
Charter of Rights and Freedoms, 104–105
Chartrand, Larry N., 141–142
chemical spills, 113–114
Chipewyan people
   convergence with Cree, 24, 25–26
   in Treaty 8 memoir, 37–38
clergy, 37
Constitution Act (1982), 104–105, 142
consultation policy, 2, 7–9, 126, 128, 135
Cowie, John, 39
Crawford, Neil, 119
credible assertion claims
   and consultation policy, 7–9
   criteria, 143
   Fort McKay Métis Nation, 133, 135–136, 145–146
Cree people
   intermarriages, 24, 26, 28
   in memoirs and reports, 22, 35, 37–38
   social organization, 24
Cree-Chipewyan Band, 67, 68–69
Crown land
   government management of, 12, 147
   and harvesting rights, 50–51
   occupation on, 77, 86, 94–95, 98, 101
culture
   bush *vs.* settlement, 24
   in impact assessments, 59, 130
   kinship and reciprocity, 29–30
   northern Indigenous, 35–36

D

Daniels, Harry, 86
Daniels, Stan, 84, 90
Dant, Noel, 81–82
Dené laws, 28
Dené people, 21, 24, 26
Department of Indian Affairs. *See also* Indian agents
   housing and land agreements, 79–81, 82, 85–86, 182*n*45
   reserve land surveys, 67
   schools and education, 69, **70**, 71–72
   and trapping policy, 13, 50, **53**, 54–55, 56
Devine, Heather, 10, 12, 27
diseases and deaths, 76–77, 109, 113–114
Droege, Thomas, 104–105
Ducharme, Betty, **45**
Ducharme, Jim, 82–84
Duckworth, Harry, 25
duty to consult. *See* consultation policy

E

economic development, 78–79, 126–127, 128–130, 156
editorial cartoons, **122**
Edmonton Bulletin, 22
Edmonton Journal, 67, 73–74, 114, 115
education. *See* schools and education
Energy Resources Conservation Board (ERCB), 108–109, 111–112, 121–124, **122**
The English River Book, 25, 26
Ens, Gerhard, 12, 138
environment
   harms, 76–77, 109, 113–115
   monitoring and reporting, 115, 120, 125
ERCB. *See* Energy Resources Conservation Board (ERCB)
Ewashko, Roy, 118
extractivism, 12, 14, 15, 107

F

Faichney, Emma (formerly Beaver), 44–45, 166n21
Faichney, Felix, 45, **103**
Faichney, Glen, 45, **103**
Faichney, Roger, 45, 128–129
Faichney family, 45, 58, 81
family groups
    key historic, 24–28, 39–47, 49
    trapping practices, 55–56, 58
First Nations. *See also* Fort McKay First Nation (FMFN)
    consultations with, 126, 128, 196n18
    game hunting preserves, 50
Fisheries Act violations, 114–115
fishing. *See* harvesting
FMFN. *See* Fort McKay First Nation (FMFN)
FMMCA. *See* Fort McKay Métis Community Association (FMMCA)
FMMN. *See* Fort McKay Métis Nation (FMMN)
Forest Reserves Act, Alberta (1931), 51
Fort Chipewyan, 7, 21, 22–23, 50, 51
Fort Chipewyan v. Alberta Government, 7–9, 153–154
Fort McKay community. *See also* Fort McKay First Nation (FMFN); Fort McKay Métis community; Fort McKay Métis Nation (FMMN); Fort McKay region
    in Alberta government proposals, 81–86, 88–89
    culture and land management, 28–31, 34
    first school, 69, **70**
    GCOS intervention, 108–113
    history project, 16–19
    housing and land tenure, 65–69, 71–73, 78–79, 86, 89–95, 96–99
    logging truck blockade, 118–121
    meetings with government, 76, **77**, 78, 79–81
    Métis/First Nation cohesion and division, 1–3, 10–11, 105–106, 116–117, 127–128, 129–130, 156–157
    movements toward prosperity, 123–125, 156–157
    per capita income, 127
    and Rural Development Program, 77–78
    Syncrude intervention, 121–123
    water contamination, 76–77, 113–115
Fort McKay Community Association, 76–78, 96, 105, 110
Fort McKay Community Committee, 110–113
Fort McKay First Nation (FMFN)
    charges against Suncor, 114–115
    in development initiatives, 124–125, 156–157
    economic improvement, 1–2, 116, 130
    housing and land tenure, 71–72, 79, 85–86, 96–99, 105–106
    membership code, 4–5, 117
    provincial and national memberships, 131
    Teck Frontier Mine Project: Fort McKay Métis Integrated Cultural Assessment, 18
    There Is Still Survival Out There, 18, 31, 42, 63
Fort McKay First Nation Group of Companies, 124, 125, 128
Fort McKay Housing Committee, 80–81, 106
Fort McKay Industrial Relations Corporation (IRC), 1, 15, 18–19, 126–128
Fort McKay Métis community
    administration and governance, 3
    authority and representation, 8–9
    economic development, 126–130
    genealogies, 24–28, 39–47
    housing and land tenure, 4, 86, 90, 95, 99–105
    and Métis Nation of Alberta, 131, 135, 146
    Mihkwâkamiwi Sîpîsis: Stories and Pictures from Métis Elders in Fort McKay, 17, 42, 43
    path to nationhood, 15–16, 130–133
    self-government development and rights, 142, 143, 145–146, 150–158
    traditional territory, 13, 31, **32**, 54–56, 58, 69
Fort McKay Métis Community Association (FMMCA), 105, 131–133, 150–151, 154–155
Fort McKay Métis Corporation (Métis Corp), 128–129
Fort McKay Métis Local 63, 1, 4, 101–104, 129, 131, 151
Fort McKay Métis Local 122, 1, 4, 42, 91–92, 99–101, 128–129
Fort McKay Métis Nation (FMMN), **103**
    establishment, 43, 130, 132–133
    Integrated Cultural Impact Assessment, 59
    Position Paper on Consultation and Self-Government, 16, 149–158
Fort McKay region. *See also* Athabasca region; trapping areas
    fort and trading posts, 22, 39
    industrialization, 74–75
    maps, **6**, 31, **32**, **53**
    population composition, 4–5, 52, 54
    reserve assignments, 67–69
Fort McKay Specific Assessment, 18, 130

Fort McKay Sustainability Centre, 5, 18.
    See also Fort McKay Industrial Relations
    Corporation (IRC)
Fort McKay Tribal Administration/Council
    on impact of oil boom, 74
    land and identity, 28–29, 65
    on trapping and trapline system, 55, 56, 58, 66
    From Where We Stand, 18, 31, 49–50
Fort McMurray, 7, 22, 24, **38**, 67, 73–74
Fort McMurray Today, 63, 73, 115, 124, 135
Fort McMurray v. Alberta Government, 7–8
Fort Pierre-au-Calumet, 21–22
Fort Wedderburn, 22, 25
Fortier, Billie, 40, **41**
Fortna, Peter, 1, 2, 3, 5, 7, 9
Fosseneuve, Louison (Shott), 39
Fox, M., 62–63
From Where We Stand: Traditional Land Use and Occupancy Study of the Fort McKay First Nation, 18, 31, 49–50
fur trade, 13, 21, 22, **23**, 24, 31, 39, 49, 107. *See also* trapline system; trapping areas
Fyfe, G. W., 79, 80

G

Gallup, Lina, 40, **41**
game preserve legislation, 50–51
Gareau, L., 77–78
GCOS (Great Canadian Oil Sands), 73, 74, 108–109, 110, 111–112. *See also* Suncor
genealogies
    key historic families, 24–28, 39–47
    study of, 12–13
Gooden, R. v., 145, 203n17
Gordon, Charles, 66
Grammond, Sébastien, 143, 144
Grande Cache Indigenous community, 16, 181n36, 183n57
Grandjambe, Theresa, 76
Green and White Zones, 86, **87**, 88
Grew, J.L., 52, 54

H

Half-Breed Scrip Commission, 10, 36–37
Hanowski, Laura, 9
harvesting
    decline and destruction, 74–76
    rights, 3–4, 7, 30–31, 50–51, 142
    seasons, 34
HBC. *See* Hudson's Bay Company (HBC)

Head, P.W., 51, 52
high modernism, 14, 108
Hirsekorn, R. v., 145, 203n17
Historic Forts and Trading Posts of the French Regime and of the English Fur Trading Companies (Voorhis), 22
housing
    and lease terms, 100–101, 102–104
    in letters to the editor, 73–74
    programs and proposals, 4, 79–84, 93–94
Hudson's Bay Company (HBC)
    journals, 31
    posts, 22, 24, 39, **40**, 67, 68
    workers and traders, 25, 26
hunting groups and practices, 24, 25, 30–31, 34. *See also* harvesting
Hyde, Rod, 69, 110

I

impact assessments, 18, 59, 127, 130
impact benefit agreements, 1–2, 7
incomes, 127, 129, 130
Indian Act, 4, 116–117. *See also* Bill C-31
Indian agents, 52, 54, 71. *See also* Department of Indian Affairs
Indian blocks, 54–55
Indigenous northern communities. *See also* Athabasca region
    industrial development impacts, 73–74
    land claim rejections, 95–96
    lifestyle and culture, 24, 35–36
    studies, 12–13, 16
    trapping industry *vs.* trapping way of life, 59–60
industrial development. *See also* oil sands development
    Alberta government vision for, 14, 107–108
    First Nations partnerships, 128
Innes, Robert Alexander, 13, 138
interventions
    blockades, 118–121
    hearings, 108–109, 110–113, 121–124
IRC. *See* Fort McKay Industrial Relations Corporation (IRC)

J

Jackson, Wayne, 102–104, 105
Janvier/Lacorde, Isadore and family, 34, 43, 44
jobs and training, 78, 83, 88, 111, 112, 124

K

Kemp, G. A., 59–60
Kennedy, Calvin, 101
Kerr, Gordon, 60–61
kinship networks. *See also* family groups
    Fort McKay, 10, 39, 46–47, 133, 154, 157
    and governance, 13, 34, 109

L

Lacorde, Ernest, 43, **44**, 78, 81, 110, 119, 166*n*21
Lacorde, Howard, 43
Lacorde family, 34, 43, 58
land. *See also* trapline system; trapping areas
    Fort McKay traditional territory, 31, **32**, 52, **53**, 54
    Indigenous relationship with, 28–29, 30–31, 34
    Provincial Lands Act (1931), 51
    speculators, 66–67
    strategic marriages for, 26
    transfer of Indigenous, 11–12
land leases
    management, 4, 89–90, 94, 99–100
    terms, 94–95, 100–104
    transfer to Fort McKay Métis Community Association, 104–105
land tenure
    government policies, 77, 81–86, **87**, 88–89, 95–99, 101–104
    impact on community development, 78–79
    reserve assignments, 67–69
    Treaty 8 terms, 65–66
languages spoken, 24, 26, 35, 43, 46
Lavoie, Moira, 8, 154, 155
Linkletter, Clive, 79
Little Red River
    community, 24–25, 26, 27, 31, 39, 46–47
    post, 22, 24
Lizotte, R. v., 144
Loberg, Carmon, 88
Lot 10 assignment and management, 69, 71–72, 79, 86, 96, 106
Lougheed, Peter, 93

M

MAA. *See* Métis Association of Alberta (MAA)
Macdougall, Brenda, 12, 28
Maclean's Magazine, 119, **120**
Madden, Jason, 136
Mair, Charles, 37–38
Manitoba Métis Federation (MMF), 139, 142
Manning, Ernest, 76, **77**
maps and mapmaking
    Fort McKay traditional territory, 31, **32**
    trapping areas, 52, **53**, 55–56, **57**
marriages
    and cultural convergence, 24, 26
    and Indian status, 116–117
Matsui, Kenichi, 10, 26
McAndrews, C. J., 82
McCormack, Patricia, 10, 16, 24, 25, 26
McDonald, Dorothy
    and Alsands, 112–113
    family and status, 110, 116
    and logging truck blockade, 118–120
    and membership code, 117
    and rejection of Fort McKay Community Plan, 97–99
    and Suncor, 114–115
    and Syncrude, 121, 123
McDonald, Phillip, 85, 110, 118
McDonald family, 39, 58, 81
McKay, Ian, 11
McKay Métis Group of Companies, 156
Métis Association of Alberta (MAA), 86, 89–94
Métis Corp (Fort McKay Métis Corporation), 128–129
Métis Government Recognition and Self-Government Agreement (MGRSA), 139–140
Métis Nation of Alberta (MNA)
    attempt to represent Fort McKay, 135–137, 146
    Local affiliates, 1, 104
    mandate and operations, 130–132, 139–140, 150–152, 153
Métis Nation of Ontario, 153
Métis National Council, 139, 157
Métis people. *See also* Fort McKay Métis community
    historical research, 12–13
    identity and rights, 7–8, 25–26, 51–52, 137–139, 141–143, 146–147, 155–156
Métis rights cases, 143–145
Métis Settlements General Council, 144, 145, 152
Mihkwâkamiwi Sîpîsis: Stories and Pictures from Métis Elders in Fort McKay, 17, 42, 43
Mildred Lake Plant, 121–123, 125
MMF. *See* Manitoba Métis Federation (MMF)
MNA. *See* Métis Nation of Alberta (MNA)
Moore, Marvin, 96–98
Moose Lake Accord, 3, 130
Morgan, Kenneth, 16

N

Natural Resources Transfer Act, 50, 71, 72
Nelson, Ken, 115
Neufeld, Soleil Cree (formerly Fortier), 40, **41**
Nicks, Trudy, 16
North West Company (NWCo), 21–22, 25
North West Mounted Police (NWMP) censuses, 26, 27
Northern Transportation Company Limited (NTCL), 43, 69, **70**
Northland Forestry logging trucks, 118

O

Oberholtzer, J. E., 82, 88
Oil Sands Developer Group (OSDG), 125–126, 128
oil sands development
    boom impacts, 73–74
    government support for, 12, 14, 107–108
    projects and proposals, 108–109, 110–113, 121–124, 128–129
Oliver, Bill, 114
Oliver, Frank, 66–67
Orr, Francis, 29–30, 60–61, **62**, 80, 121
Orr, Johnny, 30
Orr family, 44
Otipemisiwak (the people who govern themselves), 131–132, 137, 151, 157
Otipemisiwak Métis Government Constitution, 139–140

P

Pahl, Milt, 119
Parker, James M., 34
Pearson, C. L., 76
Piché family, 21, 25–26, 27, 34, 36, 38, 39, 43
Piepenburg, Roy L., 81
Poitras, Audrey, 135, 136
Pond, Peter, 21
Powder, Alphonse, 41–42, 81
Powder, Modest, 41–42, **42**
Powder, Zachary, 42, 81, 90
Powder family, 34, 41–43, 58, 94
Powley, R. v., 7–8, 142, 143–144, 145, 152
Provincial Lands Act (1931), 51

Q

Quickfall, Brian, 101–102
Quintal, Ron, **103**
    and Alberta government, 101–104
    family, 40–41
    and Métis Nation of Alberta, 131, 135, 146
    and Solv-Ex, 129–130

R

R. v. Gooden, 145, 203n17
R. v. Hirsekorn, 145, 203n17
R. v. Lizotte, 144
R. v. Powley, 7–8, 142, 143–144, 145, 152
Ray, Arthur, 10, 26
RCAP. *See* Royal Commission on Aboriginal Peoples (RCAP)
Red River Point Society
    effectiveness, 116, 117
    leases, 89, 90, 94, 99
    representatives, 42, 110
Reddekopp, G. Neil, 10, 39, 68–69, 72
Regional Municipality of Wood Buffalo, 103–104, 202n10
Registered Fur Management Areas (RFMAs), 13, 31, 55, 58, 63
Rendell, John S., 128
Renner, Rob, 101–102
reserve land assignment, 67–69, 71, 72, 79
Richards, Janice, 45, **103**
rights
    eligibility, 3–4, 50–51, 59–60
    land tenure, 66, 68, 95, 99
    local *vs.* collective authority for, 130–131, 132, 135–137, 139–146, 152
    self-governance, 104–105
Roach, T. F., 86, 89–90
Robertson, Donald, 36
Robillard, Elzear, 39, 68
Robinson, Donald F., 67–68
Ross, James, 66
Ross, John, 25
Ross, W.A., 62–63
Royal Commission on Aboriginal Peoples (RCAP), 142–143, 145

S

s.35 rights. *See* Section 35 (s.35) rights
Sanderson, George, 85
Sawchuk, Joe, 12, 138
schools and education, 69, **70**, 71–72
Scott, James C., 14
scrip
    records, 12, 25–26
    vs. treaty offering, 10, 36–38, 41, 65–66
scrip speculators, 37

Seaman, Paul, 144
Section 35 (s.35) rights, 7–8, 142–143, 152, 155
Selby, Henry, 67
self-government. *See also* rights
    Fort McKay Métis path, 15–16, 104–105, 106, 130–133
    legal frameworks, 140–142
    Métis Nation of Alberta position, 139–140
Seton, Ernest Thompson, 30–31
settler colonialism, 11–12, 14
Shields, Jack, 119
Shott, Clara (formerly Boucher), 40, 94, 110, 116, 118, 119–120
Shott family, 34, 39–41, 58, 81
Sifton, Clifford, 36
Sinclair, S. J., 78
Skead, W. B., 55–56
Smith, James G. E., 24
Solv-Ex scam, 128–129
Speaker, R. A. "Ray," 84
St. Germain, Vincent, 21
St-Onge, Nicole, 10
Strom, Harry, 84
Suncor, 113–115. *See also* GCOS (Great Canadian Oil Sands)
Supreme Court of Canada, 140, 142, 143, 152
surveys, 67–69, 79
Syncrude. *See also* Oil Sands Developer Group (OSDG)
    Mildred Lake projects, 121–124, **122**, 125
    trapline compensation, 60–61
Syncrude Expansion Review Group, 125

T

Tanner, N.E., 51–52
Tea Dances, 29–30
Teck Frontier Mine Project: Fort McKay Métis Integrated Cultural Assessment (FMFN), 18
There Is Still Survival Out There: A Traditional Land Use and Occupancy Study of the Fort McKay First Nations (FMFN), 18, 31, 42, 63
Thiesen, H.W., 51
Tourangeau, Ed, 80, 81, 85, 90–92, 94
Tourangeau family, 21, 26–27, 34, 36, 38, 39, 43, 58
training and jobs, 78, 83, 88, 111, 112, 124
transportation
    Fort McKay region, 39, 43, 74, **75**, 109
    Northland Forestry logging trucks, 118
trapline system
    disconnect with Indigenous practice, 55–56
    erosion of ownership, 59–60
    and Fort McKay way of life, 63–64
    impetus for, 49–51
    implementation, 51–55
    mapping and administration, 56, **57**, 58–59
trapping areas
    competition from white trappers, 49–50
    destruction and compensation, 60–63, 74–75
    government policies and proposals, 13–14, 52, 54–55
    Indigenous management of, 30–31, 34, 66
Treaty 8 Commission, 10, 35–38, **38**
treaty status. *See also* Bill C-31
    and Fort McKay way of life, 27
    and housing, 100–101
    vs. scrip offering, 10, 36–38, 65–66
Trudeau, Justin, 138

U

United Nations Declaration on the Rights of Indigenous Peoples (UNDRIP), 105, 141, 145, 153, 155

V

Van Dyke, Edward W., 27–28, 30, 88, 94, 99, 110
Voorhis, Ernest, 22
voyageurs, 21, 25, 26

W

wahkotowin, 28
Waquan, Loretta, **103**
waste dumps, 121
water pollution, 76–77, 113–114
Water Resources Act (1931), 51
water treatment facilities, 84, 113, 114
Weiss, Norm, 119
white settlers and home-owners, 66–67, 94–95
white trappers, 49–50, 52
Wood, Charles, 119
Wood, Margie, 43
Wood Buffalo National Park, 50
Wood Buffalo Regional Municipality, 103–104, 202n10

www.ingramcontent.com/pod-product-compliance
Lightning Source LLC
Chambersburg PA
CBHW041311240426
43661CB00065B/2901